ELEMENTARY, MY DEAR!

CAUGHT'YA!
GRAMMAR WITH A GIGGLE
FOR GRADES
1, 2, AND 3

Jane Bell Kiester

ELEMENTARY, MY DEAR!

CAUGHT'YA!
GRAMMAR WITH A GIGGLE
FOR GRADES
1, 2, AND 3

Jane Bell Kiester

 Maupin House

Elementary, My Dear!
Caught'ya Grammar with a Giggle
for Grades 1, 2, and 3

Cover Illustration: *David Dishman*
Cover Design: *M3 Design*
Book Design: *Billie J. Hermansen*

Kiester, Jane Bell, 1945-
    Elementary, my dear! : caught'ya!, grammar with a giggle for grades 1, 2, and
3 / Jane Bell Kiester.
    p. cm.
Includes bibliographical references (p.   ).
ISBN 0-929895-30-4
    1. English language--Grammar--Study and teaching (Primary) 2. Humor in education.
I. Title

LB1528 . K54 2000
372.61--dc21
                                                        99-058933

Maupin House Publishing, Inc.
PO Box 90148
Gainesville, FL 32607-0148
1-800-524-0634
Fax: 352-373-5546
info@maupinhouse.com
Maupin House publishes classroom-proven language arts resources for innovative teachers K-12. Free catalogue.

Printed in the United States of America

DEDICATION

First, this book is gratefully dedicated to Dr. Peter Bensen, chiropractor and kinesiologist *par excellence*, who still is putting my body back together after a nearly fatal car accident in August, 1997. What that drunk driver nearly destroyed, Dr. Bensen has restored enough so that I can begin to work and write again.

Thanks, Dr. Bensen, for not giving up on me when any upgrade in my health seemed doubtful. Thanks for the off-hour office visits when you took time from your family to ease my pain. Without your expertise, kindness, humor (albeit the gallows type), and perseverance, I would not have been able to finish this book.

and

This book is dedicated to all you brave and wonderful souls who love to teach the younger crowd, and especially to the exciting, innovative, dynamic K-3 teachers at Tommy Barfield Elementary School in Marco Island, Florida. Thanks for keeping me in sync with the times and for sharing your ideas and expertise.

Without you primary teachers working so hard to prepare the children so well, this book would never have been begun, and those of us who follow you and teach the older crowd wouldn't stand a chance. Thank you.

ACKNOWLEDGMENTS

First, I wish to thank my constant, loving editors and nurses this past year, my mother, Perra Bell (age 80) and my husband, Chuck Kiester. Without your editing and "tersing," not to mention encouragement, I would not dare write. Without your patient nursing, care, and chauffeuring as I recuperate so slowly, I would not be able to function. I love you.

Second, I wish to thank the six teachers at Tommy Barfield Elementary School who teach in two multiage primary-program teams. They shared their expertise, ideas, and enthusiasm. Debbie Cooper, Jody McCarty, and Esther Scuderi taught one combined kindergarten/first/second-grade class. Margo Barath, Diane Stone, and Barbara Stukey taught the second multi-age group. Thank you, ladies; you're super! Congratulations on the high Florida Writes scores at your school!

I especially wish to thank Debbie Cooper who spoke to me at length about the magic she and her colleagues weave to teach students how to write correctly and confidently. Debbie also sent me some wonderful examples of her students' work and tested parts of this book on them.

Next, I wish to thank Dr. Peter Bensen, Dr. Hal Brodsky, Joe Maruca, L.M.T., Dr. Michael Rozboril, and Stephen Schacter, C.A. Slowly, you are all helping me to regain at least part of my life, my thinking ability, my mobility, and my energy. I am very lucky to have found such a competent, bright medical team who work together for the patient's welfare. The world needs more open-minded, caring practitioners like you.

Thanks also to Dr. Cynda Crawford of Aalatash Animal Hospital for her information about skunks, rabies, and other diseases of wild animals, without which the *Putrescent Petra* story would have contained inaccurate information. I had no idea one had to kill an animal to check for rabies...

I also wish to thank Miss Kelly Alexaitis, age eight, who provided an example and her hand-writing. Thank you for not giving up. I love your paragraph even if you don't like to write! I hope your sister doesn't get too mad.

And finally, I wish to thank Robert and Julie Graddy at Maupin House, the "blithe-writer" publishing company. Thank you for helping with the boring stuff and for agreeing to include my sometimes quirky ideas. Thank you for thinking more of my fellow teachers than of your pocketbook. And, most of all, thanks for your friendship and frankness.

CONTENTS

HOW AND WHY TO USE THIS BOOK

Years ago, when the first *Caught'ya* book (intended for grades three through twelve) was published, one teacher in a parochial school had one of the early multi-age classes. This teacher said that when she did the *Caught'ya*s with her third graders, her first and second graders wanted badly to participate. She told me that she acquiesced with trepidation and found that, with the exception of an occasional tear when she "caught" a younger student with an error, her youngest students' writing fluency, vocabulary, and English skills soared! She was amazed (and very pleased) with the results.

I should not have been surprised. A teaching colleague of mine, Jeannette Hiebsch, explained it very well. She had taught first grade for many years and suddenly, with no transition or preparation, joined me in teaching eighth grade. When asked about the differences between first and eighth graders, Jeannette replied with a grin, "Well, there are three main differences between first and eighth graders. First, *I teach mostly the same things*, but the eighth graders do not need them broken down into such tiny increments. Second, the eighth graders are much bigger, and third, they don't throw up as much."

It was the difference in the increments that got me thinking. After all, I use many primary techniques (including kinesthetics, songs, and knee-to-knee conferences) to teach my eighth-grade students. I learned about these clever and universal techniques from friends who taught the primary grades and from ideas gleaned at primary conventions. I hope my eighth graders never discover that I use these first-grade teaching tools! I have already had to swear one student, whose mother teaches first grade, to silence.

After consulting with some primary teachers about their students' specific needs and capabilities it was clear that a separate book was needed to address teaching the *Caught'ya* method of English at the first-, second-, and third-grade levels. Primary teachers in about eight Florida schools have kindly tried out earlier drafts of these stories with their students. The results have been extremely positive. Let me tell you how this method of teaching came about.

History of the *Caught'ya* Method

In 1979, in a moment of desperation-led inspiration that hits most teachers from time to time, I came up with the idea of the *Caught'ya*. I had observed in my fifth-grade students' weekly journals that nothing I did to try to teach writing fluency, vocabulary, grammar, mechanics, and usage (and I had tried every method that came down the educational pike) carried over into their writing. Something had to be changed.

I cautiously implemented the *Caught'ya* method of teaching grammar, mechanics, usage, and vocabulary into my curriculum. It taught all the skills at the same time in the context of a story, *and* it taught the students how to edit. (This is really what we teachers want our students eventually to be able to do — write fluently, edit, proofread, recognize the errors, and *correct* their own work!) I crossed my fingers and hoped for success.

After only a month of implementing this system with my students, I discovered many of the errors that had plagued their papers had diminished considerably! Good vocabulary use soared as well. During editing time, students actually were editing and correcting. Because they were editing an actual story, instead of doing exercises on a worksheet or in a grammar book, my young students became aware of their own errors and were able to correct quite a few of them. And, because the vocabulary they learned was learned in the context of a story, many of the words remained in their minds, ready for use in their own writings. I saw results I had not seen when using any other method. Finally, something worked!

I changed schools and two then three, grade levels. At the middle-school level, I taught English using the *Caught'ya* method and continued to see dramatic improvement in my students' writing. Then, one day the reading teacher came to me and asked what I was doing that all the other English teachers were not doing. She had noticed that 100% of my students knew how to punctuate a quotation correctly, and she knew that I taught "regular" English. The students of other English teachers (including those in advanced classes) did not fare as well.

I was ecstatic. At the end of that same year, the results of the California Achievement test came back. My students (even my struggling compensatory students) had averaged an increase of two Stanines higher than their previous test in language mechanics and usage! That was all the proof I needed to abandon forever the traditional grammar book and skills worksheets — far fewer errors in my students' writing, more fluent writing, increased use of great vocabulary, *and* improved standardized test scores.

To put the cherry on top of the proverbial cake, students liked the method! It was short and fun. It required only ten to fifteen minutes of each period, leaving the rest of the time to spend writing or reading. Doing a *Caught'ya* began each period with a bang and a laugh, plus it had the side effect of helping to bond me even tighter to my students, thus reducing discipline problems.

More than a decade ago, a student of mine innocently expressed the problem of teaching grammar, mechanics, usage, and vocabulary in the traditional way quite succinctly: "Mrs. Kiester, I know what they're asking for in the grammar book or on a worksheet. They ask for only one skill at a time. When I write, I use all the skills and rules at the same time. It's totally different."

Why, then, given all the research that has been done on the subject since 1909, combined with the assurance that students think grammar books' exercises and worksheets were designed to bore them, have most schools continued to teach grammar directly from those two sources? They do so because we teachers want to get rid of all those egregious errors in our students' writing, and most of us had no better way to do it.

That was the boat in which I had been floating in 1979. That was the spark that led to the invention of the *Caught'ya* technique, a method that directly addresses my student's dilemma. The *Caught'yas* use "all the skills and rules at the same time," just as our students and we do when we write.

With consistent success, I continued to use the *Caught'ya* method in my classroom all during the 1980s. Indeed, I *still* am using it in my English classroom and *still* am getting results. One year, just to make sure I was including all the skills my county expected me to teach, I kept track of everything I taught. Without ever opening the grammar book or the vocabulary book my county had provided, I taught (and am still teaching) the following:

more than 300 vocabulary words/year	paragraphing
punctuation, including quotations	subjects and predicates
the eight parts of speech	subject/verb agreement
collective nouns	who/whom/that/which
titles and how to write them	avoidance of passive voice
verb-tense agreement and consistency	active verbs
correct forms of many verbs	all nine comma rules
common homophones	effective adjective and adverb use
diagramming sentences	use of infinitives
common and proper nouns	antecedent/pronoun agreement
letter-writing format	modifier agreement
use of gerunds	direct and indirect objects
recognition of phrases and clauses	participial phrases
analogies	bibliographical forms
the basic spelling rules	
subordinate clauses and punctuation therein	
irregular verbs (especially lie/lay and sit/set)	

common literary devices and writing conventions such as use
    of metaphors, similes, and description within dialogue
various types of writing (descriptive, etc.)
conjunctions, memorization, and proper use thereof
prepositions and prepositional phrases as adjectives and
    adverbs
pronoun use and overuse, and how to use them correctly
avoidance of run-on sentences and fragments
simple, compound, complex, and compound-complex
    sentences (composition thereof and punctuation therein)
plus   editing, proofreading, and the writing process

And, because teaching all this with *Caught'yas* did not take the entire time allotted for language arts, my students spent more time *writing* than ever before. Some wise reading teacher once said that students learn to read by reading. Well, they also learn to write by writing.

Now, first, second, and third graders do not need to know all the above skills, but you might be surprised at how much your students *can* master beyond your state's standard requirements for a particular grade. You will be amazed at how much great vocabulary they can successfully use (Younger children just *love* using big, juicy words.), and at how quickly they can learn to write fluently. It's all how you approach the subject and how much you demand of them. I always have found that I get out of my students what I expect of them. Thus, I always keep my expectations high.

Students who are weak in English skills especially love the *Caught'ya* method because it eliminates any feeling of failure and frustration previously associated with language arts. Since the *Caught'ya* is short (and can be made even shorter, if needed), it can be completed even by those students with short attention spans. If I have a particularly easy *Caught'ya* on the board, I like to check the papers of my weakest students first so I can praise them for making no errors that day. Other teachers who use the *Caught'ya* method with below-level students also note a marked increase in their students' standardized test scores in the area of mechanics, usage, and reading — sometimes as much as three Stanines!

After the first two *Caught'ya* books were published and distributed, Maupin House received many letters from happy teachers who had experienced success with the method. One young, brand-new teacher startled her county when her students tested twenty-two percentage points higher on the mechanics part of a standardized test, higher than any other teacher in the county, a fact she credited to the use of *Caught'yas* in her classroom. She even won a trip!

Two administrators in different Florida counties independently did some informal analyzing to determine what factors most affected scores on the Florida Writes test and on standardized tests. Because of student demographics at some of their schools, high scores were surprising. After their investigations, both of these administrators were convinced that the significant difference at the successful schools was that the majority of the teachers in those schools used *Caught'yas*.

A second-grade teacher, Kathy Lee, bought a copy of the second *Caught'ya* book and phoned me to get some information about the publication date of **Elementary, My Dear**. In the ensuing hour-long, delightful conversation (Kathy must be a wonderful teacher!), Kathy told me the story of her second-grade students who learned the word "chartreuse" in a *Caught'ya*. They still remembered the word a month later when they spied the principal of the school walking down the hall in a bright yellow-green suit.

"Do you know what color your suit is?" asked several of Kathy's kids.

"Why, it's yellow-green," replied the principal.

"No," Kathy's second graders informed the amazed principal, "it's *chartreuse*."

Needless to say, the principal was impressed with second graders knowing how to use such a word correctly. Kathy informed her that her students had learned the word from a *Caught'ya* story, "The Meanest Teacher in the World" (Mrs. Obnoxious) in the book **Caught'ya Again** (Kiester, 1993).

By the way, Kathy won Teacher of the Year for her district and was one of the five finalists in her county! Kathy told me that on the day of the ceremony, the video the officials took of her class showed her students completing a *Caught'ya*. During the filming, one of Kathy's at-risk, second-grade students regaled the class with the rule for commas in a series, while doing a *Caught'ya*.

In an elementary school where primary teachers had been adapting and using *Caught'yas* for years with their students, the fourth-grade average on the State Writing Assessment Test was 3.8 in 1998, higher than all of the middle and even most of the high schools in their county!!! *Caught'yas* work!

"Is this snake oil or a new grammar book?" you ask. Read on and find out how the *Caught'ya* method works and why so many teachers from grades one to junior college swear by it.

A Quick Overview of the *Caught'ya* Method

Even if you have already read **Caught'ya! Grammar with a Giggle** or **Caught'ya Again! More Grammar with a Giggle**, you still might want to skim this section and the subsequent, more detailed explanations in the specific chapter for your grade level before skipping ahead to the stories. An overview of the information necessary to implement the *Caught'ya* method in your classroom is repeated here. This may help those of you who have never used *Caught'yas* to decide if you like the method. In the following chapters (one each for grades one, two, and three), I have added some embellishments and alternative methods of execution that might help teachers make this non-traditional method more successful for their students.

The *Caught'ya* method teaches language skills in context in an integrated approach, making certain to cover all (and more) of your state's standards for your grade level. Essentially, a *Caught'ya* is two or three sentences of an ongoing, funny story taught from a blackboard, a piece of paper, or an overhead projector every day.

In this book, there are three separate, specifically designed stories — one each for grades one, two, and three. Each sentence in the story contains errors or omitted punctuation. The first-grade story and the first part of the second-grade story use CLOZE technique (leaving strategic blanks in words) to move Stage Three writers (letter copiers) to subsequent writing stages and make it possible for *all* students to experience success. (See the first-grade student example in **Chapter 1**.)

Each *Caught'ya* also includes at least several challenging words (for first grade, any word not on the Dolch Sight Word List) that should be new to most students. Many also contain simple literary devices (such as similes) and writing conventions. The teacher introduces and elicits the meaning of the word(s), reads the *Caught'ya* dramatically, carefully repeats any word in which there are CLOZE blanks, points out the spaces between words, reviews the need for a capital letter at the beginning of a sentence and a period at the end, and initiates a discussion as to whether the sentence begins a new paragraph in the story. Third graders even can discuss what kind of sentences are involved (simple, compound, complex).

Second- and third-grade students then write the *Caught'ya* as correctly as they can into their editing journals (fully explained in subsequent chapters). Because first graders and some second graders are not yet developmentally ready to copy several sentences and correct the errors in them, the teacher needs to cut and paste a teacher-made copy of the *Caught'ya* into their editing journals.

Meanwhile, in all three grades, the teacher walks around the room and gives immediate, tinged-with-humor (hugs included) feedback to individual students, providing mini-lessons, helping those who are not developmentally past Stage Four writing (the labelers), and urging or challenging students to find the errors on their own. While the teacher meanders around the room, students complete and correct the *Caught'ya* then, in their response journals, write about any topic they wish.

Please note that editing and response journals will be explained in much more detail in the chapter that contains the story composed especially for your grade level. You will be told several ways to make the journals, and you will be given details concerning how to establish their use in your classroom.

When nearly all of the students have completed the *Caught'ya* (and, in the case of first graders, also have drawn a picture to demonstrate comprehension of the content), have written in their response journals, and have received a comment from the teacher, the teacher returns to the board or overhead. The teacher and students again discuss the meanings of the vocabulary words, acting them out if possible.

Then, the whole class, with the teacher presiding, reads the *Caught'ya* again several times and reviews the missing punctuation and errors (or letters for the CLOZE blanks). At this point the teacher and class discuss, as much as possible, the *reasons* and *rules* for each correction, just as you do in math. Second- and third-grade students correct their errors, using simple proofreading marks.

After the entire *Caught'ya* has been corrected communally, second- and third-grade students can count the errors they missed the first time — i.e., when they attempted to correct the sentence on their own. These students then indicate the number of their initial errors in the margins of their papers. With each corrected sentence several skills have been introduced, reinforced, or practiced; a new word has been learned; and maybe the class has enjoyed a giggle about the story, the vocabulary word, or the antics of the teacher as he or she cavorted around the room and checked each student's *Caught'ya*. And, after students have the routine of this entire procedure down pat, teachers find that their classes begin the day more smoothly with fewer discipline problems.

It is important to note that at the first-grade level a *Caught'ya* takes from one-half hour to forty-five minutes because the six-year-olds take time to do the following while the teacher walks around the class: 1) cut and paste (or find the correct page in their pre-made editing journals); 2) attempt to fill in the CLOZE blanks; 3) draw a picture to show comprehension; 4) write as many words and letters as they can in a response journal. Reviewing the *Caught'ya* afterwards also takes longer due to the need for repetition and modeling of the letters for the Stage Three (and below) writers.

At the second-grade level, because of developmental maturity and because of having to copy the sentences, completing a *Caught'ya* takes almost the same amount of time as it does with a first-grade class. For some students, especially the perfectionists and the low-achievers, copying, correcting, and then writing in the response journal takes a long time, but these activities are important to their development as writers. **IMPORTANT NOTE**: If you wish to reduce the time further, or your students are taking too long to copy the usual three short sentences per *Caught'ya*, have your second graders copy only one sentence of each *Caught'ya* (you pick) and do the rest orally with the class as a whole.

And, at the third-grade level, a teacher can get around to each student in a class of thirty or more in fewer than fifteen minutes, still giving students time to write in their response journals, and then take another five to ten minutes to review the *Caught'ya*.

For continuity, you probably will want to use a *Caught'ya* every day as a routine exercise. This is a good idea, especially at the primary level in order that the students do not forget the story line. This also will make it easier to repeat skills *ad nauseam* until every student in the class masters them or begs for mercy.

Students soon get used to entering the classroom and immediately settling down to write the *Caught'ya* (or filling in the CLOZE blanks and illustrating the content of the sentences), and composing in their response journals. The *Caught'ya* routine shortens the "waste time" at the beginning of every period. Because students crave the individual feedback their teacher gives while they are working on the *Caught'ya* sentence, they usually get to work very quickly.

Unfortunately, there are always a few students (usually the older ones) who get started quickly in order to "get it over with." With a little enthusiasm, you easily can discourage this attitude by making the *Caught'ya* a fun, laugh-filled activity. Younger students tend to be more enthusiastic about the learning process, and honest older students have been known to confess in a weak moment that, even though they sometimes complain for the benefit of their peers, they really *do* enjoy doing the *Caught'yas*. Almost all students admit that they learn from them.

Sometimes students help each other with the errors in the *Caught'ya* sentence. I encourage this practice. You may hear whispered debates about whether and why a question mark is needed or hear a child reminding a friend to capitalize the first letter in a sentence — music to any teacher's ears.

For your reference, all of the skills included in the *Caught'yas* in this book (and then some) have been explained with simple examples in the **Appendix** of this book. Do not hesitate to use this for help with the explanations of each rule. It includes suggestions on how to teach some of the skills in the *Caught'yas*.

The evaluation of the *Caught'ya* sentences is equally important. It is based on whether students catch the errors and mark them on their papers when the whole class reviews the *Caught'ya*, **not** based on the number of errors made the first time, when students attempted to correct the sentence on their own. This way students, no matter how weak their English skills are, can have success with the *Caught'ya* method. Even the students with poor skills can excel if they listen and carefully correct their work. This is a wonderful inducement to pay attention.

It does not matter what grade you teach; this system works at any level as long as your students are at least Stage Three writers and can read most of a sentence. It is up to you to change and modify the details to fit the needs of *your* students. (More about this in the chapter for your particular grade level.)

Do not worry if you are an introvert or feel that you are not naturally a ham. *Caught'yas* will be successful in your classroom if *you* are at all enthusiastic about them and about the subsequent improvement in your students' writing. If it is not your style to cavort around the room, or if your students (third grade) are at that stage of trying to be too "grown up" to be silly, your being serious as you go around the room will work just as well.

All of us want feedback, and primary students are no exception. You simply have to modify the method to fit *your* personality and *your* students' likes and dislikes. Remember, many teachers have used the *Caught'ya* method with great success, and all have different personalities. No two teachers present the *Caught'yas* in exactly the same way. If you expect your students to succeed, they will!

In whatever fashion you choose to approach this method of teaching English skills, please keep in mind that the most important elements of the method are humor, enthusiasm, playing with the vocabulary, and the class discussion about the "why" of each correction.

Look at the chapter for your grade level for detailed information concerning implementation and adaptation of *Caught'yas* for your class. The story that was written specifically for your grade level also is included in that chapter. In addition, you will want to look at **Chapter 4** in which you will find nine pre-writing and writing ideas. As you use this book, I wish you and your students many giggles, a plethora of great vocabulary, and much fluent writing.

FIRST-GRADE STORY

Eggbert the Ball

Bounces by Himself

What Is Included in This Chapter

1) A how-to section, which will detail how to implement the *Caught'ya* method in your classroom. This includes some general, final notes.

2) The part of Eggbert's story to be read aloud to the class by the teacher.

3) One-hundred twenty student *Caught'ya* sentences for Eggbert's story so that you can anticipate what you will ask your children to do. These sentences can be enlarged, copied, and given, one per day, to your students, or you can use the disk that comes with this book and print out the student copies.

4) Eggbert's story for the teacher (a key) with the answers and the list of skills that are included in each *Caught'ya*.

1

How to Implement *Caught'yas* in Your First-grade Classroom

First graders who are Stage Three writers (copiers) can learn how to do *Caught'yas* and, indeed, can experience much success with them. A number of traditional first-grade teachers as well as multi-age primary-program teachers (whose classrooms include children who traditionally would be in kindergarten, first-grade, and second-grade) have informed me that *Caught'yas* work very well with their young children. They warned of only one difficulty. Several teachers reported that in the beginning of the year they had inadvertently reduced a few children to tears by cheerfully saying "*Caught'ya*" when they spotted an error in their work.

Beginning with the next page, on which you will find an encapsulated version of the eight steps to implement *Caught'yas* in the first grade, you will find the information you need to begin students on their way to fluent writing and use of good vocabulary. Each of the eight steps will be fully explained in detail.

Eight Easy Steps for First-grade *Caught'yas*

1. Write your own thematic unit, write your story, or use Eggbert's story from this chapter and buy an appropriate prop for the story.

2. Decide on skills and vocabulary words you want to be sure to include and A) Compose your own sentences; B) Use the *Caught'yas* as written in this chapter or from the editing journals on the disk; or C) Change the sentences in Eggbert's story to fit your students' needs.

3. Teach your students about editing journals and response journals and make or buy one of each for every student. Read the introduction to Eggbert's story to your class or begin the thematic unit.

4. Having introduced the *Caught'ya* vocabulary the day before, write the day's *Caught'ya* on the board or overhead. Introduce "Wonder Words" if you wish. Read the sentences dramatically, go over the vocabulary words, identify the missing letters in the CLOZE blanks, and review daily capitalization and end punctuation.

5. Your students cut and paste the day's *Caught'ya* in their editing journals (or turn to the appropriate page in their pre-made editing journal), fill in the CLOZE blanks as correctly as they can, draw a picture to illustrate the content of the sentences, and, with as many letters and words as they can, "write" something related in their response journals.

6. Walk around the room, commenting on each student's effort, giving hugs, and helping with response journals by writing model sentences.

7. Return to the board or overhead. Check the *Caught'ya* with the class, eliciting answers from students. Review the vocabulary words.

8. Collect the editing journals and make some positive, individual comments in each student's journal. Collect response journals at another time and write encouraging comments. Note errors your students made for further instruction at a later time.

The *Eight Easy Steps* Explained More Fully

STEP 1

Write your own thematic unit, write your own plot or use Eggbert's story from this chapter and buy an appropriate prop for the story.

If you have never used *Caught'ya*s, I recommend that you use Eggbert's story for the first year to get the feel of the method. If you write your own story, design it to suit your own students and their environment. Alternately, you could use thematic science or social studies units to form the sentences for the *Caught'ya*s and integrate your entire curriculum. You also could write a story with your colleagues. I know of a school where teachers wrote a story that is continued in each grade level throughout the school, somewhat like an ongoing soap opera.

Using Thematic Units

Tommy Barfield Elementary School on Marco Island, Florida, contains an unusually dedicated faculty. They offer two very successful approaches to teaching elementary students: one is a traditional, single-grade primary setting, and the other is a less traditional multi-age primary program. Most of the teachers in both groups use *Caught'ya*s, but they use them differently.

The suggestion to use thematic units instead of a story, especially with pre-writers, came from six teachers at Tommy Barfield who taught on two multi-age primary-program teams. Debbie Cooper, one of the teachers, sent me some wonderful examples of her students' work, a page of which is included at the end of this section.

The teachers at Tommy Barfield write their own *Caught'ya* sentences using thematic science or social studies content instead of stories. For example, they have had *Caught'ya*s about a unit on seeds, in which they included information about plants, trees, etc. Other *Caught'ya*s made part of a conservation unit in which they included information about forests, trunks, photosynthesis, and Smoky the Bear. These teachers also composed units about saving the earth, about pollution, and about recycling. Each unit always included some paragraphs about the food chain and various animals.

The Marco Island teachers' favorite unit, however, was one on the estuaries. This is particularly appropriate since Marco Island is part of an estuary and is situated near the Florida Everglades. The *Caught'ya*s in this unit included information on the mangroves, sea grass, mud flats, fry fish, oyster beds, beaches, loggerhead turtles (which lay eggs on the island), sharks, etc. — anything that had to do with an estuary. Of course, several field trips to the estuary were deemed necessary.

If using thematic units appeals to you, please know that it is not hard to write the sentences of the *Caught'yas* for each unit. If there are several first-grade teachers at your school, you could take turns writing them or brainstorm and write them together. I suggest you base your thematic units on the region in which your school is located in order to involve your students in the environment in which they live. Plan a field trip to complement your *Caught'ya* sentences. Even a field trip to a nearby woods can be an adventure for young students.

After you finish Eggbert's story (about the end of March if you complete one *Caught'ya* a day), using a thematic unit to finish the year is a good idea. You can model the form for your thematic *Caught'ya*s on the story in this chapter. If you have any further questions about thematic units, Debbie Cooper and her colleagues will be glad to help you out. Write to them c/o Tommy Barfield Elementary School, 101 Kirkwood Street, Marco Island, FL 33937-4305.

Using Eggbert's Story

If you use the story in this chapter about Eggbert the ball (which is *not* part of a thematic unit about which students have prior information), you will want to involve your students in the plot so that it is familiar to them before they begin working with the *Caught'ya*s. Before school starts, buy a brightly colored, patterned ball, the more unusual the pattern the better. If you can't find one with bright designs (a beach ball might be your best bet), buy a plain ball and paint it. You might want to buy or make two to have the second as a backup in case the first one breaks or disappears. Label your ball with Eggbert's name and place it prominently in your room for all to see.

For Your Plans — Time Necessary to Complete the Caught'yas

Several veteran first-grade teachers have informed me that a *Caught'ya* takes about forty-five minutes to complete. Five to ten minutes must be spent going over the *Caught'ya*, its vocabulary, and its missing letters. Then, while the teacher walks around the class, six-year-olds take at least twenty to twenty-five minutes to do the following: 1) cut and paste (or find the correct page in their pre-made editing journals); 2) attempt to fill in the CLOZE blanks; 3) draw a picture to show comprehension and; 4) write as many words and letters as they can in a response journal. Going over the *Caught'ya* afterwards also takes another ten minutes due to the need for repetition and modeling of the letters for the Stage-Three (and below) writers.

STEP 2

Decide on skills and vocabulary words you want to be sure to include and A) Compose your own sentences; B) Use the *Caught'ya*s as written in this chapter or from the pre-made editing journals on the disk; or C) Change the sentences in Eggbert's story to fit your students' needs.

Make a list of what you want to teach this year for Language Arts. If you write *Caught'ya*s using your own thematic units or story, make sure to include all that is on your list when you write your sentences. If you use Eggbert's story, you might want to read the corrected *Caught'ya*s (in the last section of this chapter) to make sure that the sentences include all the English skills that you want to cover this year. If you wish to add more sentences or take some away, you can do either in several ways (even if you use the pre-made editing journals that you made from the disk included with this book). The hallmark of the *Caught'ya* method is that each teacher can modify the sentences for his or her classes. You can do any or all of the following:

● Go over as a class the skills you decide are too difficult for your students to do individually and have students make the changes with you.

- Fill in the CLOZE blanks orally until your students have reached Stage Four of writing and can do this on their own. At Stage Four of writing, students have learned that letters represent sounds, and words and text convey meaning.

- Change the CLOZE blanks so that you can teach a digraph or blend of your choosing in a particular *Caught'ya* by simply *whiting out* the appropriate letters and putting underlines instead.

- Ask your aide or a fifth-grade student to *white out* (or put in) punctuation in each of the pre-made editing booklets made from the disk.

- Or, as your students approach writing fluency, add a short sentence on the board for them to copy.

STEP 3

Teach your students about editing journals and response journals, and make or buy one of each for every student. Read the introduction to Eggbert's story to your class or begin the thematic unit.

Use of Editing and Response Journals

Begin the year by your making and then having students decorate an editing journal and a response journal. The editing journals are for the *Caught'ya*s. The response journals are for free writing about any subject the student desires. A teacher can suggest a topic for those children who cannot think of a subject, but it should be just that, a suggestion. It is a good idea to link the suggestion to the action or vocabulary in the day's *Caught'ya*.

Young students are not developmentally ready to edit their own writing although they can revise work. By having two journals, the two concepts are separated for the time being. By the end of the year, however, you may want to ask your students to search in one of their already filled response journals for capital letters and end punctuation that need to be applied, for sentences in which to substitute strong, active verbs, and for places to insert some really "big, juicy" vocabulary words.

Making Editing and Response Journals

With this book, Maupin House Publishing offers you a computer disk that contains the *Caught'yas* for the first-grade story. When you print out the story from this disk, you will notice that the *Caught'yas* are separated, one per page. Each page includes a space for a student's name, the day, the date, and, below the *Caught'ya* sentences, enough space for the student to draw a picture in order to demonstrate comprehension of the content of the sentences. In other words, you can print out the entire story from the disk, (approximately 121 pages), run off a copy for each of your students, and staple each booklet together. In this way, you will have a pre-made editing journal for each of your first graders. The title page also leaves space for students to draw a picture in order to personalize their editing journal so as to "make it their own."

You may not want to run off all 121 pages at one time. The size of such a booklet would daunt most six-year-olds. I suggest running off and stapling ten to twenty *Caught'yas* at a time. Each time you do so, you will want to be sure to include another copy of the title page that says "Editing Journal."

You can construct the response journals from unlined newsprint (although it tears easily), 8 1/2" by 11" greenbar computer paper (without carbons), or large-lined primary paper. Old, still usable greenbar computer paper is often given away by businesses who are delighted to donate their unused, fading, outdated paper instead of throwing it out. Make construction paper covers and staple the paper inside the covers or, if you have one, use the machine that perforates the left edge and buy those big, curling-edge claws that hold a booklet together.

The students then can decorate their folders or booklets. If you do not use the pre-made editing journals from the disk, they will need to make several editing journals during the course of the year. Here is another idea. If you can find them and your budget can afford it, buy spiral notebooks with primary lines for the response journals. Paste a piece of white construction paper over the cover so that each student can decorate his or her own notebook.

Preparing Your Students for Eggbert's Story

When you are ready to begin doing *Caught'ya*s, introduce some of the more difficult words (the "big juicy words") that will appear in the first few sentences. Post them on the board. Sound them out daily. Display the ball prominently. Then read the beginning of the story of **"Eggbert the Ball Bounces by Himself,"** the part that is meant to be read aloud by the teacher. (You will find this part of the story immediately after this section.)

Read the introduction to the story many times to acquaint students with their own Eggbert and his beginnings. This activity will prime students to do the *Caught'ya*s and will introduce a few more of the oral-only vocabulary words.

STEP 4

Having introduced the *Caught'ya* vocabulary the day before, write the day's *Caught'ya* on the board or overhead. Introduce "Wonder Words" if you wish. Read the sentences dramatically, go over the vocabulary words, identify the missing letters in the CLOZE blanks, and review daily capitalization and end punctuation.

Vocabulary

This first-grade story introduces quite a bit of vocabulary. Vocabulary is the key to fluent reading, writing, and good writing-test scores. A day in advance, you will want to display the vocabulary for each *Caught'ya* and sound out the words with your class at the end of that day. This will make the words slightly familiar when students encounter them in the *Caught'ya* the next day.

Young children love using big words, yet students of all ages (depending on personal learning acuity) need to have a new word or concept repeated from fifteen to sixty times in order for mastery to take place. By introducing the vocabulary a day in advance and reviewing it repeatedly, you increase students' chances of learning the words.

Please note that as I wrote Eggbert's story, I used the Dolch sight-word list of vocabulary and added an extra word or two in each day's *Caught'ya*. This would mean that your children would be introduced to five to ten new, "big, juicy" words a week. When each new word has been used ten times in subsequent *Caught'ya*s, it is no longer highlighted as a new word. Use these words constantly when you talk. Post them on the board. Go over them frequently for recognition. Require their use in response journals. You will be surprised (and delighted) at the results!

More Vocabulary

To aid in learning excellent vocabulary, the vocabulary-conscious teachers at Tommy Barfield Elementary School have what they call a "Working Word List" which they encourage students to use in their response journals. This list includes four basic writing words (basic pre-primer words that students want to use a lot like "how"), two thematic words a day from their science and social studies units (which can be extremely difficult scientific words like "periwinkle," "estuary," and "dendrites"), the *Caught'ya* words, and a "Wonder Word" that can be "any word in the world," says Debbie Cooper. Wonder Words are just for fun.

Students not only use the basic words and the thematic words in their free writing but also illustrate their Wonder Word on a card which they keep for reference to use when they write. This daily vocabulary work increases tremendously the students' word power in the response journals and gives them more choices for free writing exercises. I highly recommend it. Good vocabulary at an early age is one of the most important keys to reading and writing well in later grades.

Copying the Caught'ya

In addition to the copy of the day's *Caught'ya* that each student has in his or her editing journal (either pre-made or pasted), you will need to copy the day's *Caught'ya* on the board or overhead, boxing the vocabulary words and writing them a second time above the *Caught'ya*. You might want to keep a list of all the vocabulary words somewhere in the classroom and add to it each day.

On a personal note: I dislike using audio-visual devices of any kind, even one as simple as an overhead. The cord trips you; the bulb burns out just as your most difficult students enter the room, and the squirt bottle (or else you have to use spit) is a tempting weapon for students to use on each other.

On the other hand, the pre-made editing journal from the disk can readily be made into transparencies for use in correcting the *Caught'yas* with your students. Thus, perhaps you first-grade teachers should consider the use of transparencies with an overhead projector, despite cord and squirt-bottle problems.

Going over the Caught'ya

Before the students begin editing their copy of the *Caught'ya*, go over the day's *Caught'ya* and vocabulary words (copied on whatever medium you choose) in great detail with the class as a whole. Get the children to participate in the process as much as possible. This is where it is especially important to challenge your students to correct the *Caught'ya*.

Dare your students, encourage them, pump them up, and do whatever it takes to intrigue them enough to work hard to:

1) fill in the CLOZE blanks

2) draw the picture underneath to show comprehension

3) write in their response journals, wrapping between lines and putting spaces between words

4) begin every sentence with a capital letter

5) put punctuation at the end of each sentence

6) learn the vocabulary words well enough to recall them when writing on their own

Please note that these generally are the standard, official state objectives for language arts for the first grade. They do not vary much from state to state.

After you read the *Caught'ya* dramatically, it is a good idea to have a few students read it again as dramatically as they can, review what happened previously in the story (for those who have been absent), and elicit the meaning of the vocabulary words in a way that will make your students remember them for more than five minutes.

Point out spaces between words. Have your students use their fingers to do this. Even beginners can listen to a daily discussion of "to indent or not to indent." I like to say, as my students and I physically move our bodies in the correct direction, "This is a paragraph and must be indented. We have to *move it over.*" The teachers who follow you will be forever grateful if students have learned the rudiments of paragraphing by the end of the first grade, especially to indent whenever someone new speaks.

STEP 5

Your students cut and paste the day's *Caught'ya* in their editing journals (or turn to the appropriate page in their pre-made editing journal), fill in the CLOZE blanks as correctly as they can, draw a picture to illustrate the content of the sentences, and, with as many letters and words as they can, "write" something related in their response journals.

Beforehand

If you do not use the editing journals made from the disk, enlarge and cut out each day's *Caught'ya* separately so that your students can trim (practicing their large-motor skills) and paste them in their editing journals. At this point, you also will want to have that overhead copy of the *Caught'ya* (or write it on the board) so that you can go over it with the class in Steps 4 and 7.

Cutting and Pasting and Doing the Caught'ya

After students have the day's *Caught'ya* pasted in their editing journals or have found the correct page in their pre-made journals, they attempt to fill in the CLOZE blanks, using the displayed vocabulary to insert any punctuation or capital letters that have been left out, and to draw a picture below the *Caught'ya*. This picture should illustrate the meaning of the sentences. (See the example of a student page at the end of this section.)

After the Caught'ya

When the *Caught'ya* is completed, encourage students to write a few sentences (letters, words, pictures) in their response journals about a topic that is an offshoot of the *Caught'ya* and urge them to try to use the vocabulary words of the day as well as the Wonder Words. For example, if Eggbert sees a dog, then the topic might be to write what the students know about dogs. Students might want to suggest a few more Wonder Words.

Multi-age and Multi-leveled Classes

As the year progresses, the more skilled students who are already at Stages Six and Seven of writing fluency (sentence makers; story makers) should try to copy the *Caught'ya* into their editing journals. These students should not illustrate the *Caught'ya* (because of the time spent copying). After they write the sentences correctly, they continue as usual by writing in their response journals and perhaps working with the Wonder Word vocabulary.

STEP 6

Walk around the room, commenting on each student's effort, giving hugs, and helping with response journals by writing model sentences.

This is where the giggles come in to play. You, Eggbert, and any teacher's aide you may be lucky enough to have, circulate around the room, stopping by each child's desk. This is the point at which you can help a child sound out a word to fill the CLOZE blank, put punctuation in the *Caught'ya* when a child simply cannot quite get the idea, or give verbal and physical encouragement. Eggbert also can "visit" briefly with each child.

As you walk around the room, touching each student, be free with help, hugs, praise (lots), comments, encouragement, and models. Help students copy their names, the date, and day of the week in their editing journals so that when they are developmentally ready, they can copy them again, this time *without* help, into their response journals. This is the time for you to give individual, mini-lessons to the children. Leave Eggbert on a child's desk for encouragement.

You may want to ask some of your weaker students (those at Stage Three of writing fluency) what they want to say in the response journal and, under any picture they have drawn, print a sentence or two of what they dictate to you. You then can have the student repeat what he/she said and what you wrote as a model.

Alternately, for your more advanced students (Stages Six and Seven writers) who may be able to write a sentence, you can respond with a sentence or two of your own on the same page in the child's response journal. Be sure to give each child a hug, a kind word, and sometimes maybe even a small treat so that they associate editing and writing with positive feelings.

STEP 7

Return to the board or overhead. Check the *Caught'ya* with the class, eliciting answers from students. Review the vocabulary words again.

When most of the class has finished, go up to the board or overhead and elicit the answers to the CLOZE blanks. Then read the *Caught'ya* sentences again to the class. Follow this by having several children read the *Caught'ya*. Write in any missing letters, punctuation, or capital letters, giving Stage Three and Four writers time to copy.

Review the vowels and vowel sounds in the sentences, especially in the new words. Introduce or review digraphs and blends. Have each child check to see that each sentence begins with a capital letter and ends with the correct punctuation. (**See "A Teaching Hint" in the next section, entitled *A Few Final Notes*.**)

Read the corrected sentences again while students edit their own work. Use choral reading techniques. Review the vocabulary again; play with it in some manner. I like to throw a Nerf ball from student to student as they repeat the words and their spellings and/or meanings. This entire review process can take as much as fifteen minutes or more with first graders, but they enjoy the activity, and most importantly, they learn.

As your students point out each correction in the *Caught'ya*, you model the appropriate proofreading symbols on the board or overhead and explain the *why* of each correction. If a mini-lesson is in order, give one. In Eggbert's story, to the left of each sentence in the teacher's version, you will find the "why" listed for each correction. If a number of your students missed a certain skill (for example mixing up "ou" and "ow"), you can launch into more explanation. Other explanations with simple examples can be found in the **Appendix**.

STEP 8

Collect the editing journals and make some positive, individual comments in each student's journal. Collect response journals at another time and write encouraging comments. Note errors your students made for further instruction at a later time.

Collect the editing and response journals every week or two for evaluation. Note words you had to supply. Note problems that students experienced. Make a comment in their response journals. You even might want to chart the number of words used in the response journals to keep track of the progress of each student's fluency and vocabulary use. At the first-grade level, you do not want to give grades, only positive feedback.

A Few Final Notes

The Number of Caught'yas

After you read the following introduction to your students, they are ready to begin the actual *Caught'yas*. The rest of the story will unfold bit-by-bit in the daily *Caught'ya* sentences. There are 120 *Caught'yas*, enough for one-a-day for the first twenty-four weeks of school. At that point (the end of March) you will want to use your students' stories, write a thematic unit (**see STEP 1**), or add some additional sentences of your own that incorporate words and skills you wish to reinforce. If you do only four *Caught'ya*s a week, you will have enough for the entire year, but I recommend completing one a day for more practice. Remember, each *Caught'ya* (plus all the vocabulary and free writing that accompanies it) will take at least forty-five minutes to complete each day, but no other language arts is necessary.

Vocabulary

For your students' practice, I have attempted to use most of the words on the basic Dolch sight-word list. Vocabulary above the basic Dolch sight-word list is in bold. It also is listed at the top of each *Caught'ya* for greater ease in sounding out new words. Most of the new words are repeated many times. Remember, after ten repetitions, words are no longer put in bold or featured at the top of the *Caught'ya* sentences.

What You Want to Teach

I suggest that you concentrate on seven basic skills (which you are required to teach in most states) and ignore or just mention the rest:

- Teach students to write and sound out the letters, digraphs, and blends.
- Teach students to put spaces between words and to wrap around the text.
- Teach students to begin sentences with capital letters.
- Teach students to put some punctuation at the end of a sentence.
- Teach students to capitalize proper nouns.
- Teach students to add "ed" to most verbs to form the past tense.
- Introduce the idea of indenting to form paragraphs.

Anything else you can teach, like the rudiments of paragraphing (when and why), is pure gravy. If first graders can master the above seven skills, it will provide a firm foundation for students to build on in subsequent grades. It is like being able to add before going on to subtraction. It really helps.

A Teaching Hint

From a primary teacher, I borrowed a way to teach students capital letters and end punctuation right from the start. Ask students to nod or stamp their feet at a capital letter in the *Caught'ya* and clap their hands for a period. Your students should do this twice — once when you initially go over the *Caught'ya* and the second time when you go over it with the class.

It also is very effective to ask students to "stand up and move it over" whenever a new paragraph is needed in a *Caught'ya*. I even use a "raspberry" (tongue only slightly out) for commas and a "click" sound accompanied by appropriate hand signals for a quote. By using their bodies in these very effective kinesthetic-learning exercises, students recall the rules better — usually remembering to include end punctuation and capital letters when they write their own compositions. Before the end of the year, the more advanced students even may learn to indent.

What Is Not Included in This Story

Note that since first graders usually are not developmentally ready to deal with them, no commas or quotation marks have been omitted from the students' copy of the sentences as they are in the *Caught'ya*s for subsequent grades. Even so, if you have included the skills in your writing workshops and the students have practiced placing quotation marks in their writing, about April or May you may want to ask students to insert quotation marks. Simply eliminate the quotation marks before you give students the *Caught'ya* sentences and ask them to insert quotes where needed.

Note, too, that I have not pointed out the parts of speech. You can use the *Caught'ya* sentences to do so if you feel that your students are ready and able to recognize some of them, but this is not a first-grade skill. All eight parts of speech (noun, interjection, preposition, pronoun, adverb, verb, adjective, conjunction) have been used repeatedly in this story. You might ask the class to find an example of a noun or a verb, but you probably will not want to go any further than that. A good time to do this is when you examine the *Caught'ya* with the class .

A Practical Note

There are three sets of the *Caught'ya* sentences for the first-grade story. The first set that follows these notes is a copy of the sentences you will be presenting to your students. It is intended for you as a quick perusal so that you will know what you will be teaching. It could also be enlarged, copied, and printed out for use with your students if you do not want to print out the version on the disk. The second set is the teacher's key. It comes complete with notes to help you with your teaching. It also lists the corrections you may wish to go over with your students. The third set is the one on the disk that accompanies this book. These are to be printed out, copied, and made into editing booklets for your students to use.

Names in the Story

You will have to write your name and the names of your students in the appropriate blanks when they occur. Fifty-four blanks have been left for the names of your students since you will want to use each child's name more than once. Most of these blanks are in the second half of the story.

Verb Tense

Since this story is told in the past tense, you may want to teach that form before beginning the *Caught'ya*s. You may want to teach the forms of irregular verbs as they occur.

Enjoy!

Enjoy this method with your students. I wish you much good writing and many hugs and giggles!

19. Mangroves provide a habitat and food for animals _above_ and below the water.

Actual work of first grade student in Editing Journal

2

Text to Be Read Aloud by the Teacher

Read the following to the class at the beginning of the year (Step 3) to introduce the background of the story. Vocabulary that is way beyond primer level is in bold type the first time each word is used. Since this part of the story is intended for oral reading by an adult, these words are pointed out only to warn you of their level of difficulty. Words with hearts (❤) after them are repeated frequently in the *Caught'ya* itself.

Eggbert the Ball

Bounces❤ by Himself

It was dark in the toy store. It was quiet. Toys sat on long gray **shelves❤**. On the wall, a clock tick tocked. The clock tick tocked so softly you could **barely** hear it. The **toy store❤** was closed and locked up for the night.

Suddenly, at the end of one of the rows of shelves, near the far wall of the store, a light **flickered** on and off, on and off like Tinkerbell. There was a sound like a small bell. Something rolled on a shelf and fell to the floor with a small thump.

Whatever it was sat there a minute. Then it **bounced❤**, slowly at first, then faster and faster and higher and higher. It **arrived** at the front of the store. It bounced one more time up into the big front window of the store. There it stopped. It made a noise from the **valve❤** in its side. **(Show a valve and explain its use.)** The noise sounded like a **sigh❤**.

What had bounced all on its own without boy or girl hands to move it? What had sighed? What was in the big window of the toy store? A ball!

This ball was round like all other balls. It did not look much different from all other balls. This ball was... ***(Insert your own description of the ball you have in your classroom.)***

But, this was no ordinary ball. This ball was **special❤**. This ball had a name — **Eggbert❤**. This ball could bounce all by itself! This ball could think. This ball even could **understand** people talk! Eggbert was special.

Now, Eggbert did not know how or why he was different from all the other balls. He just was. One minute he had been on the shelf with all the other balls. He did not think. He could not move. Then a light had flickered on and off like Tinkerbell. All of a sudden Eggbert could think. He could move by himself.

Now, Eggbert had rolled and bounced himself to the big front window of the store. He wanted to see what was outside the store. You see, none of the toys knew what was outside the store. They saw the inside of a **factory**. Then they saw the inside of a big brown box. Then they saw the inside of the toy store. No toy in the store had ever been outside in the big world.

This was why the minute Eggbert knew he could bounce all by himself, he bounced his way to the front **window❤**. He had always **envied** the lucky toys who sat in the window. *They* could see outside.

Eggbert sat the rest of the night in the toy store window. He was **waiting**. He did not know what he was waiting for. But, Eggbert waited anyway......

Stop reading out loud here.

3
Student *Caught'ya* Sentences for First Grade

This section is for your quick reference. You will want to use it so that you easily can see what you are giving your students to correct. Use the sentences provided on the disk to print, copy, and make editing booklets for your students. If you lack the equipment to do this, you can enlarge, put one per page, and copy the sentences in this section.

Eggbert the Ball

Bounces by Himself

1. **sat, inside, outside**

    Eggbert **sat** and s___ t. It was dark **inside**. It w___s black **outside**.

2. **outside, high**

    The ___lack **outside** went away. The sun came up. It looked like a big ball, a ___ig yellow ___all **high** in the sky.

3. **bright**

    The ___un wa___ **bright** and pretty. The ___un was big and yellow. Eggbert looked around.

4. **outside, window, boys, girls**

    Eggbert looked **outside** the **window**. He l___ ___ked and l___ ___ked. Eggbert saw **boys** and **girls** run by.

> **Note to Teachers:** *Put in the names of three of your students in the blanks in #5 before you run off copies for your students or put names on the board for students to copy.*

5. **people**

    Big, tall **people** went by. Short, f___t **people** w___nt by. _____ and _____ and _____ r___n by. No one s___w Eggbert.

6. **stopped, window, boys, girls**

   No one **stopped** to look in the **window**. Eggbert looked and l___ ___ked. He saw **boys** and **girls**. He s___ ___ dogs and c___ts.

7. **boy, girl, whiskers**

   A **boy** ran by. A **girl** r___n by. A big dog r___ ___ by. A bl___ck and white c___t with long white **whiskers** l___ ___ked at Eggbert.

8. **meow, outside, inside**

   It said, "**Meow**." The c___t was **outside**. Eggbert w___s not ___ ___tside. He w___s **inside**.

9. **wanted, roll, bounce, boys, girls, feel**

   Eggbert **wanted** to **roll** and **bounce** with the **boys** and **girls**. He want___d to go with th___m. He **wanted** to **feel** th___ sun.

10. **roll, bounce, outside**

    "I w___nt to be with them," Eggbert said. "I w___ ___t to **roll** and **bounce** with th___ ___. I w___ ___ ___ to see the **outside**."

11. **sighed, door, store**

    Eggbert **sighed**. He s___gh___d and s___ ___ ___ed. Then a tall man c___me to the **door** of the **store**.

12. **opened, door, toy store, window**

    The t___ ___ ___ man **opened** the **door**. He c___me in the **toy store**. He did n___t see Eggbert in the b___g **window**.

13. **back, store, bounced, times, himself**

    The man w___nt to the **back** of the **store**. Eggbert saw him look around. Eggbert **bounced** up and down, ___p and down, up and d___ ___ ___ thr___ ___ (3) **times**. The m___n did n___t se___ Eggbert bounce by **himself**.

14. **sighed, wanted**

    Eggbert **sighed** and s___ ___ ___ed. He **wanted** the man to see him. The man did not see him. The man d___d not see E___ ___ ___ ___ ___t.

15. **hear, toy store**

    The man did n___t **hear** Eggbert. The man w___rked in the **toy store**. He liked to w___rk in the **toy st___ ___e**. It was f___n.

16. **sat, window, dark, outside, night**

    Eggbert **sat** in the **window** all day. Then it g___t **dark outside**. Eggbert **s___t** in the **w___ndow** all **night**.

17. **heard, hear, sigh**

    No one saw Eggbert. No one **heard** E___ ___ ___ ___ ___t. Only a black and white cat look___d at Eggb___ ___ ___t. Can you **hear** a b___ ___ ___ **sigh**?

18. **lonely, night, bounced, window, store**

    Eggbert w___s very sad. Eggbert w___ ___ very **lonely**. One **night** he **bounced** out of the **window** into the **store**.

19. **bounce, roll, night, boys, girls**

    "I will **bounce** and **roll**," Eggbert said one **night**. "The man will see m___. **Boys** and **girls** will s___ ___ me."

20. **found, floor, back, window, talk**

    One d___y the m___n **found** Eggbert on the **floor**. He p___t Eggbert **back** in the **window**. He d___d n___t **talk** to Egg___ ___ ___t.

21. **found, high, shelf, back, window**

    One day the man **found** E___ ___bert **high** ___p on a **shelf**. He p___t Eggbert **back** in the **window**.

22. **every, found, window, strange**

    Every day the man **found** Eggbert out of the **window**. What a **strange** b___ll! Where would the b___ ___ ___ be **every** day wh___n the m___n c___me to w___rk?

23. **back, window, night, bounced**

    Every day the man put Eggbert **back** in the **window**. Ev___ ___ ___ **night** Eggbert **bounced** out of the **w___ ___ ___ ___w**.

24. **special, bounced, times**

    "This ball is **special**," the man said.
    Eggbert **bounced** up and down, up and d___ ___ ___, up and d___ ___ ___ thr___ ___ (3) **times** to say, "Yes."

25. **bounce, nice, himself**

    Did the **nice** m___n see Eggbert **bounce** by **himself**? No. Egg___ ___ ___t w___s s___d.

26. **nice, lady, store, a lot, teacher**

 One day a **nice lady** c___m___ in the **store**. She looked **a lot** l___k___ your **teacher**. Who was she? What did she want?

27. **lady, nice, kind, excited**

 This **lady** looked n___ ___ ___. She l___ ___ ___ ___ ___ **kind**. Eggbert w___ ___ **excited**.

28. **lady, toy store, back, front**

 The **lady** l___ ___ked ar___ ___nd the **toy store**. She l___ ___ ___ed in the **back** of the **store**. She l___ ___ked in the **front** of the **store**.

29. **sighed, bounced**

 Eggbert **sighed** and s___ ___ ___ **ed**. He **bounced** up and d___ ___n. "Please see me. Pl___ ___se s___ ___ me," he wanted to say. "Please take m___ with you. Pl___ ___se t___ ___ ___ me with you."

> **Note to teachers:** *In the next ten Caught'yas, some of the beginning capital letters have been left out for students to insert.*

30. **lady, heard, sigh, through, valve**

 The **lady** saw E___ ___ ___ ___ ___t. she saw him b___ ___nce up and d___ ___n. She **heard** him **sigh through** his **valve**.

> **Note to teachers:** *Insert the name of your school in Caught'ya #31.*

31. **lady, buy, special, classroom, children**

 the **lady** said to the man in the store, "I want to **buy** this ball. this ball is **special**. To Eggbert she s___ ___d, "How my **children** at _____ School would like to have y___ ___ in th___ ___r **classroom**!"

32. **rolled, left, right, joy**

 Eggbert **rolled** up and d___ ___n. he r___ ___ ___ed to the **left** and then to the **right**. He was happy. he was fu___ ___ of **joy**.

33. **someone, noticed, talked, could, talk, back**

 why was E___ ___bert ha___ ___y? **Someone noticed** him. **someone talked** to h___m. Eggbert wi___ ___ed he **could talk back**.

34. **sighed, air, through, valve, hiss, snake, lady, excited**

eggbert **s___ghed**. He let **air** come **through** h___s **valve** wi___ ___ a **hiss** l___ke a **snake**. the **lady** heard him, and she was very **excited**.

35. **talk, cried, hiss, snake, roll, else**

"Oh, y___ ___ **talk**," she **cried** ___ ___t with joy. "you **hiss** like a **snake**, and y___ ___ b___ ___nce and **roll** all by y___ ___rself. What **else** can you d___?" she asked Eggbert.

36. **times, lady, rolled, hiss, feet, home**

Eggbert bounced five **times**. he b___ ___nced right up to the kind **lady**, **r___lled** onto her **feet**, and let ___ ___t a **hiss**. ___ ___ ___ ___ ___ ___t wanted the **lady** t___ take him **home** with her.

37. **lady's, feet, higher, arms**

eggbert bounced again, right on the **lady's feet**. Then he b___ ___ ___ ___ ___ ___ two times, even **higher**. on the next bounce, Eggbert j___mped into the nice **lady's arms**.

38. **lady, cost, hissed, rolled, lady's, arms, tag**

"oh," s___ ___d the **lady** to Eggbert. "I want to buy you. how much do you **cost**?"

Eggbert **hissed**. he **rolled** ar___ ___nd in the **lady's arms** so she c___ ___ld see his **tag**.

Note to teachers: *Put your name on the board so that students can copy it in the blanks in Caught'yas #39, #40, #41, #47, #50, #51, #52, #54, #55, #57, #60, #64, #74, and #85. Or, if you are blowing these up or typing a new copy, insert your name before running copies for your students.*

---

39. **lady, tag, going, hiss, children**

"your name is Eggb___rt," said the **lady**. "It says so right on your **tag**. "h___llo, ___ ___ ___ ___ ___ ___t. My name is _____. you are **going** to laugh, **hiss**, and play with my **children**."

Note #1 to teachers: *After this point in the student Caught'yas no sentence has a capital letter at its beginning. If your students are not yet ready to put in the capital letter on their own, simply pen it in on the student copy before you copy it for your class. In addition, prepositions will no longer be pointed out. You might want to have your students recite them as they occur.*

Note #2 to teachers: *It is important to target the use of strong, active verbs in children's writing at a very early age. Practice and awareness at age six becomes habit at age eight. From this point on, the use of strong, active verbs will be noted. "Dead" or weak verbs are the following: am, are, be, had, has, have, is, was, were, any verb ending in "ing," and the sense verbs which substitute as verbs of being (see, hear, smell, taste, feel). Strong verbs are all other verbs! It is sad, though, that most children use only the "dead" verbs in their writing. The use of strong, active verbs immediately improves any story or essay. After practice, first graders can produce some really good work using active verbs.*

---

40. **paid, took, arms, bag, knew, store**

_____ **paid** for Eggbert and **took** h___m outs___de ___n her **arms**. she d___d not put eggbert in a **bag**. she **knew** he wanted to see outs___de the **store**.

41. **car, doors, back, window**

_____ and Eggbert we___ ___ out of the toy ___ ___ore, and ___ ___ey got into a li___ ___le ye___ ___ow **car** with ___ ___een **doors**. _____ put E___ ___bert in the **back** so that he cou___ ___ see out ___ ___e big **back window**.

42. **shelf, window, explained**

"just don't roll off of the **shelf**," s___ ___d the lady to eggbert. "if you ro___ ___ off the **shelf**, you won't be able to see out the **w___ ___ ___ ___w**," she **explained**.

43. **shelf, carefully, window**

e___ ___ber___ bounced ___ ___ree (3) li___ ___le bounces to ___ay, "Yes." he bou___ ___ ___ ___ very **carefu___ ___y**. he did not wa___ ___ to fall off this **shelf**. *this* s___ ___ ___f had a **window** to the ou___ ___ide.

44. **other, cars, road, slowly**

eggbert looked and loo___ ___ ___. he saw **other cars** r___de down the **road**. some went very fast. some w___ ___ ___ very **slowly**.

45. **people, other, window**

eggbert liked the slow cars b___st. he could see **people** and dogs inside them. he d___d n___t see **other** b___lls. a big brown d___g in a big blue car p___t its head out the **window**.

46. **barked, rode, bark, back, hissed**

it **barked** at eggbert as he **rode** by.
"**bark**. b___ ___k," the dog s___ ___d.
eggbert w___ ___ted to **bark back** at the dog. he b___ ___ ___ced, and he **hissed**, but he could not b___ ___k.

47. **bark**

oh, Eggbert," s___ ___d _____, "You are a b___ ___ ___. you are not a d___ ___. ba ___ ___ s do not **b___ ___k**.

48. **name, waved, back, window, car, wave**

    eggbert saw a little girl in a big red car. her **name** was _____. the girl **waved** and laughed to see the ball in the **back wind___ ___** of a little yell___ ___ and green **car**. eggbert wanted to **wave** and l___ ___gh, too.

49. **times, waves, tried, sounded, hiss**

    he ___ounce___ up and down, u___ a___d do___ ___, ten **times**. This is how a ba___ ___ **waves** to ___ou. eggbe___ ___ **tried** to lau___ ___, but it **sounded** like a **hi___ ___**.

50. **air, hiss, flat**

    "oh, eggbert," said _____. "you will run out of **air** if you **hiss** and **h___ ___ ___**.
    eggbert *was* looking a little **flat**

51. **window, building, school**

    "here we are," said _____.
    eggbert looked out the back **window**. he saw a big r___ ___ **building**. it w___ ___ a **school**

52. **school, live, classroom, shelf**

    "___ ___is is our **s___ ___ ool**," said _____ to eggbert. "you w___ll **live** here in my **classroom**. i have a **shelf** jus___ for you

53. **doors, front, school, excited**

    the lady stopped the li___ ___le ye___ ___ow car with the green **doors**. she sto___ ___ed right in **front** of the red **school**. e___ ___bert was very **excited**

54. **excited, hissed, flat, picked, back**

    eggbert was so **excited**. he bounced, and he **hissed**. he **hi___ ___ed** so much, he was almost **flat** when _____ **picked** him up from the **back** of the car

55. flat, hissed, fix, blow, air, valve

"you made y___ ___rself **flat**," said _____. "you **hissed** t___ ___ much. i can **fix** that. i will **blow air** into y___ ___r **valve** "

56. could, flat, poor

eggbert **could** not hiss. he was too **flat**. **poor** eggbert **could** not bounce. he was too ___ ___**at**. do you go **f**___ ___ ___ when you try to talk

57. school, hall, door, a lot, desks

_____ walked into the r___d **school**. she took ___ ___ ___ ___ ___ ___t d___ ___n a long **hall**. she open___ ___ a br___ ___n **door**. eggbert s___w **a lot** of little **desks**

58. classroom, boys, girls, every, love

"this is our **classroom**," s___e said. "**boys** a___ ___ **girls** co___e here eve___ ___ day. they will p___ay w___ ___ ___ you. they w___ ___ ___ **love** you "

59. desk, papers, covered, mess, teacher's

then she walked up to a big **desk**. many **papers covered** the de___ ___. the **desk** w___ ___ a **mess**. is your **teacher's** de___ ___ a **mess**? is your **de**___ ___ a **mess**

60. messy, desk, children, classroom, things, heard, noises

_____ put eggbert on her **messy desk**. "s___ ___n," she s___ ___d, "many **children** will come into this **classr**___ ___**m**."

eggbert l___ ___ked ar___ ___nd the **classr**___ ___**m**. he saw many funny **things**. he h___ ___rd fu___ ___y **noises**

61. picture, classroom

what did eggbert see? draw a **picture** (with some words) of your **classroom** to sh___ ___ what eggbert saw. h___ ___ many wind___ ___s did ___ ___ ___ ___ ___ ___t see

62. a lot, desks, tried, flat

eggbert saw **a lot** of **desks**. how many **d**___ ___ ___**s** did eggbert see "i want to bou___ ___e on every **desk**," e___ ___bert said to hi___ ___elf he **tried** to bou___ ___e, but he could not. eggbert was too **flat**

63. lady, need, air, valve, blew

the nice **lady** saw eggbert try to b___ ___nce. "oh," she s___ ___d, "I **need** to put **air** into y___ ___ "

the lady put eggbert's **valve** up to her lips. she **blew**, and she **bl**___ ___

64. fix, blew, air, valve, rolled, tickled

"this will **fix** you," she said to eggbert as she **blew air** into his **valve**.
eggbert **rolled** in her hands. it **tickled** when _____ **blew air**
into his **valve**. he grew and gr___ ___ as she **bl**___ ___

65. papers, sorry, tickle, times

the nice lady p___cked up some **papers** fr___m h___r desk. one **p**___**p**___**r**
was right under ___ggbert.
"i'm **sorry**," she said to eggb___rt. "d___d that **tickle** you "
eggbert bounced up and ___ ___ ___ ___ three **times** to say, "Y___s "

66. talk, snake

the nice lady laughed. e___ ___bert lau___ ___ed, too, with a li___ ___le hiss.
he wa___ ___ed to say, "Tha___ ___ you," but he cou___ ___ not **talk**. he could
only hi___ ___ like a **snake**

67. left, classroom, waved, desk

then the k___ ___ ___ lady **left** the **classroom**. as she went out the
d___ ___r, she **waved** to eggbert.
"g___ ___d-bye," she s___ ___d. "don't fall off ___ ___ ___ **desk** "

68. tomorrow, door, closed, quiet, classroom

then she s___ ___d, "i will be back **tomorrow** when the sun comes up.
be a good ba___ ___ "
___ ___en the **door closed**, it was **quiet** in the **classroom**.
___ ___ ___ ___ ___ ___t was all by hims___ ___ ___

69. door, lonely, classroom, behind

he was lonely. then eggbert saw a **door** ins___de the **classroom**. ___ ___ere
d___d it go? w___ ___t was **behind** the **d**___ ___r? w___o was **beh**___ ___ ___
the **door**

70. desk, thought, tomorrow

"today was a big day for a ball who has never been out___ ___ ___ ___. i
will sleep here on the b___g **desk**," **thought** eggbert. "then i w___ll look
ar___ ___nd **tomorrow**. i can b___ ___nce and h___ss again now that i am round
and full of air ag___ ___n "

71. teacher's, next, morning, loud, bell, woke, fell, desk

and eggbert w___ ___t to sleep right there on the **teacher's desk**.
and the **next morning** a **loud bell woke** up ___ ___ ___ ___ ___ ___t. and it
was v___ ___y **loud**. and eggbert was so surpris___d, he **fell** off the **d**___ ___ ___

72. **bell, rang, rolled, teacher's, desk, still, classroom**

when the **bell rang** again, eggbert **rolled** ___nder the t___ ___ ___ ___er's **desk.** he was **still** there when _____ came into the **classroom**

73. **ready, students**

"where are you, eggbert?" she called when she d___d n___t see the b___ll. "i want to wash you. i m___st g___t you **ready** f___r my **students**   "

74. **everywhere, desks, shelves, bathroom**

_____ looked **everywhere** for ___ ___ ___bert. she looked under all the little **desks.** she looked on all the **shelves**. she looked in the **bath**___ ___ ___ ___, too

75. **classroom, teacher**

she did not s___ ___ eggbert. "where is that ball?" she said
    just then _____, _____, and _____ c___m___ into the **classroom**
    "what are you looking for?" _____ asked her **teacher**

76. **teacher, surprise**

"i am looki___ ___ for eggbert," said the **tea**___ ___**er**
"who is e___ ___bert?" a___ ___ed _____.
"eggbert is a **surprise**," said _____

77. **teacher**

"do you want me to help you look?" asked _____
"yes," said the **teacher**
"can i help, too?" asked _____ and _____ as they walked in the door
"yes, you can help, too," said the **teacher**

78. **everywhere, funny-looking, thing, teacher**

the six l___ ___ked **everywhere**. just then _____ and _____ came in the classr___ ___m d___ ___r.
"what is that **funny-looking** r___ ___nd **thing** under your desk?" _____ asked his **teacher**

79. **teacher**

"that must be eggb___ ___t," said the **teach**___ ___. "come out, eggbert   "
eggb___ ___t rolled out from und___ ___ her desk.
"oh, what a pretty ball!" said _____ and _____ togeth___ ___

80. **bell, rang, children, a lot, noise**

the **bell rang** again, and many **children** ran into the classroom. the **bell made a lot** of **noise**. _____ and _____ made **a lot** of **noise**. ___ ___ ___ ___ ___ ___t rolled under the t___ ___ ___ ___ er's desk again

81. **scared, bell, start, school, friends**

"come ___ ___t, eggbert," said the t___ ___cher. "do not be **scared**. it is only the **bell** to **start school**," she s___ ___d. "here are many new **friends**. they want to play with y___ ___ ”

82. **children, sat, quiet, meet, friend**

all the **children sat** at their desk___. they were very, very **qu___ ___t**. they wanted to meet eggbert. they wanted to **meet** th___ ___r new **fr___ ___nd**

83. **children, high**

eggbert rolled out from under the big desk of the teacher. he bounced up and down, up and d___ ___ ___ so he could see all the **children**. he b___ ___ ___ ___ ___ ___ so **high**, he went right onto the teacher___ ___ desk

84. **high, children**

there, up **high** on the big desk, eggbert could see all the **children**. all the **children** c___ ___ld see egg___ ___ ___ t, too

"it's a ball," said _____

85. **special**

"it's a very **special** ball," said _____, the teacher. this is eggbert. ___ ___ ___ ___ ___ ___t can bounce all by h___ ___ ___ ___ ___ ___ ”

86. **through, valve, noises, snake**

eggbert hissed **through** his **valve** to say, "hello ”

"oh, he can make **noises**, too," said _____

"there is a **snake** inside the ball," said _____

87. **snake, friend**

"no, there is no ___**nake** ins___ ___ ___ the ball, ” ___aid the teacher. "that i___ eggbert___ ___ way to ___ay, 'Hello.' he want___ to be your **friend** ”

88. **patted**

eggbert boun___ ___ ___ off the teacher___ ___ desk. he rol___ ___ ___ and boun___ ___ ___ all around the classroom. he b___ ___ ___ ___ ___ ___ by _____ and by _____. they **patted** him

89. **kiss, tickled, sneezed, through, valve, sounded, kitten**

_____ gave eggbert a **kiss**. it **tickl**___ ___. he **sneez**___ ___ **through** his **valve**. it **sound**___ ___ like the **sneeze** of a little **kitten**

90. **boys, a lot, threw**

everyone lau___ ___ ___ ___. _____ and _____, two **boys** who l___ k___d to play **a lot**, pick___ ___ up eggbert and **threw** him around the classroom. eggbert l___k___d that. it was f___ ___

91. **hit, wall, hard**

the boys threw eggbert faster and f___ ___ ___ ___ ___. eggbe___ ___ liked to fly around the room, but he did not like it when he **hit** the **wall hard**. it hu___ ___

92. **ouch, hit, wall, hard, sorry**

"**ouch**," he ___issed w___en ___e ___**it** t___e **wall** ___**ard**
"**sorry**," _____ and _____ said. "we will not do t___at again "

93. **mad, boys, wall, hard, threw, hit, slowly**

eggbert was not **mad** at the **boys**. but, he did not l___ ___ ___ to hit the **wall hard** because it h___ ___ ___. after that, the **boys threw** eggbert more **slowly**. he did not **hit** the **wall** ag___ ___ ___

94. **kiss**

the rest of the day was fun. ___ ___ ___bert rolled a___ ___ ___ ___ ___ the class___ ___ ___ ___. he bounced up to give _____ a ball **kiss**. (What is a ball **kiss** like?)

95. **lap, surprised**

then he b___ ___nced into _____'s **lap**.
"oh," she said, **surprised**. are you g___ ___ng to help me with my work "
eggbert rolled ar___ ___nd in her arms

96. **working, hard**

eggbert bounced d___ ___ ___ and rolled up to _____ desk. he was **working hard**. he did not see eggbert.
___ ___ ___ ___ ___ ___t hissed a "Hello." he then rolled to the next desk

97. **need, bath, dirty, bathroom**

_____ pi___ ___ed up eggbert. "you **need** a **bath**," she told him. "you are a very **dirty** ball. i will ca___ ___y you into the **ba**___ ___**room** and wa___ ___ you "

98. idea, a lot, took, bathroom

"___hat a good **idea**," said the teacher. "i ___anted to ___ash eggbert today, too. he rolled around **a lot** "

_____ and _____ **took** eggbert into the **bathroom**

99. sink, smelly, soap, getting

they washed ___ ___ ___ ___ ___ ___t in the **sink** with some **smelly soap**. it was gr___ ___n **soap**. eggbert did not like the gr___ ___ n **soap**, but he did like **getting** cl___ ___n

100. funny-looking, thing, next, sink, square, tank, water

eggbert saw a **funny-looking thing next** to the **sink**. what was it? it ___ ___ ___ round with a **square tank** at the back. there ___ ___ ___ **water** in it. what ___ ___ ___ it

101. time, watched

eggbert did not have **time** to look. soon he was clean. _____ and _____ put him on the teacher's desk. from the big d___ ___ ___, eggbert **watched** the class work and play, ___ ___ ___ ___ and ___ ___ ___ ___

102. walls, hit

when the class went outside, eggbert w___ ___ ___ out, too. _____, _____, _____, and _____ played with eggbert. they pl___ ___ ___ ___ ball with eggbert. outside, there were no **walls** for eggbert to **hit**

103. happy, bell, rang, end, surprised

wh___ ___ the class went in___ ___ ___ ___, eggbert w___ ___t in, too. eggbert was **happy**. wh___ ___ the **bell** r___ ___g at the **end** of the day, eggbert was **surprised**

104. children, left, waved, good-bye, wave

all the **ch___ldren left** the cl___ssr___ ___m. th___y **waved good-bye** to eggbert. eggbert g___ve the **children** a ball **wave**. (H___w does s a ball **wave** to you)

105. times, wave, waves

eggbert ___ounced up and down, u___ and ___own ___en (10) **times**. this is ___ow a ___all **waves**. (How do you **wave**? can you show egg___ert how you wave)

106. children, home, good-bye, blew, air

      after the **children** went **home** for the day, e___ ___ ___ert and the teacher said, "**Good-bye**." the tea___ ___er said, "**Good-bye**," and eggbert hi___ ___ed. before she went **home**, the tea___ ___er **blew** more **air** into e___ ___ ___ert

107. special, children, love, tomorrow

      "you're a **special** ball," she said. "my **children love** you. be a good ball. g___ to sl___ ___p on my desk, and w___ will be back **tomorrow** "

108. night, lonely

      that **night**, eggbert was **lonely** again. he could not sleep. he rolled around the classroom. he bounced onto _____ desk

109. messy, bathroom, dark

      the teacher___ ___ desk was **messy**. eggbert rolled into the **bathroom**. it was **dark** inside. the li___ ___ ___ was off

110. toilet, wet

      eggbert bounced up and ___ ___, higher and ___ ___ ___ ___ ___ ___. he ___ ___ ___ ___ ___ ___ ___ right into the **toilet**! it was **wet** and cold

111. toilet, water, slept, night

      eggbert could not bounce out of the **toilet**. he could not ___ ___ ___ ___ ___ ___ out of **water**. he **slept** in the **toilet** all **night**. it was wet and c___ ___ ___

112. school, early, door

      the next morning the teacher and _____, _____, and _____ came to **school early**. they open___ ___ the **door** of the classroom. they look___ ___ and look___ ___, but they did not see eggbert

113. shelves, cubbies

      where was he? _____ looked in all the **shelves** and **cubbies**. _____ looked under all the desks. the teacher ___ ___ ___ ___ ___ ___ up high

114. heard, splash, bathroom, children

      it was not funny. where was eggbert? then _____ **heard** a **splash** in the **bathroom**. all four **children** ran into the **bath**___ ___ ___ ___

115. toilet, sink, smelly, soap

there was eggbert in the **toilet**.
"this is no place for a ball," said _____. she picked
___ ___ ___ ___ ___ ___t up from the t___ ___ ___ ___t and washed him
in the **sink** with the **smelly** green **soap**
"ewww," said _____

116. rest, happy, kiss, boy, girl

the **rest** of the ___ ___ildren came into the class___ ___ ___ ___. eggbert
was **happy** again. he bounced up to give a ball **kiss** to every **boy** and **girl**.
all day he ___ ___ ___ ___ ___ ___ ___ and r___ ___ ___ ___ ___ around the
___ ___ ___ ___ ___room

117. bell, rang, end, good-bye, idea

when the **bell rang** at the **end** of the d___ ___, eggbert did not want to say
"**Good-bye**." the children did not want to say "G___ ___ ___-___ ___ ___ "
"i have an **idea**," s___ ___ ___ the kind teacher

118. idea, lonely, night

___ ___at was the teacher's **idea**? would eggbert be **lonely** again? ___ ___ere
could ___ ___ ___ ___ ___ ___t sleep every **night**

119. home, tonight, tomorrow, next

"i know what to do," said _____. eggbert can come **home** with me
tonight. he can go h___ ___ ___ with _____ **tomorrow night**. who will
t___ ___ ___ eggbert **home** the **next** n___ ___ ___ ___

120. idea, night, home, boy, girl, happy

That was the teacher's **idea**, too. every day eggbert b___ ___ ___ ___ ed,
r___ ___ ___ ed, read, w___ ___ ___ed, and pl___ ___ed at **school**. every **night** he
went **home** with a **boy** or **girl**. ___ ___ ___ ___ ___ ___t was a very **happy**
___ ___ ___ ___

The End

**Now make up your own story about Eggbert and your class. Where will Eggbert be
found next? Where will he bounce?**

4

Teacher *Caught'ya* Sentences for First-grade Story

On the following pages you will find a key for the first-grade story about Eggbert. There are far more skills included in each *Caught'ya* than the average first grader would be able to tackle. Teach only the skills that are developmentally appropriate for your class.

Change the explanations on the left of the *Caught'ya* to words your students can understand and learn. Only *you* know your students and their abilities. Most first-grade students are not yet ready to edit; others are.

One final note about the answers to the student *Caught'ya*s that follow: the underlined parts of words or words were left blank in the children's version.

1. **sat, inside, outside**

   Paragraph – beginning of story
   Capitalization – sentences begin with a capital letter; capitalize proper nouns
   Punctuation – sentences always have end punctuation
   Vowels – short "a"
   Verb tense – "sat" is past tense of irregular verb "to sit"; "was" is past tense of irregular verb "to be"

   > Eggbert **sat** and s<u>a</u>t. It was dark **inside**. It w<u>a</u>s black **outside**.

2. **outside, high**

   No paragraph – continuation of story
   Capitalization – sentences begin with a capital letter
   Punctuation – sentences always have end punctuation
   Commas – need a comma to separate repeated information
   Vowels – short "a"
   Consonants – initial "b" sound
   Verb tense – add "ed" to most verbs to put in past tense; "went" is past tense of irregular verb "to go"; "came" is past tense of irregular verb "to come"

   > The <u>b</u>lack **outside** went away. The sun came up. It looked like a big ball, a <u>b</u>ig yellow <u>b</u>all **high** in the sky.

3. **bright**

   No paragraph – same subject
   Capitalization – sentences begin with a capital letter; capitalize proper nouns
   Punctuation – sentences always have end punctuation
   Vowels – short "u"
   Consonants – "s" sound
   Verb tense – add "ed" to most verbs to put them in the past tense; "was" is past tense of irregular verb "to be"

   > The <u>s</u>un wa<u>s</u> **bright** and pretty. The <u>s</u>un was big and yellow. Eggbert looked around.

4. **outside, window, boys, girls**

No paragraph – same subject
Capitalization – sentences begin with a capital letter; capitalize proper nouns
Punctuation – sentences always have end punctuation
Vowels – "oo" digraph; short "a"
Plural rules – make most nouns plural by adding "s"
Verb tense – add "ed" to most verbs to put in past tense; "saw" is past of irregular verb
    "to see"

       Eggbert looked **outside** the **window.** He l<u>oo</u>ked and l<u>oo</u>ked. Eggbert saw **boys** and **girls** run by.

5. **people**

> **NOTE:** *You need to insert the names of three students.*

No paragraph – same subject
Capitalization – sentences begin with a capital letter; capitalize proper nouns
Punctuation – sentences always have end punctuation
Commas – needed between 2 adjectives where 2nd adj. is not age, size, or color
Vowels – short "e"; short "a"
Verb tense – "went" is past tense of irregular verb "to go"; "saw" is past tense of irregular
    verb "to see"
Skills – name recognition

       Big, tall **people** went by. Short, f<u>a</u>t **people** w<u>e</u>nt by. **(Put student name here)** and **(put student name here)**, and **(put student name here)** r<u>a</u>n by. No one s<u>aw</u> Eggbert.

6. **stopped, window, boys, girls**

No paragraph – same subject
Capitalization – sentences begin with a capital letter; capitalize proper nouns
Punctuation – sentences always have end punctuation
Vowels – "oo" digraph; short "a"
Plural rules – add "s" to most nouns
Verb tense – add "ed" to most verbs to put in past tense; "saw" is past tense of irregular
    verb "to see"
Spelling rule – note the double "p" in "stopped" (consonant/vowel/consonant + suffix =
    consonant must be doubled)
Concept – repeating words

       No one **stopped** to look in the **window.** Eggbert looked and l<u>oo</u>ked. He saw **boys** and **girls.** He s<u>aw</u> dogs and c<u>a</u>ts.

7. **boy, girl, whiskers**

No paragraph – same subject
Capitalization – sentences begin with a capital letter; capitalize proper nouns
Punctuation – sentences always have end punctuation
Vowels – short "a"; "oo" digraph in middle of word
Plural rules – add "s" to most nouns
Verb tense – add "ed" to most verbs to put in past tense; "ran" is past tense of irregular verb "to run"
Literary device – point out alliteration of "white whiskers"

> A **boy** ran by. A **girl** ran by. A big dog ran by. A black and white cat with long white **whiskers** looked at Eggbert.

8. **meow, outside, inside**

No paragraph – same subject
Capitalization – sentences begin with a capital letter; capitalize proper nouns
Punctuation – sentences always have end punctuation; quotation marks around what is said out loud
Commas – quote
Vowels – short "a"; "ou" blend
Verb tense – "said" is past tense of irregular verb "to say"; "was" is past tense of irregular verb "to be"
Literary device – Onomatopoeia (a word that imitates a sound.)

> It said, "**Meow.**" The cat was **outside.** Eggbert was not outside. He was **inside.**

9. **wanted, roll, bounce, boys, girls, feel**

Paragraph – new idea
Capitalization – sentences begin with a capital letter; capitalize proper nouns
Punctuation – sentences always have end punctuation
Vowels – short "e"
Plural rules – add "s" to most nouns
Verb tense – add "ed" to most verbs to put in past tense

> Eggbert **wanted** to **roll** and **bounce** with the **boys** and **girls**. He **wanted** to go with them. He wanted to **feel** the sun.

10. **roll, bounce, outside**

Paragraph – person speaking
Capitalization – sentences begin with a capital letter; capitalize proper nouns; always capitalize "I"
Punctuation – sentences always have end punctuation; note use of quotation marks around what is said out loud
Vowels – short "e" in "em"; short "a" in "an"
Verb tense – change to present tense in quote; "said" is past tense of irregular verb "to say"

> "I want to be with them," Eggbert said. "I want to **roll** and **bounce** with them. I want to see the **outside.**"

11. **sighed, door, store**

    Paragraph – new person speaking (narrator)
    Capitalization – sentences begin with a capital letter; capitalize proper nouns
    Punctuation – sentences always have end punctuation
    Vowels – long "i" in "igh"; long "a" with silent "e"
    Verb tense – add "ed" to most verbs to put in past tense
    Literary device – rhyme

> Eggbert **sighed.** He s<u>igh</u><u>e</u>d and **s<u>igh</u><u>e</u>d.** Then a tall man c<u>a</u>me to the **door** of the **store.**

12. **opened, door, toy store, window**

    No paragraph – same subject, referring to same person
    Capitalization – sentences begin with a capital letter
    Punctuation – sentences always have end punctuation
    Vowels – short "a" in "all"; short "o"; short "i"; long "a"
    Verb tense – add "ed" to most verbs to put in past tense; "came" is past tense of irregular verb "to come"
    Literary device – rhyme

> The t<u>a</u>ll man **opened** the **door.** He c<u>a</u>me in the **toy store.**
> He did n<u>o</u>t see Eggbert in the b<u>i</u>g **window.**

13. **back, store, bounced, times, himself**

    No paragraph – same subject, same speaker
    Capitalization – sentences begin with a capital letter; capitalize proper nouns
    Punctuation – sentences always have end punctuation
    Commas – need a comma to separate repeated information
    Vowels – "ow" sound in "down"; short "u"; double long "e"; short "a," "e," and "o"; long "e" when vowel is repeated; "ou" digraph
    Plural rules – add "s" to most nouns (times)
    Verb tense – add "ed" to most verbs to put in past tense
    Skills – reflexive pronouns (himself)

> The man w<u>e</u>nt to the **back** of the **store.** Eggbert saw him look around. Eggbert **bounced** up and down, <u>u</u>p and down, up and d<u>ow</u>n thr<u>ee</u> (3) times. The m<u>a</u>n did n<u>o</u>t s<u>ee</u> Eggbert bounce by **himself.**

14. **sighed, wanted**

    No paragraph – same subject, same speaker
    Capitalization – sentences begin with a capital letter; capitalize proper nouns
    Punctuation – sentences always have end punctuation
    Vowels – short "a" and "i"; long "i"
    Verb tense – add "ed" to most verbs to put in past tense
    Skills – learning how to spell name

> Eggbert **sighed** and **s<u>igh</u>ed.** He **wanted** the man to see him. The man did not see him. The man d<u>i</u>d not see Eggbert.

15. hear, toy store

No paragraph – same subject, referring to same person
Capitalization – sentences begin with a capital letter; capitalize proper nouns
Punctuation – sentences always have end punctuation
Vowels – "or" sound; review of short vowel sounds
Verb tense – add "ed" to most verbs to put in past tense; "was" is past tense of the irregular verb "to be"
Prepositions – You might want to find a list of prepositions (in the **Appendix** of this book) and begin to have your students memorize them. This is a useful tool. ("in" in this *Caught'ya*)

> The man did n<u>o</u>t **hear** Eggbert. The man w<u>o</u>rked in the **toy store.** He liked to w<u>o</u>rk in the **toy st<u>or</u>e.** It was f<u>u</u>n.

16. sat, window, dark, outside, night

Paragraph – change of topic and person
Capitalization – sentences begin with a capital letter
Punctuation – sentences always have end punctuation
Vowels – review of short vowel sounds
Verb tense – add "ed" to most verbs to put in past tense; "sat" is past tense of irregular verb "to sit"; "got" is past tense of irregular verb "to get"
Prepositions – review and learn (outside, in)

> Eggbert **sat** in the **window** all day. Then it g<u>o</u>t **dark outside.** Eggbert s<u>a</u>t in the w<u>i</u>ndow all **night.**

17. heard, hear, sigh

No paragraph – same subject, same speaker
Capitalization – sentences begin with a capital letter; capitalize proper nouns
Punctuation – sentences always have end punctuation; note question needs end punctuation of question mark
Vowels – "oo" digraph; short vowel review
Verb tense – add "ed" to most verbs to put in past tense
Spelling rule – "no one" is 2 words
Skills – name recognition; homophone "hear/here"

> No one saw Eggbert. No one **heard** Eggbert. Only a black and white cat look<u>e</u>d at Eggb<u>e</u>rt. Can you **hear** a b<u>all</u> **sigh**?

18. lonely, night, bounced, window, store

Paragraph – change of topic
Capitalization – sentences begin with a capital letter; capitalize proper nouns
Punctuation – sentences always have end punctuation
Vowels – short "a"; long "o" when followed by consonant/silent "e"
Verb tense – add "ed" to most verbs to put in past tense; "was" is past tense of irregular verb "to be"
Prepositions – review and continue to learn (out, of, into)

> Eggbert w<u>a</u>s very sad. Eggbert w<u>a</u>s very **lonely.** One **night** he **bounced** out of the window into the **store.**

19. **bounce, roll, night, boys, girls**

Paragraph – new speaker
Capitalization – sentences begin with a capital letter; capitalize proper nouns; always capitalize "I"
Punctuation – sentences always have end punctuation; note use of quotation marks around what is said out loud
Commas – quote
Vowels – final "e" in two-letter word = long "e"; double "e" = long "e"
Plural rules – add "s" to most nouns
Verb tense – future tense with "will"; "said" is past tense of irregular verb "to say"

> "I will **bounce** and **roll**," Eggbert said one **night**. "The man will see m<u>e</u>. **Boys** and **girls** will s<u>ee</u> me."

20. **found, floor, back, window, talk**

Paragraph – different topic; refers to different person
Capitalization – sentences begin with a capital letter; capitalize proper nouns
Punctuation – sentences always have end punctuation
Vowels – long "a" if followed by "y"; review of short vowels
Consonants – "lk" sound
Verb tense – add "ed" to most verbs to put in past tense
Skills – name recognition

> One d<u>a</u>y the m<u>a</u>n **found** Eggbert on the **floor**. He p<u>u</u>t Eggbert **back** in the **window**. He d<u>i</u>d n<u>o</u>t **talk** to Egg___ ___ ___ ___.

21. **found, high, shelf, back, window**

No paragraph – same topic; same person
Capitalization – sentences begin with a capital letter; capitalize proper nouns
Punctuation – sentences always have end punctuation
Vowels – short "a"; short "u"
Verb tense – "found" is past tense of irregular verb "to find"; "put" is past tense of irregular verb "to put"
Prepositions – review and continue to learn (up, on, in)
Skills – name recognition

> One day the man **found** Eggbert **high** <u>u</u>p on a **shelf**. He p<u>u</u>t Eggbert **back** in the **window.**

22. **every, found, window, strange**

Paragraph – change of time
Capitalization – sentences begin with a capital letter; capitalize proper nouns
Punctuation – sentences always have end punctuation; use of exclamation mark for emphasis; question mark needed at end of question
Vowels – short vowel review; long vowel with silent "e" at end of word
Verb tense – "found" is past tense of irregular verb "to find"; "came" is past tense of irregular verb "to come"; use of "would" as conditional
Literary device – deliberate use of fragment ("What a strange ball!)

Every day the man **found** Eggbert out of the **window**. What a **strange** ball! Where would the b<u>all</u> be **every** day wh<u>e</u>n the m<u>a</u>n c<u>a</u>me to w<u>or</u>k?

23. back, window, night, bounced

No paragraph – same topic
Capitalization – sentences begin with a capital letter; capitalize proper nouns
Punctuation – sentences always have end punctuation
Vowels – "ow" sound and how it varies
Verb tense – add "ed" to most verbs to put in past tense; "put" is past tense of irregular verb "to put"
Prepositions – review and continue to learn (out, of, in)
Skills – word recognition

> Every day the man put Eggbert **back** in the **window**. Ev<u>ery</u> **night** Eggbert **bounced** out of the **w<u>in</u>dow.**

24. special, bounced, times

2 Paragraphs – new person speaking; topic change
Capitalization – sentences begin with a capital letter; capitalize proper nouns
Punctuation – sentences always have end punctuation; note use of quotation marks around what is said aloud
Commas – quote
Vowels – other "ow" sound; double "e" as long "e"
Verb tense – switch to present tense in quote; "said" is past tense of irregular verb "to say"; add "ed" to most verbs to put in past tense
Prepositions – review and continue to learn (out, of, into)

> "This ball is **special**," the man said.
> Eggbert **bounced** up and down, up and d<u>own</u>, up and d<u>own</u> thr<u>ee</u> (3) **times** to say, "Yes."

25. bounce, nice, himself

No paragraph – same subject
Capitalization – sentences begin with a capital letter; capitalize proper nouns
Punctuation – sentences always have end punctuation; note question mark at end of question
Vowels – review short vowel sounds
Verb tense – add "ed" to most verbs to put in past tense; "was" is past tense of irregular verb "to be"
Prepositions – review and continue to learn (by)
Literary device – note deliberate use of fragment in narrator aside)"No"
Skills – name recognition

> Did the **nice** m<u>a</u>n see Eggbert **bounce** by **himself**? No. Eggbert w<u>a</u>s s<u>a</u>d.

26. **nice lady, store, a lot, teacher**

Paragraph – change of topic
Capitalization – sentences begin with a capital letter; capitalize proper nouns
Punctuation – sentences always have end punctuation; need question mark after question
Vowels – silent "e" at end of word renders vowels long
Verb tense – "came" is past tense of irregular verb "to come"; add "ed" to most verbs to
    put in past tense; "was" is past tense of irregular verb "to be"

> One day a **nice lady** came in the **store**. She looked **a lot** like your **teacher.**
> Who was she? What did she want**?**

27. **lady, nice, kind, excited**

No paragraph – same topic; same speaker
Capitalization – sentences begin with a capital letter; capitalize proper nouns
Punctuation – sentences always have end punctuation
Vowels – short "a"; long "i" when followed by consonant/silent "e"
Verb tense – add "ed" to most verbs to put in past tense; "was" is past tense of irregular
    verb "to be"
Skills – word recognition

> This **lady** looked **nice**. She looked **kind**. Eggbert was **excited**.

28. **lady, toy store, back, front**

No paragraph – same topic; same speaker
Capitalization – sentences begin with a capital letter; capitalize proper nouns
Punctuation – sentences always have end punctuation
Vowels – "oo" digraph; "ou" blend
Verb tense – add "ed" to most verbs to put in past tense
Prepositions – review and continue to learn (around, in, of)
Skills – word practice

> The **lady** looked around the **toy store.** She looked in the **back** of the **store.** She
> looked in the **front** of the store.

29. **sighed, bounced**

Paragraph – new speaker
Capitalization – sentences begin with a capital letter; capitalize proper nouns
Punctuation – sentences always have end punctuation; note use of quotes around what is
    said out loud
Commas – quote
Vowels – long "i" with "gh"; "ow" sound; review long vowel rules
Verb tense – add "ed" to most verbs to put in past tense; switch to present tense for quote
Prepositions – review and continue to learn (up, down, with)

> Eggbert **sighed** and sighed. He **bounced** up and down. "Please see me.
> Please see me," he wanted to say. "Please take me with you. Please take me
> with you."

30. **lady, heard, sigh, through, valve**

    Paragraph – change of topic
    Capitalization – sentences begin with a capital letter; capitalize proper nouns
    Punctuation – sentences always have end punctuation
    Vowels – "ow" sound; "ou" digraph"; "ea" digraph;
    Verb tense – "saw" is past tense of irregular verb "to see"; "heard" is past tense of irregular verb "to hear"
    Prepositions – review and continue to learn (up, down, through)
    Verbs – introduce sense verbs
    Skills – name recognition

    > The **lady** saw Eggbert. She saw him bounce up and down. She **heard** him **sigh through** his **valve.**

31. **lady, buy, special, classroom, children**

    Paragraph – new speaker
    Capitalization – sentences begin with a capital letter; capitalize proper nouns; always capitalize "I"
    Punctuation – sentences always have end punctuation; note use of quotes around what is said out loud; note use of exclamation mark for emphasis
    Commas – quote
    Vowels – "ai" and "ei" digraphs; "ou" digraph
    Verb tense – add "ed" to most verbs to put in past tense; "was" is past tense of irregular verb "to be"; switch to present tense for quote
    Prepositions – review and continue to learn (up, down, with)
    Skills – name recognition; learn homophone "their" as possessive pronoun

    > The **lady** said to the man in the store, "I want to **buy** this ball. This ball is **special.** To Eggbert she said, "How my **children** at **(put your school name here)** would like to have you in their **classroom!**"

32. **rolled, left, right, joy**

Paragraph – change of topic
Capitalization – sentences begin with a capital letter; capitalize proper nouns
Punctuation – sentences always have end punctuation
Vowels – "ow" sound
Consonants – "ll" sound in "roll" and "full"
Verb tense – add "ed" to most verbs to put in past tense; "was" is past tense of irregular
    verb "to be"
Prepositions – review and continue to learn (to, of)
Concept – go over "left" and "right"

        Eggbert **rolled** up and d<u>ow</u>n. He **rolled** to the **left** and then to the **right.** He
was happy. He was fu<u>ll</u> of **joy.**

33. **someone, noticed, talked, could, talk, back**

No paragraph – same topic; same speaker
Capitalization – sentences begin with a capital letter; capitalize proper nouns
Punctuation – sentences always have end punctuation; need for question mark after
    question
Vowels – short "a" and "i"
Consonants – "lk" sound; double consonants; "w"; "sh" blend
Verb tense – add "ed" to most verbs to put in past tense; "was" is past tense of irregular
    verb "to be"; switch to present tense for quote; "could" as conditional ("maybe")
    tense needed after "if"

        Why was Eggbert ha<u>pp</u>y? **Someone noticed** him. **Someone talked** to h<u>i</u>m.
Eggbert wi<u>sh</u>ed he **could talk back.**

34. **sighed, air, through, valve, hiss, snake, lady, excited**

> **NOTE:** *Since this Caught'ya has so many vocabulary words (although many are repeats), you may want to use this as a vocabulary lesson.*

Paragraph – change of idea
Capitalization – sentences begin with a capital letter; capitalize proper nouns
Punctuation – sentences always have end punctuation
Commas – comma in a compound sentence (see **Appendix**)
Vowels – review of short vowels and long vowels
Consonants – "th" blend
Verb tense – add "ed" to most verbs to put in past tense; "was" is past tense of irregular
    verb "to be"; "heard" is past tense of irregular verb "to hear"
Prepositions – review and continue to learn (up, down, with)
Literary device – simile

        Eggbert **si<u>gh</u>ed**. He let **air** come **through** h<u>i</u>s **valve** wi<u>th</u> a **hiss** l<u>i</u>ke a **snake.**
The **lady** heard him, and she was very **excited.**

35. **talk, cried, hiss, snake, roll, else**

Paragraph – new person speaking
Capitalization – sentences begin with a capital letter; capitalize proper nouns
Punctuation – sentences always have end punctuation; note use of quotes around what is
    said out loud; question needs question mark at end (note placement in quotation)
Commas – after interjection ("Oh"); compound sentence
Vowels – "ou" digraph; "ou" blend; "o" at end of word as "ooooo" sound
Consonants – "lk"; double consonant sounds
Verb tense – add "ed" to most verbs to put in past tense; "was" is past tense of irregular
    verb "to be"; switch to present tense for quote
Prepositions – review and continue to learn (with, by)
Skills – reflexive pronouns (myself, yourself, etc.)

"Oh, you **talk**," she **cried** out with joy. "You **hiss** like a **snake**, and you bounce and **roll** all by yourself. What **else** can you do?" she asked Eggbert.

36. **times, lady, rolled, hiss, feet, home**

Paragraph – narrator speaking
Capitalization – sentences begin with a capital letter; capitalize proper nouns
Punctuation – sentences always have end punctuation
Commas – verb series
Vowels – "ou" blend; "o" at end of word as "ooooo" sound
Consonants – double "l" sound
Verb tense – add "ed" to most verbs to put in past tense
Prepositions – review and continue to learn (up, out, with)
Skills – name recognition

Eggbert bounced five **times**. He bounced right up to the kind **lady**, **rolled** onto her **feet**, and let out a **hiss**. Eggbert wanted the **lady** to take him **home** with her.

37. **lady's, feet, higher, arms**

No paragraph – same topic; same speaker
Capitalization – sentences begin with a capital letter; capitalize proper nouns
Punctuation – sentences always have end punctuation
Commas – extra information
Vowels – "ou" blend; short "u"
Verb tense – add "ed" to most verbs to put in past tense
Skills – possessive of singular noun; introduce parts of the body

Eggbert bounced again, right on the **lady's feet**. Then he bounced two times, even **higher**. On the next bounce, Eggbert jumped into the nice **lady's arms.**

38. **lady, cost, hissed, rolled, lady's, arms, tag**

2 Paragraphs – new speaker; change to narrator
Capitalization – sentences begin with a capital letter; capitalize proper nouns; always capitalize "I"
Punctuation – sentences always have end punctuation; note use of quotes around what is said out loud; question mark needed at end of question
Commas – quote
Vowels – "ai," digraph; "ou" blend; "ou" digraph
Verb tense – "said" is past tense of irregular verb "to say"; add "ed" to most verbs to put in past tense; switch to present tense for quote

"Oh, "said the **lady** to Eggbert. "I want to buy you. How much do you · **cost?**"

Eggbert **hissed**. He **rolled** around in the **lady's arms** so she could see his **tag.**

39. **lady, tag, going, hiss, children**

Paragraph – new speaker
Capitalization – sentences begin with a capital letter; capitalize proper nouns
Punctuation – sentences always have end punctuation; note use of quotes around what is said out loud
Commas – quote; series of verbs
Vowels – long "i" with "gh"; short "e" review
Verb tense – switch to present tense for quote
Abbreviation – name
Skills – name recognition

"Your name is Eggbert," said the **lady**. "It says so right on your **tag**. "Hello, Eggbert. My name is **(put your name here)**. You are **going** to laugh, **hiss**, and play with my **children."**

NOTE #1: *After this point in the student Caught'yas no sentence has a capital letter at its beginning. If your students are not yet ready to put in the capital letter on their own, simply pen it in on the student copy before you copy it for your class. In addition, prepositions no longer will be pointed out. You might want to have your students recite them as they occur.*

NOTE #2: *It is important to target the use of strong, active verbs in children's writing at a very early age. Practice and awareness at age six becomes habit at age eight. From this point on, the use of strong, active verbs will be noted. "Dead" or weak verbs are the following: am, are, be, had, has, have, is, was, were, any verb ending in "ing," and the sense verbs which substitute as verbs of being (see, hear, smell, taste, feel). Strong verbs are all other verbs! Sadly, though, most children use only the "dead" verbs in their writing. The use of strong, active verbs immediately improves any story or essay. After practice, first graders can produce some really good work using active verbs.*

40. paid, took, arms, bag, knew, store

Paragraph – change of place
Capitalization – sentences begin with a capital letter; capitalize proper nouns
Punctuation – sentences always have end punctuation
Vowels – long and short vowel review
Verb tense – add "ed" to most verbs to put in past tense; "was" is past tense of irregular
  verb "to be"
Prepositions – review and continue to learn (for, outside, in)
Abbreviations – name
Skills – name recognition

> **(Put your name here) paid** for Eggbert and **took** him outside in her **arms**.
> She did not put Eggbert in a **bag**. She **knew** he wanted to see outside the **store.**

41. car, doors, back, window

No paragraph – same topic
Capitalization – sentences begin with a capital letter; capitalize proper nouns
Punctuation – sentences always have end punctuation
Commas – compound sentence (see **Appendix**)
Vowels – short and long vowel review
Consonants – go over consonant blends ("nt," "st," "th," "gr," "ld"); review double
  consonants
Verb tense – "went" is past tense for irregular verb "to go"; "got" is past tense for irregular
  verb "to get"
Abbreviation – name
Coordinating conjunctions – It is good to have your students memorize the coordinating
  conjunctions: for, and, nor, but, or, yet, so. Once these are memorized, students can
  learn not to capitalize them in a title, not to begin a sentence with one and to put a
  comma before one if there is a complete sentence on either side (a compound
  sentence)
Skills – name recognition; color recognition; strong verb use

> **(Put your name here)** and Eggbert went out of the toy store, and they got
> into a little yellow **car** with green **doors. (Put your name here)** put Eggbert in
> the **back** so that he could see out the big **back window.**

42. shelf, window, explained

Paragraph – new speaker
Capitalization – sentences begin with a capital letter; capitalize proper nouns
Punctuation – sentences always have end punctuation; note use of quotes around what is
  said out loud
Commas – quote; long introductory adverb (subordinate clause)
Vowels – "ai" digraph; "ow" sound as long "o"
Consonants – double consonant sounds like "ll"
Verb tense – switch to present tense for quote; add "ed" to most verbs to put in past tense
Skills – word recognition

> "Just don't roll off of the **shelf**," said the lady to Eggbert. "If you roll off the
> **shelf**, you won't be able to see out the **window**," she **explained.**

43. **shelf, carefully, window**

Paragraph – new speaker (narrator)
Capitalization – sentences begin with a capital letter; capitalize proper nouns
Punctuation – sentences always have end punctuation; note use of quotes around what is
    said out loud
Commas – quote
Consonants – review; plosive "t" sound; consonant blends; double consonants
Verb tense – add "ed" to most verbs to put in past tense; "had" is past tense of irregular
    verb "to have"
Skills – strong verb
Literary device – use of italics for emphasis

> Eggbert bounced three little bounces to say, "Yes." He bounced very
> **carefully**. He did not want to fall off this **shelf**. *This* **shelf** had a **window** to
> the outside.

44. **other, cars, road, slowly**

Paragraph – new topic
Capitalization – sentences begin with a capital letter; capitalize proper nouns
Punctuation – sentences always have end punctuation
Vowels – diphthong "oo"; long "i" with silent "e"; short "e"
Consonants – practice "k," "d," and "nt"
Verb tense – add "ed" to most verbs to put in past tense; "went" is past tense of irregular
    verb "to go"
Skills – word recognition; strong verb use; putting "ed" to make past tense

> Eggbert looked and looked. He saw **other cars** ride down the **road**. Some
> went very fast. Some went very **slowly.**

45. **people, other, window**

No paragraph – same topic
Capitalization – sentences begin with a capital letter; capitalize proper nouns
Punctuation – sentences always have end punctuation
Vowels – short vowel review
Consonants – initial "b," "c," "d," and "p" sounds
Verb tense – add "ed" to most verbs to put in past tense;
Skills – strong verb use

> Eggbert liked the slow cars best. He could see **people** and dogs inside them. He
> did not see **other** balls. A big brown dog in a big blue car put its head out the
> **window.**

46. **barked, rode, bark, back, hissed**

No paragraph – same topic; 2 Paragraphs – new persons speaking
Capitalization – sentences begin with a capital letter; capitalize proper nouns
Punctuation – sentences always have end punctuation; use of quotes around what is said
    out loud
Commas – quote; compound sentence; compound sentence
Consonants – initial "b" and "c" and "d" sounds
Verb tense – add "ed" to most verbs to put in past tense; "rode" is past tense of irregular
    verb "to ride"; "said" is past tense of irregular verb "to say"
Skills – word practice; strong verb use
Literary device – Onomatopoeia (a word that imitates a sound)

> It **barked** at Eggbert as he **rode** by.
> "**Bark. Bark**," the dog s<u>ai</u>d.
> Eggbert w<u>an</u>ted to **bark back** at the dog. He b<u>ou</u>nced, and he **hissed**, but he could not **ba<u>rk</u>.**

47. **bark**

Paragraph – new person speaking
Capitalization – sentences begin with a capital letter; capitalize proper nouns
Punctuation – sentences always have end punctuation; use of quotes around what is said
    out loud
Commas – quote
Vowels – "ai" digraph; short vowel review
Consonants – initial "b" and "d" sounds; double consonants
Verb tense – use of present tense for quote; add "ed" to most verbs to put in past tense;
    "said" is past tense of irregular verb "to say"
Skills – word practice; name recognition; making a noun plural by adding "s"

> Oh, Eggbert," s<u>ai</u>d **(put your name here)** "You are a b<u>all</u>. You are not a d<u>og</u>. Ba<u>ll</u>s do not **bark.**

48. **name, waved, back, window, car, wave**

Paragraph – new person speaking (narrator)
Capitalization – sentences begin with a capital letter; capitalize proper nouns
Punctuation – sentences always have end punctuation
Commas – always put commas around "too" if the meaning is "also"
Vowels – "ow" sound; "au" digraph
Consonants – initial "b" and "c" and "g" sounds
Verb tense – add "ed" to most verbs to put in past tense; "was" is past tense of irregular
    verb "to be"; "saw" is past tense of irregular verb "to see"
Skills – name recognition; strong verb use

> Eggbert saw a little girl in a big red **car**. Her **name** was **(put student name here)**. The girl **waved** and laughed to see the ball in the **back window** of a little yell<u>ow</u> and green **car**. Eggbert wanted to **wave** and l<u>au</u>gh, too.

49. times, waves, tried, sounded, hiss

> Paragraph – topic change
> Capitalization – sentences begin with a capital letter; capitalize proper nouns
> Punctuation – sentences always have end punctuation
> Commas – repeated information; compound sentence
> Vowels – "y"
> Consonants – double consonant sounds; plosive "t"
> Verb tense – add "ed" to most verbs to put in past tense; switch to present tense for
>   narrator aside; "tried" is past tense of verb "to try"; "came" is past tense of verb "to
>   come"
> Skills – word practice; strong verbs
> Literary device – narrator aside; simile

> He bounced up and down, up and down, ten **times**. This is how a ball
> **waves** to you. Eggbert **tried** to laugh, but it **sounded** like a **hiss**.

> **NOTE:** *From here on, students are responsible for inserting end punctuation in some of the*
> *sentences.*

50. air, hiss, flat

> 2 Paragraphs – new person speaking; narrator aside
> Capitalization – sentences begin with a capital letter; capitalize proper nouns
> Punctuation – sentences always have end punctuation; use of quotes around what is said
>   out loud
> Commas – quote
> Vowels – short vowel review
> Consonants – double consonant sounds; plosive "t"
> Verb tense – add "ed" to most verbs to put in past tense; "said" is past tense of irregular
>   verb "to say"; "was" is past tense of irregular verb "to be"
> Skills – word recognition
> Literary device – narrator aside

> "Oh, Eggbert," said **(put your name here)**. "You will run out of **air** if you
> **hiss** and **hiss**.
> Eggbert *was* looking a little **flat.**

51. window, building, school

> 2 Paragraphs – new persons speaking
> Capitalization – sentences begin with a capital letter; capitalize proper nouns
> Punctuation – sentences always have end punctuation; use of quotes around what is said
>   out loud
> Commas – quote
> Vowels – short vowel review
> Consonants – double consonant sounds; plosive "t"; "s"
> Verb tense – use of present tense for quote; add "ed" to most verbs to put in past tense;
>   "said" is past tense of irregular verb "to say"; "was" is past tense of irregular verb "to
>   be"; "saw" is past tense of irregular verb "to see"
> Skills – name recognition; homophone "hear/here"; color recognition

"Here we are," said **(put your name here)**.

Eggbert looked out the back **window**. He saw a big r<u>e</u>d **building**. It w<u>a</u>s a **school.**

52. school, live, classroom, shelf

Paragraph – new person speaking
Capitalization – sentences begin with a capital letter; capitalize proper nouns; always
    capitalize "I"
Punctuation – sentences always have end punctuation; use of quotes around what is said
    out loud
Commas – quote
Vowels – short vowel review; "y"
Consonants – double consonant sounds; consonant blends; plosive "t"
Verb tense – switch to present tense for quote

"<u>Th</u>is is our **school**," said **(put your name here)** to Eggbert. "You wi<u>ll</u> **live**
here in my **classroom**. I have a **shelf** jus<u>t</u> for you.

53. doors, front, school, excited

Paragraph – new person speaking (narrator)
Capitalization – sentences begin with a capital letter; capitalize proper nouns
Punctuation – sentences always have end punctuation
Consonants – double consonant sounds; plosive "t" and "p"
Verb tense – add "ed" to most verbs to put in past tense; "was" is past tense of irregular
    verb "to be"
 Skills – name recognition; strong verb; color recognition

The lady stopped the li<u>tt</u>le ye<u>ll</u>ow car with the green **doors**. She sto<u>pp</u>ed
right in **front** of the red **school**. Eggbert was very **excited.**

54. excited, hissed, flat, picked, back

Paragraph – new subject
Capitalization – sentences begin with a capital letter; capitalize proper nouns
Punctuation – sentences always have end punctuation
Commas – compound sentence; long introductory phrase
Consonants – double consonant sounds; plosive "t"
Verb tense – add "ed" to most verbs to put in past tense; "was" is past tense of irregular
    verb "to be"
Skills – name recognition; strong verb use

Eggbert was so **excited**. He bounced, and he **hissed**. He **hissed** so much, he
was almost **flat** when **(put your name here)** **picked** him up from the **back** of
the car.

55. **flat, hissed, fix, blow, air, valve**

Paragraph – new person speaking
Capitalization – sentences begin with a capital letter; capitalize proper nouns; always capitalize "I"
Punctuation – sentences always have end punctuation; use of quotes around what is said out loud
Commas – quote
Vowels – short vowel review; "ow" sound; "ou" digraph; double "o" at end of word
Consonants – double consonant sounds; plosive "t"
Verb tense – add "ed" to most verbs to put in past tense; "said" is past tense of irregular verb "to say"; "was" is past tense of irregular verb "to be"; future tense with "will"
Skills – word recognition; strong verb use

> "You made yourself **flat**," said **(put your name here)**. "You **hissed** too much. I can **fix** that. I will **blow air** into your **valve**."

56. **could, flat, poor**

Paragraph – new person speaking (narrator)
Capitalization – sentences begin with a capital letter; capitalize proper nouns
Punctuation – sentences always have end punctuation; need for question mark at end of question
Vowels – short vowel review
Consonants – "f" and "t"; "fl" blend
Verb tense – add "ed" to most verbs to put in past tense; "was" is past tense of irregular verb "to be"; use of present tense in narrator aside
Skills – word recognition
Literary device – narrator aside

> Eggbert **could** not hiss. He was too **flat. Poor** Eggbert **could** not bounce. He was too **flat**. Do you go **flat** when you try to talk**?**

57. **school, hall, door, a lot, desks**

Paragraph – change of topic
Capitalization – sentences begin with a capital letter; capitalize proper nouns
Punctuation – sentences always have end punctuation
Vowels – short vowel review; "ow" sound; long vowel review
Verb tense – add "ed" to most verbs to put in past tense; "took" is past tense of irregular verb "to take"; "saw" is past tense of irregular verb "to see"
Spelling rule – "a lot" is two words
Skills – strong verb use; color recognition; adding "ed" to make past tense of regular verbs

> **(Put your name here)** walked into the red **school**. She took Eggbert down a long **hall**. She opened a brown **door**. Eggbert saw **a lot** of little **desks.**

58. **classroom, boys, girls, every, love**

Paragraph – new person speaking
Capitalization – sentences begin with a capital letter; capitalize proper nouns
Punctuation – sentences always have end punctuation; use of quotes around what is said
   out loud
Commas – quote
Vowels – short vowel review ; "y"
Consonants – beginning and middle single consonant sounds; "pl" and "th" blends;
   initial "w" sound
Verb tense – use of present tense in quote; "said" is past tense of irregular verb "to say";
   "was" is past tense of irregular verb "to be"; future tense with "will"
Skills – word recognition

   "This is our **classroom**," she said. "**Boys** and **girls** come here **every** day.
   They will play with you. They will **love** you."

59. **desk, papers, covered, mess, teacher's**

Paragraph – new person speaking (narrator)
Capitalization – sentences begin with a capital letter; capitalize proper nouns
Punctuation – sentences always have end punctuation; need for question mark after
   question
Consonants – final double consonants
Verb tense – add "ed" to most verbs to put in past tense; "was" is past tense of irregular
   verb "to be"; use of present tense for narrator aside
Skills – possessive of singular noun; word recognition
Literary device – narrator aside

   Then she walked up to a big **desk**. Many **papers covered** the desk. The **desk**
   was a **mess**. Is your **teacher's desk** a **mess**? Is your **desk** a **mess**?

60. **messy, desk, children, classroom, things, heard, noises**

2 Paragraphs – new topics
Capitalization – sentences begin with a capital letter; capitalize proper nouns
Punctuation – sentences always have end punctuation; use of quotes around what is said
   out loud
Commas – introductory adverb, quote
Vowels – review common digraphs
Consonants – double consonant sounds; plosive "t"
Verb tense – add "ed" to most verbs to put in past tense; "said" is past tense of irregular
   verb "to say"; future tense with "will"
Skills – name recognition; word recognition

   (Put your name here) put Eggbert on her **messy desk**. "Soon," she said,
   "many **children** will come into this **classroom**."
   Eggbert looked around the **classroom**. He saw many funny **things**. He
   heard funny **noises**.

61. **picture, classroom**

Paragraph – new person speaking (narrator aside)
Capitalization – sentences begin with a capital letter; capitalize proper nouns
Punctuation – sentences always have end punctuation; need for question mark after question
Vowels – "ow" sound and how it varies
Consonants – final "w"
Verb tense – switch to present tense for narrator aside
Skills – word recognition; put "s" to make most nouns plural
Literary device – narrator aside

What did Eggbert see? Draw a **picture** (with some words) of your **classroom** to sh<u>ow</u> what Eggbert saw. H<u>ow</u> many wind<u>ow</u>s did Eggbe<u>rt</u> see?

62. **a lot, desks, tried, flat**

3 Paragraphs – new topic; new person speaking; narrator again
Capitalization – sentences begin with a capital letter; capitalize proper nouns; always capitalize "I"
Punctuation – sentences always have end punctuation; use of quotes around what is said out loud; question mark needed at end of question
Commas – compound sentence; quote
Vowels – "ou" blend
Consonants – consonant blends, particularly "nc" and "gg"; plosive "t"
Verb tense – switch to present tense for quote; "said" is past tense of irregular verb "to say"; "was" is past tense of irregular verb "to be"
Spelling rule – "a lot" is two words
Skills – word recognition; counting; reflexive pronouns (myself, himself, etc.)

Eggbert saw **a lot** of **desks**. How many **desks** did Eggbert see?
"I want to bou<u>nc</u>e on every **desk**," Eggbert said to hi<u>ms</u>elf.
He **tried** to bou<u>nc</u>e, but he could not. Eggbert was too **flat.**

63. **lady, need, air, valve, blew**

2 Paragraphs – change of topic; new person speaking (narrator)
Capitalization – sentences begin with a capital letter; capitalize proper nouns; always capitalize "I"
Punctuation – sentences always have end punctuation; use of quotes around what is said out loud
Commas – quote; always put a comma after an interjection; compound sentence
Vowels – digraphs; "ew" sound
Verb tense – switch to present tense for quote; "saw" is past tense of irregular verb "to see"; "said" is past tense of irregular verb "to say"; "blew" is past tense of irregular verb "to blow"
Skills – possessive of singular noun; word recognition

The nice **lady** saw Eggbert try to b<u>ou</u>nce. "Oh," she s<u>ai</u>d, "I **need** to put **air** into y<u>ou</u> ."
The lady put Eggbert's **valve** up to her lips. She **blew**, and she **bl<u>ew</u>.**

64.   fix, blew, air, valve, rolled, tickled

2 Paragraphs – new person speaking; return to narrator
Capitalization – sentences begin with a capital letter; capitalize proper nouns
Punctuation – sentences always have end punctuation; use of quotes around what is said
     out loud
Commas – quote
Vowels – "ew" sound
Consonants – consonant blends (lots in this *Caught'ya*)
Verb tense – use of future tense with "will"; "said" is past tense of irregular verb "to say";
     "grew" is past tense of irregular verb "to grow"
Skills – word recognition; use of strong verbs
Literary device – rhyme

> "This will **fix** you," she said to Eggbert as she **blew air** into his **valve.**
>   Eggbert **rolled** in her hands. It **tickled** when **(put your name here) blew
> air** into his **valve.** He grew and gr<u>ew</u> as she bl<u>ew.</u>

65.   papers, sorry, tickle, times

3 Paragraphs – new topic; new person speaking; back to narrator
Capitalization – sentences begin with a capital letter; capitalize proper nouns
Punctuation – sentences always have end punctuation; use of quotes around what is said
     out loud; question mark needed at end of question
Commas – quote
Vowels – review short vowels; review long vowels
Consonants – "ck" blend
Verb tense – add "ed" to form past tense of regular verbs; "said" is past tense of irregular
     verb "to say"; "was" is past tense of irregular verb "to be"
Skills – word recognition; contractions

> The nice lady p<u>i</u>cked up some **papers** fr<u>o</u>m h<u>er</u> desk. One **paper** was right
> under <u>E</u>ggb<u>er</u>t.
>   "I'm **sorry**," she said to Eggbert. "D<u>i</u>d that **tickle** you?"
> Eggbert bounced up and <u>down</u> three **times** to say, "Y<u>e</u>s."

66.   talk, snake

Paragraph – new subject
Capitalization – sentences and quotes begin with a capital letter
Punctuation – sentences always have end punctuation; use of quotes around what is said
     out loud
Commas – quote; commas needed around "too" if meaning is "also"
Vowels – "ou" blend
Consonants – double consonant blends (there are lots in this *Caught'ya*)
Verb tense – add "ed" to form past tense of regular verbs;
Skills – word recognition
Literary device – alliteration

> The nice lady laughed. Eggbert laug<u>h</u>ed, too, with a li<u>tt</u>le hiss. He wa<u>n</u>ted to
> say, "Tha<u>nk</u> you," but he cou<u>l</u>d not **talk.** He could only hi<u>ss</u> like a **snake.**

67. left, classroom, waved, desk

2 Paragraphs – new topic; new person speaking
Capitalization – sentences and quotes begin with a capital letter; capitalize proper nouns
Punctuation – sentences always have end punctuation; use of quotes around what is said
   out loud; question mark needed at end of question
Commas – complex sentence with subordinate clause at beginning; quote
   (see **Appendix**)
Vowels – review common digraphs
Consonants – double consonant sounds
Verb tense – "left" is past tense of irregular verb "to leave"; "said" is past tense of irregular
   verb "to say"; "went" is past tense of irregular verb "to go"
Skills – word recognition; contractions

> Then the k<u>i</u>nd lady **left** the **classroom**. As she went out the d<u>oor</u>, she **waved**
> to Eggbert.
> "G<u>oo</u>d-bye," she s<u>ai</u>d. "Don't fall off <u>the</u> **desk**."

68. tomorrow, door, closed, quiet, classroom

No paragraph – same person speaking; Paragraph – new topic
Capitalization – sentences begin with a capital letter; capitalize proper nouns; always
   capitalize "I"
Punctuation – sentences always have end punctuation; use of quotes around what is said
   out loud
Commas – complex sentence with subordinate clause at beginning; quote
Vowels – review common digraphs
Consonants – "wh" blend
Verb tense – use of future tense with "will"; "said" is past tense of irregular verb "to say";
   "was" is past tense of irregular verb "to be"
Skills – word recognition; reflexive pronouns (myself, himself, etc.)

> Then she s<u>ai</u>d, "I will be back **tomorrow** when the sun comes up. Be a good
> ba<u>ll</u>."
> <u>Wh</u>en the **door closed**, it was **quiet** in the **classroom**. <u>Eggbe</u>rt was all by
> hims<u>elf</u>.

69. door, lonely, classroom, behind

No paragraph – same topic
Capitalization – sentences and quotes begin with a capital letter; capitalize proper nouns;
Punctuation – sentences always have end punctuation; question mark needed at end of
   question
Vowels – review of short and long vowels
Consonants – "wh" blend
Verb tense – switch to present tense for quote; "saw" is past tense of irregular verb "to
   see"; "was" is past tense of irregular verb" to be"
Skills – word recognition; question words
Literary device – narrator aside

> He was lonely. Then Eggbert saw a **door** ins<u>i</u>de the **classroom**. <u>Wh</u>ere d<u>i</u>d it go?
> Wh<u>at</u> was **behind** the d<u>oo</u>r? <u>Wh</u>o was **beh<u>i</u>nd** the door?

70. **desk, thought, tomorrow**

> Paragraph – new person speaking
> Capitalization – sentences and quotes begin with a capital letter; capitalize proper nouns; always capitalize "I"
> Punctuation – sentences always have end punctuation; use of quotes around what is said out loud
> Commas – quote
> Vowels – review long and short vowels; "ou" blend and "ai" digraphs
> Consonants – consonant blends; "th" blend
> Verb tense – add "ed" to end of regular verbs to put in past tense; "was" is past tense of irregular verb "to be"; use of future tense with "will"; use of present tense for quote
> Skills – word recognition

> "Today was a big day for a ball who has never been outside. I will sleep here on the big **desk**," **thought** Eggbert. "Then I will look around **tomorrow**. I can bounce and hiss again now that I am round and full of air again."

71. **teacher's, next, morning, loud, bell, woke, fell, desk**

> **NOTE:** *It is wise to teach first graders to NOT begin a sentence with a coordinating conjunction (and, or, nor, for, so, but, yet). You could have students memorize these conjunctions in a song or by chanting. Then you can tell them to never begin a sentence with one. In a few years, good writers can put them back, but until students learn the judicious use of a fragment, for effect, it is not wise to do so. How many times have you seen a paper where every sentence begins with "and"? You may omit the "and" in the student copy if you feel your students are not yet ready for this or leave it in and tell students that four words need to be taken out. Challenge them to find those words.*

> 2 Paragraphs – new topic; time change
> Capitalization – sentences begin with a capital letter; capitalize proper nouns
> Punctuation – sentences always have end punctuation
> Commas – long introductory phrase
> Vowels – review long and short vowels; "ou" blend and "ai" digraphs
> Consonants – consonant blends; "nt," "th," and "sk" blends
> Verb tense – "went," "woke," and "was" are past tense of irregular verbs "to go," "to wake," and "to be"
> Skills – never begin a sentence with a conjunction (and); some strong verbs

> Eggbert went to sleep right there on the **teacher's desk**
> The **next morning** a **loud bell woke** up Eggbert. It was very **loud**. Eggbert was so surprised, he **fell** off the **desk.**

72. **bell, rang, rolled, teacher's, desk, still, classroom**

Paragraph – new time
Capitalization – sentences begin with a capital letter; capitalize proper nouns
Punctuation – sentences always have end punctuation
Commas – complex sentence with subordinate clause at beginning (see **Appendix**)
Vowels – short "u"
Consonants – consonant blends; "th" blend
Verb tense – add "ed" to end of regular verbs to put in past tense; "was" is past tense of
    irregular verb "to be";
Skills – singular possessive; use of strong verbs

> When the **bell rang** again, Eggbert **rolled** <u>u</u>nder the **teacher's desk**. He was **still** there when **(put your name here)** came into the **classroom.**

73. **ready, students**

Paragraph – new person speaking
Capitalization – sentences and quotes begin with a capital letter; capitalize proper nouns
Punctuation – sentences always have end punctuation; use of quotes around what is said
    out loud; question mark needed at end of question
Comma – direct address
Vowels – review short vowels; "ou" blend and "ea" digraphs
Consonants – "w"; "wh" blend
Verb tense – add "ed" to end of regular verbs to put in past tense; use of present tense for
    quote
Skills – word recognition; plurals are formed by adding "s"

> "Where are you, Eggbert?" She called when she d<u>i</u>d n<u>o</u>t see the b<u>a</u>ll. "I want to wash you. I m<u>u</u>st g<u>e</u>t you **ready** f<u>o</u>r my **students.**"

74. **everywhere, desks, shelves, bathroom**

Paragraph – new topic, new speaker (narrator)
Capitalization – sentences begin with a capital letter; capitalize proper nouns
Punctuation – sentences always have end punctuation
Comma – always before "too" meaning "also"
Consonants – "l"
Verb tense – add "ed" to end of regular verbs to put in past tense
Spelling rule – "too" meaning "also" has two "o's"
Skills – word recognition; compound words

> **(Put your name here)** looked **everywhere** for <u>E</u>ggbert. She looked under all the little **desks.** She looked on all the **shelves.** She looked in the **bath<u>r</u>oom,** too.

NOTE: *After this point there are fifty more blanks in which you can insert the names of your students. There no longer will be a reminder to do so. You will want to use each student's name several times.*

75. **classroom, teacher**

No paragraph – continuation; 2 Paragraphs – narrator; new person speaking
2 Paragraphs – new person speaking
Capitalization – sentences and quotes begin with a capital letter; capitalize proper nouns
Punctuation – sentences always have end punctuation; use of quotes around what is said
    out loud; question mark needed at end of question .
Commas – noun series; quote
Vowels – review long vowels
Consonants – "wh" blend
Verb tense – add "ed" to end of regular verbs to put in past tense; "said" is past tense of
    irregular verb "to say"; use of present tense for quote
Skills – name recognition

> She did not s<u>ee</u> Eggbert. "Where is that ball?" she said.
>   Just then _____, _____, and _____ c<u>ame</u>
> into the **classroom.**
>   "What are you looking for?" _____ asked her **teacher.**

76. **teacher, surprise**

3 Paragraphs – new persons speaking
Capitalization – sentences and quotes begin with a capital letter; capitalize proper nouns;
    always capitalize "I"
Punctuation – sentences always have end punctuation; use of quotes around what is said
    out loud; question mark needed at end of question
Commas – quote
Consonants – consonant blends and doubled consonants
Verb tense – add "ed" to end of regular verbs to put in past tense; "said" is past tense of
    irregular verb "to say"; use of present tense for quote
Skills – new paragraph needed every time someone new speaks; name recognition

> "I am look<u>ing</u> for Eggbert," said the **tea<u>ch</u>er.**
> "Who is Eggbert?" a<u>sk</u>ed _____.
> "Eggbert is a **surprise**," said _____.

77. **teacher**

4 Paragraphs – new persons speaking
Capitalization – sentences and quotes begin with a capital letter; capitalize proper nouns;
    always capitalize "I"
Punctuation – sentences always have end punctuation; use of quotes around what is said
    out loud; question mark needed at end of question
Commas – quote; always put commas around "too" if the meaning is "also"
Verb tense – add "ed" to end of regular verbs to put in past tense; "said" is past tense of
    irregular verb "to say"; use of present tense for quote
Skills – new paragraph needed every time someone new speaks; name recognition

> "Do you want me to help you look?" asked _____.
> "Yes," said the **teacher.**
> "Can I help, too?" asked _____ and _____ as they walked in
> the door.
> "Yes, you can help, too," said the **teacher.**

78.   everywhere, funny-looking, thing, teacher

2 Paragraphs – narrator; new person speaking
Capitalization – sentences and quotes begin with a capital letter; capitalize proper nouns
Punctuation – sentences always have end punctuation; use of quotes around what is said
    out loud; question mark needed at end of question
Vowels – "oo" digraph and "ou" blend; review short vowels
Consonants – consonant blends and doubled consonants
Verb tense – add "ed" to end of regular verbs to put in past tense; "came" is past tense of
    irregular verb "to come"; use of present tense for quote
Skills – new paragraph needed every time someone new speaks; name recognition

> The six looked **everywhere**. Just then _____ and _____
> came in the classroom door.
>   "What is that **funny-looking** round **thing** under your desk?" _____
> asked his **teacher.**

79.   teacher

3 Paragraphs – new persons speaking (second is narrator)
Capitalization – sentences and quotes begin with a capital letter; capitalize proper nouns
Punctuation – sentences always have end punctuation; use of quotes around what is said
    out loud
Commas – quote; direct address
Vowels – "er" sound
Verb tense – add "ed" to end of regular verbs to put in past tense; "said" is past tense of
    irregular verb "to say"
Skills – new paragraph needed every time someone new speaks; name recognition

> "That must be Eggbert," said the **teacher.** "Come out, Eggbert."
> Eggbert rolled out from under her desk.
>   "Oh, what a pretty ball!" said _____ and _____
> together.

80.   bell, rang, children, a lot, noise

Paragraph – new person speaking (narrator)
Capitalization – sentences begin with a capital letter; capitalize proper nouns
Punctuation – sentences always have end punctuation
Commas – compound sentence
Verb tense – add "ed" to end of regular verbs to put in past tense; "rang" is past tense of
    irregular verb "to ring"; "ran" is past tense of irregular verb "to run"
Spelling rule – "a lot" is 2 words
Skills – possessive of singular noun; name recognition; use of strong verbs

> The **bell rang** again, and many **children** ran into the classroom. The **bell**
> **made a lot** of **noise.** _____ and _____ made **a lot** of
> **noise.** Eggbert rolled under the teacher's desk again.

81. **scared, bell, start, school, friends**

Paragraph – new person speaking
Capitalization – sentences and quotes begin with a capital letter; capitalize proper nouns
Punctuation – sentences always have end punctuation; use of quotes around what is said
    out loud
Commas – direct address; quote
Vowels – "oo" digraph; "ea" digraph; "ou" digraph and blend;
Verb tense – "said" is past tense of irregular verb "to say"; imperative tense used to order
    someone around
Spelling rule – "i" before "e" except after "c"; n<u>ei</u>ghbor, w<u>ei</u>gh, and th<u>ei</u>r are w<u>ei</u>rd
Skills – new paragraph needed every time someone new speaks

"Come <u>out</u>, Eggbert," said the t<u>ea</u>cher." Do not be **scared**. It is only the **bell** to **start school**," she s<u>ai</u>d. "Here are many new **friends**. They want to play with y<u>ou</u>."

82. **children, sat, quiet, meet, friend**

Paragraph – new person speaking (narrator)
Capitalization – sentences begin with a capital letter; capitalize proper nouns
Punctuation – sentences always have end punctuation
Comma – repeated word
Vowels – "ie" and "ei" digraphs
Consonants – "s"
Verb tense – add "ed" to end of regular verbs to put in past tense; "sat" is past tense of
    irregular verb "to sit"; "were" is past tense of irregular verb "to be"
Spelling rule – "i" before "e" except after "c," and "neighbor" and "weigh" and "their" are
    "weird"
Skills – new paragraph needed every time someone new speaks;

All the **children sat** at their desk<u>s</u>. They were very, very **quiet**. They wanted to meet Eggbert. They wanted to **meet** th<u>ei</u>r new **friend.**

83. **children, high**

Paragraph – change of place
Capitalization – sentences begin with a capital letter; capitalize proper nouns
Punctuation – sentences always have end punctuation
Commas – repeated information; pause
Vowels – "ou" blend; long "i" when followed by "ght"; "ow" sound spelled "ou"
Consonants – "nc" blend
Verb tense – add "ed" to end of regular verbs to put in past tense; "went" is past tense of
    irregular verb "to go"
Skills – possessive of singular noun; use of strong verbs

Eggbert rolled out from under the big desk of the teacher. He bounced up and down, up and d<u>ow</u>n so he could see all the **children**. He b<u>ou</u>nced so **high**, he went right onto the teacher<u>'s</u> desk.

84. **high, children**

   No paragraph – same place and topic; Paragraph – new person speaks
   Capitalization – sentences and quotes begin with a capital letter; capitalize proper nouns
   Punctuation – sentences always have end punctuation; use of quotes around what is said out loud
   Commas – quote; extra information; always put commas around "too" if it means "also"
   Vowels – "ou" digraph and "ou" blend; review short vowels
   Consonants – consonant blends ("sk" and "rt"); doubled consonants
   Verb tense – use of present tense for quote
   Skills – contraction "it's" means "it is"; new paragraph needed every time someone new speaks; name recognition

> There, up **high** on the big desk, Eggbert could see all the **children**. All the **children** could see Eggbert, too.
> "It's a ball," said _____.

85. **special**

   Paragraph – new person speaking
   Capitalization – sentences and quotes begin with a capital letter; capitalize proper nouns
   Punctuation – sentences always have end punctuation; use of quotes around what is said out loud
   Commas – quote; appositive (extra information about a noun)
   Verb tense – "said" is past tense of irregular verb "to say"; use of present tense for quote
   Skills – contraction "it's" = "it is"; new paragraph needed every time someone new speaks; name recognition; reflexive pronouns (himself)

> "It's a very **special** ball," said _____, the teacher. This is Eggbert. Eggbert can bounce all by himself."

86. **through, valve, noises, snake**

   3 Paragraphs – new person speaking (first one is narrator)
   Capitalization – sentences and quotes begin with a capital letter; capitalize proper nouns
   Punctuation – sentences always have end punctuation; use of quotes around what is said out loud
   Commas – quote; always put a comma after an interjection; always put commas around "too" if the meaning is "also"
   Vowels – "oi" blend; review long vowel with silent "e"
   Consonants – doubled consonants
   Verb tense – add "ed" to end of regular verbs to put in past tense; "said" is past tense of irregular verb "to say"; use of present tense for quote
   Skills – new paragraph needed every time someone new speaks; name recognition

> Eggbert hissed **through** his **valve** to say, "Hello."
> "Oh, he can make **noises**, too," said _____.
> "There is a **snake** inside the ball," said _____.

87. snake, friend

Paragraph – new person speaking
Capitalization – sentences and quotes begin with a capital letter; capitalize proper nouns
Punctuation – sentences always have end punctuation; use of quotes around what is said
    out loud; quote within a quote; question mark needed at end of question
Commas – introductory word; quote
Vowels – long vowels with silent "e"
Consonants – "s" sound
Verb tense – use of present tense for quote; "said" is past tense of "to say"
Spelling rule – "i" before "e".....
Skills – possessive of singular noun; new paragraph needed every time someone new
    speaks; quote within a quote

> "No, there is no **snake** inside the ball," said the teacher. "That is Eggbert's way to say, 'Hello.' He wants to be your **friend**."

88. patted

Paragraph – new topic (narrator speaking)
Capitalization – sentences begin with a capital letter; capitalize proper nouns
Punctuation – sentences always have end punctuation
Vowels – "ou" blend making "ow" sound; review short vowels
Consonants – consonant blends and doubled consonants
Verb tense – add "ed" to end of regular verbs to put in past tense
Spelling rule – when adding suffix to consonant/vowel/consonant, double the last
    consonant; compound words
Skills – possessive of singular noun; name recognition; strong verb use

> Eggbert bounced off the teacher's desk. He rolled and bounced all around the classroom. He bounced by _____ and by _____. They **patted** him.

89. kiss, tickled, sneezed, through, valve, sounded, kitten

No paragraph – same topic (Eggbert moving around room)
Capitalization – sentences and quotes begin with a capital letter; capitalize proper nouns;
    always capitalize "I"
Punctuation – sentences always have end punctuation; use of quotes around what is said
    out loud
Verb tense – add "ed" to end of regular verbs to put in past tense; "gave" is past tense of
    "to give"
Skills – adding "ed" to make a verb past tense; use of strong verbs
Literary device – simile; strong verb use

> _____ gave Eggbert a **kiss**. It **tickled**. He **sneezed through** his **valve**. It **sounded** like the **sneeze** of a little **kitten**.

90. **boys, a lot, threw**

Paragraph – change of topic
Capitalization – sentences begin with a capital letter; capitalize proper nouns
Punctuation – sentences always have end punctuation
Vowels – review long vowels with silent "e"
Consonants – consonant blends and doubled consonants
Verb tense – add "ed" to end of regular verbs to put in past tense; "came" is past tense of
    irregular verb "to come"; "threw" is past tense of irregular verb "to throw"; "was" is
    past tense of irregular verb "to be"
Spelling rule – "a lot" is 2 words
Skills – "ed" suffix puts regular verbs in past tense; name and word recognition

> Everyone laugh<u>ed</u>. _____ and _____, two **boys** who
> li<u>ke</u>d to play **a lot**, pick<u>ed</u> up Eggbert and **threw** him around the classroom.
> Eggbert li<u>ke</u>d that. It was <u>fun.</u>

91. **hit, wall, hard**

Paragraph – new action
Capitalization – sentences begin with a capital letter; capitalize proper nouns
Punctuation – sentences always have end punctuation; use of quotes around what is said
    out loud
Commas – compound sentence
Vowels – review short vowels
Consonants – "h" sound; consonant blends ("rt" and "st")
Verb tense – add "ed" to end of regular verbs to put in past tense; "threw" is past tense of
    irregular verb "to throw"
Skills – new paragraph needed every time someone new speaks; strong verbs; word
    recognition

> The boys threw Eggbert faster and <u>faster</u>. Eggbe<u>rt</u> liked to fly around the
> room, but he did not like it when he **hit** the **wall hard.** It hu<u>rt</u>.

92. **ouch, hit, wall, hard, sorry**

2 Paragraphs – new persons speaking
Capitalization – sentences and quotes begin with a capital letter; capitalize proper nouns
Punctuation – sentences always have end punctuation; use of quotes around what is said
    out loud
Commas – quote
Consonants – "h"
Verb tense – add "ed" to end of regular verbs to put in past tense; "said" is past tense of
    irregular verb "to say"; use of future tense
Skills – new paragraph needed every time someone new speaks; name recognition

> "**Ouch**," he <u>h</u>issed w<u>h</u>en <u>h</u>e **hit** the **wall hard.**
> "**Sorry**," _____ and _____ said. "We will not do <u>th</u>at
> again."

93. **mad, boys, wall, hard, threw, hit, slowly**

Paragraph – new person speaking (narrator)
Capitalization – sentences begin with a capital letter; capitalize proper nouns
Punctuation – sentences always have end punctuation
Commas – introductory phrase
Vowels – review short vowels; review long vowels with silent "e"; "ai" digraph
Verb tense – "threw" is past tense of irregular verb "to throw"; "was" is past tense of
    irregular verb "to be"
Skills – do not begin a sentence with a coordinating conjunction (and, or, nor, for, so,
    but, yet); name recognition; review coordinating conjunctions

> Eggbert was not **mad** at the **boys**. He did not like to hit the **wall hard**
> because it hurt. After that, the **boys threw** Eggbert more **slowly**. He did not **hit**
> the **wall** again.

94. **kiss**

Paragraph – time change
Capitalization – sentences begin with a capital letter; capitalize proper nouns
Punctuation – sentences always have end punctuation; question mark needed at end of
    question
Vowels – "ou" blend; review short vowels
Consonants – consonant blends and doubled consonants
Verb tense – add "ed" to end of regular verbs to put in past tense; use of present tense for
    narrator aside; "was" is past tense of irregular verb "to be"
Skills – words within words; name recognition
Literary device – narrator aside in parentheses

> The rest of the day was fun. Eggbert rolled around the classroom. He
> bounced up to give _____ a ball **kiss**. (What is a ball **kiss** like?)

95. **lap, surprised**

No paragraph – same subject; 2 Paragraphs – new person speaking, 2nd is narrator
Capitalization – sentences and quotes begin with a capital letter; capitalize proper nouns
Punctuation – sentences always have end punctuation; use of quotes around what is said
    out loud; question mark needed at end of question
Comma – interjection; quote
Vowels – "oi" and "ou" blends
Verb tense – add "ed" to end of regular verbs to put in past tense
Skills – singular possessive; new paragraph needed every time someone new speaks;
    name recognition; strong verbs (narrator)

> Then he bounced into _____'s **lap.**
>   "Oh," she said, **surprised**. Are you going to help me with my work?"
>   Eggbert rolled around in her arms.

96. working, hard

No paragraph – same topic; Paragraph – someone speaking
Capitalization – sentences and quotes begin with a capital letter; capitalize proper nouns
Punctuation – sentences always have end punctuation; use of quotes around what is said out loud; question mark needed at end of question
Vowels – "ow" sound
Verb tense – add "ed" to end of regular verbs to put in past tense; "was" is past tense of irregular verb "to be"
Skills – possessive of singular noun; new paragraph needed every time someone new speaks; name recognition

> Eggbert bounced d<u>ow</u>n and rolled up to _____'s desk. He was **working hard**. He did not see Eggbert.
> <u>Eggber</u>t hissed a "Hello." He then rolled to the next desk.

97. need, bath, dirty, bathroom

Paragraph – new action and person speaking
Capitalization – sentences and quotes begin with a capital letter; capitalize proper nouns; always capitalize "I"
Punctuation – sentences always have end punctuation; use of quotes around what is said out loud; question mark needed at end of question
Consonants – consonant blends ("ck," "ld," "sh," "th"); doubled consonants
Verb tense – add "ed" to end of regular verbs to put in past tense; use of present tense for quote; "told" is past tense of irregular verb "to tell"
Skills – new paragraph needed every time someone new speaks; name recognition

> _____ pi<u>ck</u>ed up Eggbert. "You **need** a **bath**," she told him. "You are a very **dirty** ball. I will ca<u>rr</u>y you into the **ba<u>th</u>room** and wa<u>sh</u> you."

98. idea, a lot, took, bathroom

2 Paragraphs – new person speaking (second is narrator)
Capitalization – sentences and quotes begin with a capital letter; capitalize proper nouns; always capitalize "I"
Punctuation – sentences always have end punctuation; use of quotes around what is said out loud
Commas – quote; always before "too" meaning "also"
Vowels – "oo" digraph
Consonants – "w" sound
Verb tense – add "ed" to end of regular verbs to put in past tense; "said" is past tense of irregular verb "to say"; "took" is past tense of verb "to take"
Spelling rule – "a lot" is two words; compound words
Skills – new paragraph needed every time someone new speaks; name recognition

> "<u>W</u>hat a good **idea**," said the teacher. "I <u>w</u>anted to <u>w</u>ash Eggbert today, too. He rolled around **a lot**."
> _____ and _____ **took** Eggbert into the **bathroom.**

99. sink, smelly, soap, getting

No paragraph – same topic
Capitalization – sentences begin with a capital letter; capitalize proper nouns
Punctuation – sentences always have end punctuation
Comma – compound sentence
Vowels – "ea" digraph; double "e" = long "e"
Consonants – consonant blends and doubled consonants
Verb tense – add "ed" to end of regular verbs to put in past tense; "was" is past tense of
    irregular verb "to be"
Skills – new paragraph needed every time someone new speaks; color recognition; word
    recognition
Literary device – rhyme

> They washed <u>Eggbert</u> in the **sink** with some **smelly soap**. It was gr<u>ee</u>n **soap**.
> Eggbert did not like the gr<u>ee</u>n **soap**, but he did like **getting** cl<u>ea</u>n.

100. funny-looking, thing, next, sink, square, tank, water

No paragraphs – same topic
Capitalization – sentences begin with a capital letter; capitalize proper nouns
Punctuation – sentences always have end punctuation; question mark needed at end of
    question
Vowels – review short vowels
Consonants – consonant blends and doubled consonants
Verb tense – "saw" is past tense of irregular verb "to see"; "was" is past tense of irregular
    verb "to be"
Skills – word recognition
Literary device – narrator aside for humor

> Eggbert saw a **funny-looking thing next** to the **sink**. What was it? It <u>was</u> round
> with a **square tank** at the back. There <u>was</u> **water** in it. What <u>was</u> it?

101. time, watched

No paragraph – same topic
Capitalization – sentences begin with a capital letter; capitalize proper nouns
Punctuation – sentences always have end punctuation
Commas – repetition
Vowels – "ay" digraph; review short vowels
Consonants – "sk" and "rk" blends
Verb tense – add "ed" to end of regular verbs to put in past tense; "was" is past tense of
    irregular verb "to be"; "put" is past tense of irregular verb "to put"
Skills – name recognition; word recognition

> Eggbert did not have **time** to look. Soon he was clean. _____ and
> _____ put him on the teacher's desk. From the big d<u>esk</u>, Eggbert
> **watched** the class work and play, <u>work</u> and <u>play</u>.

102. **walls, hit**

Paragraph – change of place
Capitalization – sentences begin with a capital letter; capitalize proper nouns
Punctuation – sentences always have end punctuation
Commas – subordinate clause at beginning; noun series; introductory word
Vowels – "ay" digraph
Consonants – "nt" blend
Verb tense – add "ed" to end of regular verbs to put in past tense; "went" is past tense of irregular verb "to go"; use of present tense for quote; "were" is past tense of irregular verb "to be"
Skills – noun/verb agreement ("were no wall<u>s</u>"); form past tense with suffix "ed"; name recognition

When the class went outside, Eggbert w<u>ent</u> out, too. _____,
_____, _____, and _____ played with Eggbert.
They pl<u>ay</u>ed ball with Eggbert. Outside, there were no **walls** for Eggbert to **hit.**

103. **happy, bell, rang, end, surprised**

Paragraph – place change
Capitalization – sentences begin with a capital letter; capitalize proper nouns
Punctuation – sentences always have end punctuation
Commas – complex sentences with subordinate clause at beginning
Vowels – vowel sounds with "n" ("an" and "en"); long "i" when silent "e"
Consonants – "n"; "wh" blend
Verb tense – add "ed" to end of regular verbs to put in past tense; "rang" is past tense of irregular verb "to ring"; "was" is past tense of verb "to be"
Spelling rules – the difference between "when" and "went"
Skills – word recognition

Wh<u>en</u> the class went in<u>side</u>, Eggbert w<u>ent</u> in, too. Eggbert was **happy**. Wh<u>en</u> the **bell r<u>ang</u>** at the **end** of the day, Eggbert was **surprised.**

104. **children, left, waved, good-bye, wave**

No paragraph – continuation of topic
Capitalization – sentences begin with a capital letter; capitalize proper nouns
Punctuation – sentences always have end punctuation; question mark needed at end of question
Vowels – short vowel review; "oo" and "oe" digraphs
Verb tense – add "ed" to end of regular verbs to put in past tense; "left" is past tense of irregular verb "to leave"
Skills – strong verbs (all of them)
Literary device – narrator aside in parentheses

All the **ch<u>i</u>ldren left** the cl<u>a</u>ssr<u>oo</u>m. The<u>y</u> **waved good-bye** to Eggbert. Eggbert g<u>a</u>ve the **children** a ball **wave**. (H<u>o</u>w does a ball **wave** to you**?**)

105. times, wave, waves

No paragraph – same topic
Capitalization – sentences and quotes begin with a capital letter; capitalize proper nouns
Punctuation – sentences always have end punctuation
Consonants – consonant review
Verb tense – add "ed" to end of regular verbs to put in past tense; use of present tense for narrator aside
Skills – word recognition
Literary device – narrator aside in present tense and parentheses

> Eggbert bounced up and down, up and down ten (10) **times**. This is how a ball **waves**. (How do you **wave**? Can you show Eggbert how you wave?)

106. children, home, good-bye, blew, air

Paragraph – new time
Capitalization – sentences and quotes begin with a capital letter; capitalize proper nouns
Punctuation – sentences always have end punctuation; use of quotes around what is said out loud
Commas – quote; complex sentence with subordinate clause at beginning
Consonants – consonant review; double consonants
Verb tense – add "ed" to end of regular verbs to put in past tense; "went" is past tense of irregular verb "to go"; "said" is past tense of verb "to say"; "blew" is past tense of verb "to blow"
Skills – hyphen use in two words acting as one

> After the **children** went **home** for the day, Eggbert and the teacher said, "**Good-bye**." The teacher said, "**Good-bye**," and Eggbert hissed. Before she went **home**, the teacher **blew** more **air** into Eggbert.

107. special, children, love, tomorrow

Paragraph – new person speaking
Capitalization – sentences and quotes begin with a capital letter; capitalize proper nouns
Punctuation – sentences always have end punctuation; use of quotes around what is said out loud
Commas – quote; compound sentence
Vowels – long vowel sounds (end of 2 letter word, doubled)
Verb tense – add "ed" to end of regular verbs to put in past tense; use of present tense for quote; use of imperative
Skills – contraction "you're" = "you are"

> "You're a **special** ball," she said. "My **children love** you. Be a good ball. Go to sleep on my desk, and we will be back **tomorrow**."

108. night, lonely

Paragraph – narrator speaking
Capitalization – sentences begin with a capital letter; capitalize proper nouns
Punctuation – sentences always have end punctuation
Verb tense – add "ed" to end of regular verbs to put in past tense; "was" is past tense of
    irregular verb "to be"
Skills – possessive of singular noun; name recognition; strong verb use

> That **night**, Eggbert was **lonely** again. He could not sleep. He rolled around
> the classroom. He bounced onto _____'s desk.

109. messy, bathroom, dark

No paragraph – same topic
Capitalization – sentences begin with a capital letter; capitalize proper nouns
Punctuation – sentences always have end punctuation
Vowels – long "i" followed by "ght"
Consonants – "ght" (go over other words like "night," right," might")
Verb tense – add "ed" to end of regular verbs to put in past tense; "was" is past tense of
    irregular verb "to be"
Skills – possessive of singular noun

> The teacher's desk was **messy**. Eggbert rolled into the **bathroom**. It was **dark**
> inside. The light was off.

110. toilet, wet

No paragraph – same topic
Capitalization – sentences begin with a capital letter; capitalize proper nouns
Punctuation – sentences always have end punctuation
Comma – pause
Consonants – "gh" blend
Verb tense – add "ed" to end of regular verbs to put in past tense; "was" is past tense of
    irregular verb "to be"
Skills – word recognition
Literary device – humor

> Eggbert bounced up and up, higher and higher. He bounced right into the
> **toilet**! It was **wet** and cold.

111. toilet, water, slept, night

No paragraph – same topic
Capitalization – sentences begin with a capital letter; capitalize proper nouns
Punctuation – sentences always have end punctuation
Verb tense – add "ed" to end of regular verbs to put in past tense; "slept" is past tense of
    irregular verb "to sleep"; "was" is past tense of verb "to be"
Skills – word recognition; negatives

> Eggbert could not bounce out of the **toilet**. He could not bounce out of **water**.
> He **slept** in the **toilet** all **night**. It was wet and cold.

112. **school, early, door**

Paragraph – time change
Capitalization – sentences begin with a capital letter; capitalize proper nouns
Punctuation – sentences always have end punctuation
Commas – noun series; compound sentence
Verb tense – add "ed" to end of regular verbs to put in past tense; "came" is past tense of irregular verb "to come" "was" is past tense of verb "to be"
Skills – name recognition; add "ed" suffix to form past tense of regular verbs; strong verb use

The next morning the teacher and _____, _____, and _____ came to **school early.** They open<u>ed</u> the **door** of the class-room. They look<u>ed</u> and look<u>ed</u>, but they did not see Eggbert.

113. **shelves, cubbies**

Paragraph – slight change of topic
Capitalization – sentences begin with a capital letter; capitalize proper nouns
Punctuation – sentences always have end punctuation; question mark needed at end of question
Verb tense – add "ed" to end of regular verbs to put in past tense; "was" is past tense of irregular verb "to be"
Spelling rule – form plurals of nouns that end in consonant/y by getting rid of the "y" and adding "ies"
Skills – name recognition; word recognition

Where was he? _____ looked in all the **shelves** and **cubbies**. _____ looked under all the desks. The teacher <u>looked</u> up high.

114. **heard, splash, bathroom, children**

No paragraph – continuation
Capitalization – sentences begin with a capital letter; capitalize proper nouns
Punctuation – sentences always have end punctuation; question mark needed at end of question
Verb tense – add "ed" to end of regular verbs to put in past tense; "heard" is past tense of irregular verb "to hear"; "was" is past tense of verb "to be"; "ran" is past tense of the verb "to run"
Spelling – compound words
Skills – word recognition; name recognition

It was not funny. Where was Eggbert? Then _____ **heard** a **splash** in the **bathroom**. All four **children** ran into the **bath<u>room</u>.**

115. **toilet, sink, smelly, soap**

No paragraph – continuation; 2 Paragraphs – new persons speaking
Capitalization – sentences and quotes begin with a capital letter; capitalize proper nouns
Punctuation – sentences always have end punctuation; use of quotes around what is said out loud
Commas – quote
Verb tense – add "ed" to end of regular verbs to put in past tense; "said" is past tense of irregular verb "to say"; use of present tense for quote
Skills – word recognition; name recognition; new paragraph needed every time someone new speaks; strong verb use

> There was Eggbert in the **toilet**.
> "This is no place for a ball," said _____. She picked Eggbert up from the **toilet** and washed him in the **sink** with the **smelly** green **soap.**
> "Ewww," said _____.

116. **rest, happy, kiss, boy, girl**

Paragraphs – resuming narration
Capitalization – sentences begin with a capital letter; capitalize proper nouns
Punctuation – sentences always have end punctuation;
Vowels – review short vowels; "oo" digraph
Consonants – doubled consonants
Verb tense – add "ed" to end of regular verbs to put in past tense; "came" is past tense of irregular verb "to come"; use of present tense for quote; "was" is past tense of irregular verb "to be"
Spelling – compound words; plurals of words not ending in "s"
Skills – word recognition; compound words; adding the suffix "ed" to form past tense

> The **rest** of the children came into the classroom. Eggbert was **happy** again. He bounced up to give a ball **kiss** to every **boy** and **girl**. All day he bounced and rolled around the classroom.

117. **bell, rang, end, good-bye, idea**

2 Paragraphs – time change; new person speaking
Capitalization – sentences and quotes begin with a capital letter; capitalize proper nouns; always capitalize "I"
Punctuation – sentences always have end punctuation; use of quotes around what is said out loud
Commas – complex sentence with subordinate clause at beginning; quote
Vowels – "ay" digraph; "oo" digraph; "ai" digraph
Verb tense – add "ed" to end of regular verbs to put in past tense; "rang" is past tense of irregular verb "to ring"
Skills – word recognition; new paragraph needed every time someone new speaks;

> When the **bell rang** at the **end** of the day, Eggbert did not want to say "**Good-bye.**" The children did not want to say "**Good-bye.**"
> "I have an **idea**," said the kind teacher.

118. idea, lonely, night

Paragraph – narrator aside
Capitalization – sentences begin with a capital letter; capitalize proper nouns
Punctuation – sentences always have end punctuation; question mark needed
Consonants – "wh" blend
Verb tense – add "ed" to end of regular verbs to put in past tense; "was" is past tense of
    irregular verb "to be"
Skills – name recognition; possession of singular noun
Literary device – narrator aside

> <u>Wh</u>at was the teacher's **idea**? Would Eggbert be **lonely** again? <u>Wh</u>ere could <u>Eggbe</u>rt sleep every **night**?

119. home, tonight, tomorrow, next

Paragraph – new person speaking
Capitalization – sentences and quotes begin with a capital letter; capitalize proper nouns;
    always capitalize "I"
Punctuation – sentences always have end punctuation; use of quotes around what is said
    out loud; question mark needed at end of question
Commas – quote
Vowels -long vowels with silent "e"; long "i" with "ght"
Verb tense – use of present tense for quote
Spelling rule – difference between homophones know/no
Skills – word recognition; new paragraph when someone new speaks; name recognition

> "I know what to do," said _____. Eggbert can come **home** with me **tonight**. He can go **home** with _____ **tomorrow night**. Who will <u>ta</u>ke Eggbert **home** the **next ni**g**ht**?

120. idea, night, home, boy, girl, happy

Paragraph – new topic
Capitalization – sentences and quotes begin with a capital letter; capitalize proper nouns
Punctuation – sentences always have end punctuation; use of quotes
Commas – always put commas around "too" if it means "also"
Vowels – review short and long vowels
Consonants – review consonants
Verb tense – add "ed" to end of regular verbs to put in past tense; "went" is past tense of
    irregular verb "to go"; "was" is past tense of irregular verb "to be"
Skills – word recognition

> That was the teacher's **idea**, too. Every day Eggbert b<u>ounce</u>d, <u>rolle</u>d, read, w<u>orke</u>d, and pl<u>aye</u>d at **school**. Every **night** he went **home** with a **boy** or **girl**. <u>Eggbe</u>rt was a very **happy** <u>ball</u>.

The End

**Now make up your own story about Eggbert and your class.
Where will Eggbert be found next? Where will he bounce?**

CHAPTER
2
SECOND-GRADE STORY

Putrescent Petra

Finds Friends

What is Included in This Chapter

1) A how-to section which will detail how to implement the *Caught'ya* method in your classroom. This includes some general, final notes.

2) One-page, quick lesson plans for teaching the *Caught'yas*.

3) The part of Petra's story to be read aloud to the class by the teacher.

4) One-hundred twenty *Caught'ya* sentences for Petra's story. These include the sentences to be put on the board or overhead for the students **(B)** the corrected sentences **(C)** a list of skills included in each *Caught'ya*, and some teaching suggestions.

5) Example of a page from a second-grade boy's editing journal. The *Caught'yas* are from a thematic unit on estuaries.

1

How to Implement *Caught'yas* in Your Second-Grade Classroom

Caught'yas can be enjoyed by all second graders who can write a sentence. If you teach a standard single-grade second-grade class, simply follow the directions in this section in order to set up a successful *Caught'ya* program for students.

If you teach in a multi-age classroom, you can use Petra's story in this chapter, the first-grade story about Eggbert in **Chapter 1**, or a story of your own. The key is to choose a story that *all* your students can use. For younger students whose writing skills are less developed, no matter what story you use, you may want to follow the model in **Chapter 1**, making a copy of each day's *Caught'ya* for them to paste in their editing journals (more about this later). More fluent writers can copy the same *Caught'yas* by themselves.

In a traditional second-grade classroom, students at the beginning of the year may not be capable of copying and writing sentences. Hence, you may temporarily want to adopt the cut-and-paste technique suggested in **Chapter 1**, using the *Caught'ya* sentences in Petra's story in this chapter. To do this, simply type, in large font, the first ten to thirty *Caught'yas*. Leave out only capital letters and end punctuation. Make copies of each *Caught'ya*, one per student, and daily ask students to paste them into their editing journals before working to add the missing capital letters and punctuation.

As soon as you think your students can copy the daily sentences from the board or over-head, cease providing them with the printed copy and instead, have them copy each *Caught'ya* into their editing journals in the traditional manner of completing *Caught'yas*.

Petra's story has been "classroom tested" in both multi-age and traditional classrooms. It currently is being used by a teacher at an elementary school in a small, affluent city (with no pockets of poverty). It also is being tested by second-grade teachers in a rural school with 95% free- and reduced-lunch students. The results from both schools were positive.

On the next page, you will find an encapsulated version of the ten steps to implementing *Caught'yas* in the second grade. You will find information you need to begin students on their way to fluent writing and the use of good vocabulary. Each of the ten steps then is explained in detail.

Ten Easy Steps for Second-grade *Caught'yas*

1. Write your own plot or choose the story in this chapter that was written especially for second graders. Buy a prop (a stuffed skunk).

2. Decide on skills and vocabulary words you want to be sure to include and A) Compose your own sentences; B) Use the *Caught'ya*s as written in Petra's story; C) Change the sentences in Petra's story to fit your students' needs; or D) Pick only one of the sentences in each *Caught'ya* for your students to copy, then plan to do the others orally with the class.

3. Teach your students about editing journals and response journals and make one each for every student. Read to your class the introduction and prepare your students for Petra's story.

4. Write the day's *Caught'ya* incorrectly (**Sentence B**) on the board or overhead. Read the sentences dramatically, going over the vocabulary words and reviewing paragraphing, capitalization, and end punctuation.

5. Students write the *Caught'ya* as correctly as they can, and then, with as many sentences as they can, write in their response journals about something related to the *Caught'ya*.

6. Walk around the room, helping students with the *Caught'ya*, giving individual mini lessons, commenting on each student's effort, giving hugs, and aiding with response journals by offering suggestions and writing a few comments or questions of your own.

7. Return to the board or overhead and check the *Caught'ya* with the class, eliciting answers from students and reviewing the vocabulary words.

8. Students mark mistakes with proofreading symbols (if possible).

9. Students count and indicate number of errors in the margin.

10. Collect the editing journals and make some positive, individual comments in each student's journal. Collect response journals at another time. Write additional encouraging comments, and note errors your students made.

The *Ten Easy Steps* Explained More Fully

STEP 1

Write your own plot or choose the story in this chapter that was written especially for second graders. Buy a prop (a stuffed skunk).

What Caught'yas to Use

If you have never used *Caught'ya*s before, I recommend that you use Petra's story for the first year to get the feel of the method. *Putrescent Petra Finds Friends* was written especially to appeal to second graders. It contains lots of stinky and smelly things as well as kids and animals who save the day. Studying animals is a part of most second-grade curricula, so this story will blend with your science units.

Then, after you have finished Petra's story, you might want to branch out and write your own story to suit your own students and their environment. You can brainstorm with fellow teachers. You could use themes from science or social studies units to form the sentences for the *Caught'ya*s and integrate your entire curriculum. (See **Chapter 1**, **Step 1**.) You also could write a story with your colleagues. I know of a school where teachers wrote a story that is continued in each grade level throughout the school, somewhat like an ongoing soap opera.

Before Using Petra's Story

If you use Petra's story, you first will want to involve your students in the plot so that it is familiar to them before they begin editing it. Before school starts, buy a stuffed skunk. You might want to buy several to have a backup in case the first one walks off or disappears. Put a label on this stuffed skunk with Petra's name and place it in a prominent place in your classroom. This will generate interest. A trip to the library to find out about skunks might be a good idea.

If You Finish Petra's Story Early

After you read the introduction to the class, the rest of the story will unfold bit by bit in the daily *Caught'ya* sentences. There are 120 of them, enough for one per day for the first twenty-four weeks of school. If you do one a day, which gives consistent practice to ensure better skills mastery, you'll need approximately thirty more of them (figuring ten days of field trips, assemblies, standardized tests, etc.).

Having to come up with some of your own *Caught'yas* gives you the flexibility to add sentences anywhere you wish, extra sentences that incorporate words and skills you wish to reinforce. You have an automatic diagnostic tool in your students' response journals! (Explanation in **Step 3**.) From reading these journals, you will know what skills need more emphasis, and you easily can give more detail to the basic story line to add more practice in these skills. (See the **Appendix** for an alphabetized list of skills.) Petra's story is very simple, and there are plenty of places where more detail or conversation can be added without changing the story line.

On the other hand, if you have not added sentences, and you run out of *Caught'yas* at the beginning of April, you might ask your students to write additional adventures for Petra. These stories can be used as *Caught'yas* for the rest of the year. Using students' writing for actual *Caught'yas* can be very effective since it automatically programs the errors they still are making.

For Your Plans — Time Necessary to Complete the Caught'yas

I am told by second-grade teachers that each *Caught'ya* should take at least thirty-five to forty-five minutes to complete. This is because students not only copy (sometimes a very slow process for seven-year-olds) and correct the *Caught'ya*, but they write in their response journals as well.

Teachers tell me that they need ten minutes to read the *Caught'ya* aloud and introduce the vocabulary. Students consume another fifteen to twenty minutes copying and correcting the *Caught'ya* in their editing journals and writing a few sentences in their response journals.

You will use those same fifteen minutes to walk around the room, looking over students' work, giving mini-lessons, and interacting with them. With you at the blackboard or overhead, the whole class spends a final ten minutes reviewing vocabulary, going over some skills, and correcting the *Caught'ya*. This amount of time is needed no matter whose *Caught'ya* sentences you use.

STEP 2

**Decide on skills and vocabulary words you want to be sure to include and
A) Compose your own sentences; B) Use the *Caught'yas* as written in Petra's story;**

C) Change the sentences in Petra's story to fit your students' needs; or D) Pick only one of the sentences in each *Caught'ya* for your students to copy, then plan to do the others orally with the class.

Skills to Be Included

All the skills that most states require second-grade teachers to cover have been included in Petra's story, but you also may wish to make a list of some additional skills you want to include. Keep this list (and a list of the required skills) on your desk all year for reference. If you write *Caught'ya*s based on your science or social studies units or if you write your own story, make sure to include in your sentences all the skills that are required for second-grade English in your state plus the extra ones on your list.

If you use Petra's story in this chapter, you might want to read all the corrected *Caught'ya*s **(C)** as well as all the skills listed to the left of each *Caught'ya* to make sure that the pre-written sentences include all those additional, non-required English skills that you want to cover this year.

Although most skills and many "big juicy" vocabulary words are repeated many times in the 120 *Caught'ya*s of this story, you might want to check for any basic skills your students may need repeated even more often. The *Caught'ya*s in Petra's story are generic and are designed for the "average" (if there is such a thing) second-grade student. If you teach gifted classes or classes in which more than half of your students are educationally below level, you may want to make the sentences more or less difficult according to the needs of your particular students.

Vocabulary

Remember that if you write your own sentences, you will want to insert at least one "big juicy" vocabulary word in each *Caught'ya* that you write. The difficulty of the word doesn't matter. Just write the sentences and then find a good place in each sentence to substitute a more sophisticated word. One of those little electronic spell checkers or thesauruses is perfect for finding delicious synonyms. Young children *love* to use these words; the bigger the better!! (Remember the "chartreuse" story in **How and Why to Use This Book**?)

Changing the Caught'yas

Changing the existing sentences or composing a few more of your own is easy. Check your students' writing efforts to see which skills need to be taught and which skills need more practice. For example, let's say in March your students need more practice writing quotation marks in a conversation. Keeping loosely to the plot of the story you chose, simply add a few more simple conversations for students to correct, in appropriate places, of course.

On the other hand, below-level students in need of basic skills may have to keep working only on putting a capital letter at the beginning of a sentence and punctuation at the end of it. You can simplify the existing sentences before you put these on the board or overhead, or you can put in missing commas, etc. on the papers of those weaker students as you stop by to see if you "caught" them.

In a nutshell, if you wish to add more or take away something, you can do either in several ways. This is the hallmark of the *Caught'ya* method — each teacher can modify the sentences for his or her classes. You can do any or all of the following:

● Go over as an entire class the skills you decide are too difficult for your students to do individually and have students make the changes with you as you write on the board or overhead.

- Pick only one of the sentences in each *Caught'ya* for your students to copy. This may be needed if your students are particularly slow copiers at the beginning of the year. Do the rest orally as a class.

- Add or delete punctuation from a *Caught'ya* before you put it on the board or overhead, depending on your students' developmental level.

- Rewrite the *Caught'ya* sentences in Petra's story in order to include fewer or more skills.

- As your students' copying ability and writing fluency increase, add another short sentence to each *Caught'ya*.

STEP 3

Teach your students about editing journals and response journals and make one of each for every student. Read to your class the introduction and prepare your students for Petra's story.

Use of Editing and Response Journals

Slowly begin your students on their *Caught'ya* journey into fluent writing and the use of good vocabulary by making or by having each child make an editing journal and a free-writing, response journal. Demonstrate their use.

The editing journals are for the *Caught'ya*s. These are the journals into which students copy the daily sentence and correct it. The response journals are for use after a student finishes copying and correcting the *Caught'ya*. These response journals are for free writing about any subject the student desires. You can suggest a topic for those children who cannot think of a subject, but it should be just that, a suggestion. It is a good idea to link the suggestion to the action or vocabulary in the day's *Caught'ya*.

Beginning second graders are not developmentally ready to edit their own writing, although they can rewrite. By having two journals, the two concepts are separated for the time being. Halfway through the year, you may want to ask your students to search in one of their already filled response journals for capital letters and end punctuation that need to be changed or inserted, for sentences in which to substitute strong, active verbs, and for places to add some really "big, juicy" vocabulary words.

Making Editing and Response Journals

You can construct the editing and response journals from unlined newsprint (although it tears easily), 8 1/2" by 11" greenbar computer paper (without carbons), or large-lined primary paper. Old, still usable computer paper often is given away by businesses who are delighted to donate their unused, fading, outdated paper instead of throwing it out. Make construction paper covers and staple the paper inside the covers or, if you have one, use the machine that perforates the left edge and buy those big, curling-edge claw binders that hold a booklet together.

The students then can decorate their folders or booklets. They will need to make several editing and response journals during the course of the year. Another idea for both journals, if you can find them and your budget can afford it, is to buy spiral notebooks with primary lines and paste a piece of white construction paper over the cover so that each student can decorate his or her own notebook.

Preparing Your Students for Petra's Story

When you are ready to begin doing *Caught'ya*s, introduce some of the more difficult words (the big juicy words) that will appear in the first few *Caught'ya*s. Post them on the board. Sound them out daily. Display the stuffed skunk prominently.

A thematic unit on skunks and their cousins also might be in order. Second graders love animals. I know a second-grade teacher who has her students enthralled about snails, of all things! Her students read about them, study them, develop a snail colony, and finally sell them at the end of the year. Why not investigate skunks?

After investigating skunks a bit, students will be primed for and interested in *Putrescent Petra*. They also will become familiar with some of the technical words that appear in the narrative. Most importantly, they are ready to begin the *Caught'ya* story.

After these initial introductions, you are ready to read the beginning of *Putrescent Petra Finds Friends*, the part that is meant to be read aloud by the teacher. Read this introduction many times to acquaint your students with Petra and her beginnings and with skunks in general. This introductory story line (that leaves the reader hanging) primes your students to do the *Caught'ya*s and also introduces a few of the vocabulary words that will be repeated in the *Caught'ya*s that follow.

STEP 4

Write the day's *Caught'ya* incorrectly (Sentence B) on the board or overhead. Read the sentences dramatically, going over the vocabulary words and reviewing paragraphing, capitalization, and end punctuation.

Overhead vs. Blackboard

Personally, I dislike using audio-visual devices of any kind, even one as simple as an overhead. The cord trips you, the bulb burns out just as your most difficult students enter the room, and the squirt bottle (or else you have to use spit) is a tempting weapon for students to use on each other.

Another problem with the use of an overhead is that the uncorrected sentence needs to be written on the transparency in permanent marker so that you can use an erasable overhead marker when you correct the sentence without erasing the uncorrected sentence. Once written in permanent marker, the incorrect sentences cannot be changed in order to play with quotations or to add another phrase with a comma or two.

On the other hand, with the use of the overhead, you do have the sentences already copied for subsequent years. It also affords you time for a few more sips of coffee and deep breaths before beginning the next subject or ushering in your class. At the primary level, you do not usually change classes and the skills to be included are basic with little room for changes. This, too, makes the overhead more practical. The choice (and dilemma) is yours.

Introducing Each Day's Caught'ya

Whichever mode of presentation you choose, copy the day's *Caught'ya*, box the vocabulary words and leave out the punctuation you want your students to insert on their own.

When you put the sentence on the board or overhead (the sentence marked "**B**" for board), list beside it, or on the board somewhere, what you want your students to do with the *Caught'ya*. At first you may ask students only to add capital letters and end punctuation. Children could be asked to write a synonym or two for one or more of the words or to define the vocabulary word. You can require them to identify the part of speech of an underlined word. What do *your* students need to practice?

This is where it is especially important to challenge your students to correct the sentences. Dare them, make funny bets with them, do whatever it takes to intrigue your students enough to work hard to correct the sentence, to find any literary device (mostly similes), and to learn the vocabulary words well enough to recall them when writing their own compositions.

What to Include in the Introduction to a Day's Caught'ya

It is a good idea to do the following:

- Read the *Caught'ya* sentences dramatically
- Review what happened previously in the story (for those who have been absent)
- Elicit the meaning of the vocabulary words in a way that will make your students remember them for more than five minutes (or make someone look it up for the class)
- Point out any literary device like similes or alliteration and elicit other examples
- Warn of any difficult skill that is included (like the comma in a compound sentence)

Paragraphs

A discussion of "to paragraph or not to paragraph" also might be in order even with beginning second graders. Students must learn to paragraph early so that they do not have problems later. Those teachers who follow you will be extremely grateful if you can teach your students the rudiments of basic paragraphing, especially the use of a new paragraph every time someone new speaks.

STEP 5

Students write the *Caught'ya* as correctly as they can, and then, with as many sentences as they can, write in their response journals about something related to the *Caught'ya*.

Editing Journal Work

After you instruct students to write the sentences in their editing journals as correctly as they can, you should see them hard at work. First, students should write their names, the day of the week (to practice spelling), the date (copied from the board), and the number of the *Caught'ya* on the line above today's sentences. Encourage students to read and reread the sentences to try to catch all the errors. This is practice for what they will be required to do in subsequent grades when they are developmentally ready to edit and proofread their own papers.

Response Journal Work

After copying and correcting the *Caught'ya*, students focus on writing several sentences or a paragraph in their response journals. This free writing may be about any subject a student wishes; however, most second graders need a suggestion for topic. Use a word or action from the day's *Caught'ya* for this purpose. For example, *Caught'ya* #10 reads: "Petra, however, was not alarmed. She was not afraid of anything except owls and those noisy, big, shiny things on the hard black path that sometimes did not stop for skunks." Topics for response journals could be any one of the following:

- Write about a time you were alarmed or afraid.
- Write all you know about owls. Why do you think Petra is afraid of them?

- What are the "noisy, big, shiny things" that do not stop for skunks? Try to write about a time you rode in one. Then, imagine if you were a skunk.

- What else might scare Petra?

Each *Caught'ya* contains enough information to generate topics for the response journals. You might even want to ask your class, after they have read the *Caught'ya*, to suggest a topic for the day's entry in the response journal.

STEP 6

Walk around the room, helping students with the *Caught'ya*, providing individual mini-lessons, commenting on each student's effort, giving hugs, and aiding with response journals by offering suggestions and writing a few comments or questions of your own.

What to Do as You Go around the Classroom

As your students attempt to write the *Caught'ya* sentences as correctly as they can (or just one of them if they are not yet capable of more), you walk around to each student and do some of the following:

- Give a hug of encouragement to each student on task

- Tease those students you know are being lazy

- Issue a challenge to your top students

- Goad good-naturedly those who are slow starters but could work faster

- Offer individual encouragement to your weaker writers

- Provide a ten-second mini-lesson to those who are not up-to-level on skills

- Skim the sentences in the response journals of those who have finished the *Caught'ya* and are already writing, and write a brief comment as well.

Using the Stuffed Skunk

You may want to have your stuffed skunk accompany you as you walk around the room checking your students' *Caught'ya*s and reading their response journals. Petra can do the teasing with you. She can sit on the desk of a particularly good child. She can go to the hospital for a temporary stay with a sick one. This involves students even more in the story. Petra can become the class mascot.

You also will need to explain that while they can pet Petra, the stuffed skunk, they should not touch or approach wild skunks. In the following story, the children never approach Petra even though she is declared to be clear of rabies. They remain friends from a distance.

Tricks to Time Management

Time yourself very carefully. After practice, you will find it takes about ten minutes to circulate around a class of thirty students. There is, however, a trick to this — several tricks in fact.

If your classes are large, as happens all too frequently, you will see only part of a *Caught'ya* sentence in the first papers you examine. If you wait to circulate around the many desks until all your students have completed the *Caught'ya* in their editing journals and have begun writing in their response journals, you could have pandemonium and boredom on your hands. (More suggestions to avoid this problem can be found later in this section.) Instead, simply glance at the first few words of the *Caught'ya* and praise those who have not yet made errors. Then, as students' sentences are more and more complete, look for only *one* thing such as the capitalization of a proper noun.

As you amble around the room glancing at your students' *Caught'ya*s, choose the most difficult correction in the *Caught'ya* because many of your students probably will miss it at first glance. If that error still exists in a student's paper, tease quickly (I say, "*Caught'ya*") and move on. If, on the other hand, a student has found and corrected the error, take a few more seconds to check the rest of the sentences. In this way, you can move very quickly around the room. I sometimes hum a tune (one at least thirty years old) as I circulate, stopping only occasionally to praise a student whose *Caught'ya* has no errors. My students hate my hummed rendition of "She'll Be Coming Round the Mountain" the most.

It is a good idea to time yourself for the first few weeks or so, in order to see that you don't spend too much time with this step. At the second-grade level, you may find that it takes your students too long to copy all of the sentences of a *Caught'ya*. (There are usually two and sometimes three of them.) If your students have this problem, ask them to copy only one of the sentences in each *Caught'ya* (the one you picked out beforehand in **STEP 2**) and do the others orally as a class.

Keeping It Fair and Keeping Students Occupied

Keep in mind to vary where you begin checking the papers. I start at the right side of the room for even-numbered *Caught'ya*s and the left side of the room for odd-numbered *Caught'ya*s. This keeps me straight and the feedback fair since the first few that I check never have the *Caught'ya*s and the response journals completed.

It is a good idea, of course, to have the day's reading or math assignment already posted on the board so that if a few of your top students finish correcting the *Caught'ya* and finish writing in their response journals, they can put their journals aside for a few minutes and begin working math problems or read until you make it around the entire classroom. It also is a good idea to have your students become accustomed to the routine of switching immediately to the next activity when they finish the *Caught'ya* and response journal. You can establish this routine at the beginning of the year. Harry Wong in his tapes and books offers some wonderfully practical ideas for establishing classroom routines.

The reality of today's classroom, assignment on board or not, practiced routine or not, is that most students do not like to switch to a new activity before bringing closure to the previous one. They will wait for you to finish going around the room and will jabber when finished with the *Caught'ya* and response journal. Read on, though. I offer one more solution.

If you have a particularly rowdy class, give feedback to only half of the class each day, again varying the side of the room, so that each student gets the feedback once every two days. In my experience, however, students dislike this practice and will look at the board to find something constructive to do so that I can complete my rounds of the entire class daily. Of course, second graders are still young enough to fall into line with the old ploy: "I like the way John is working so quietly..."

STEP 7

Return to the board or overhead and check the *Caught'ya* with the class, eliciting answers from students and reviewing the vocabulary words.

After the students have written the *Caught'ya* sentences as correctly as they can and noted any part of speech or synonym you asked for, and after you have circulated around the room giving feedback to each child, return to the blackboard or overhead and have the class tell you how to correct the sentences.

As your students point out each correction, you supply the appropriate proofreading symbols on the board or overhead and go over the *why* of each correction. If a mini-lesson is in order, give one. In this book, to the left of each sentence in the story, you will find the *why* listed for each correction. If a plethora of your students missed a certain skill (capitalizing a proper noun, for example), you can launch into a brief explanation and elicit other examples.

Teaching Suggestions

It is always a good idea to use something different (especially humor) in your explanations. For example, when I teach the difference between the intransitive verb "to rise" (does not take an object) and the transitive verb "to raise" (always takes an object), I use props, including myself, and rise from unusual places like the trash can. I ask the students to rise and to raise various objects. They laugh and think that I may be crazy, but the next time in their writing, they might use the correct form of the verb and even smile as they do it.

I use mnemonic devices because they work. I find that students learn difficult material much faster with the use of mnemonics (like **FANBOYS** to learn the seven coordinating conjunctions and songs to learn the helping verbs).

From a primary teacher, I borrowed a way to teach students capital letters and end punctuation from the start. Ask students to nod or stamp their feet at a capital letter in the *Caught'ya* and clap their hands for a period. Your students should do this twice daily — once when you initially review the *Caught'ya* and the second time when you review it with the class.

It is also very effective to ask students physically to "stand up and move it over" whenever a new paragraph is needed in a *Caught'ya*. I like to use a "raspberry" (tongue only slightly out) for commas and a "click" sound accompanied by appropriate hand signals for a quote. By using their bodies in these very effective kinesthetic-learning exercises, students recall the rules better and usually remember to include end punctuation and capital letters when they write their own compositions. The more advanced students may even learn to indent on their own before the end of the year. More teaching suggestions can be found in the **Appendix**.

I am sure that you already use all kinds of similar techniques to wrest your students' attention from their friends and the latest computer games in order to teach them English. (I was told by one fifth-grade teacher that he has his students sing an opera of the irregular verbs!) This is the step where you put such innovative ideas to good use. Because of the *Caught'ya*, you already should have their attention.

Vital Advice

My only advice (which comes from painful experience) is to keep your explanations bizarre, funny, and *short*. Teach no more than one point a day and keep it to fewer than three to five minutes, even with a class of gifted students. Absorbing correct English usage, mechanics, and grammar must be done in short, but intense, bursts if retention and carry-over are to take place. This is especially true in the second grade.

Repetition is the key. Keep on plugging a little bit each day, and keep on repeating *ad nauseam* until your students get the point and, most importantly, begin to use it correctly in their writing. I think that the much used quote about "All's fair in love and war" should be amended to say, "All's fair in love, war, and the teaching of correct English to young children."

Students mark mistakes with proofreading symbols (if possible).

As you go over the *Caught'ya* sentence at the board or overhead, students should try to use very simple proofreading symbols to correct any error they did not catch when they corrected the *Caught'ya* on their own. Encourage the children to indicate these corrections with a colored pencil, pen, or marker in a hue different from the one with which they wrote the sentences. You may want to make sure that there is one in each student's desk just for this purpose. Use the students' work in their response journals as a barometer on improvement in writing. I think you will be pleasantly surprised at the unconscious carry-over from *Caught'yas* to free writing.

Proofreading Symbols

Listed below are a few of the most commonly used proofreading symbols. These are the simplest ones. Ease young students into using them by introducing them one at a time, very slowly during the year. If you think students are not developmentally ready to handle the use of proofreading symbols, don't introduce them or use only one or two all year.

Symbol	Meaning	Symbol	Meaning
¶	Indent	¶ (crossed out)	Take out indent
∧	Add words here	ℓ	Take out, delete
≡ (under letter)	Capitalize	A (slashed)	Make a small letter
⟶	Move word	(the⟶and)	Reverse order
◯	Add punctuation (whatever is inside circle)		

Students count and indicate number of errors in the margin.

Students count the number of errors they did not catch when they attempted to correct the sentence on their own. They indicate the number in the right-hand margin. This process has two advantages. It makes students leave a good, healthy, right-hand margin, and it provides them with immediate feedback. Remind students to make all corrections, notations, and notes in a color different from the one they used to write the *Caught'ya* itself. Again, this is a study technique that makes it easier for students to see where they need to concentrate.

Encourage, cajole, forbid, threaten — do anything you can think of to keep your students honest. I do not recommend grading the *Caught'yas* of second graders in the traditional way (explained in **Chapter 3**). This would discourage budding writers. Thus, since second-grade students receive only comments and a grade for completion of the *Caught'yas*, it would be pointless for students to try to hide errors and correct them surreptitiously as the answers are divulged. Moreover, cheating would only hinder a student from learning from his/her mistakes.

Collect the editing journals and make some positive, individual comments in each student's journal. Collect response journals at another time. Write additional encouraging comments. For further instruction at a later time, note errors your students made.

Collecting the Journals and Dealing with Absentees

Keeping an editing journal and a response journal helps your students organize themselves and learn to keep track of booklets they use daily. This trains them for later grades when they have to keep notebooks and keep one piece of paper with a week's worth of *Caught'ya*s on it. It also helps you keep track of students' writing progress. Collect these journals as often as you wish. I suggest once a week.

Since there are no student texts for the *Caught'ya* method, it is difficult for students to make up missed *Caught'ya*s. Check your gradebook for those children who have been absent. Write "absent" in their journals for the days they missed and do not require them to make up those days' *Caught'ya*s.

Editing Journals

After collecting the journals, just glance at them to see that each child is completing the *Caught'ya*s. Look for daily format. Each *Caught'ya* should have the heading you wish to require (name, date, and day) for practice with spelling. It works best when an entire school adopts the same heading, making it much easier for the students to follow this routine in future grades.

Make a positive comment on each editing journal to congratulate every child on mastering a skill, like consistently capitalizing the first word in a sentence. Editing should be a positive experience. I suggest using "smiley faces" liberally. No grades need be given except a check for completion.

Using Response Journals to Chart Progress

Next, look at each child's response journal. These are the real indicators of progress and improvement in writing fluency. You might want to keep a chart for each child to indicate skills mastered (capitalization and end punctuation, for example), number of more sophisticated

Student's Name _____

Week	Basic Skills Mastered and Used	Extra Skills Mastered and Used	Vocabulary Used	# of Sentences per Entry	Comments
Sept.13-17					
Sept. 20-24					
9/27-10/2					
Oct. 5-9					
etc.....					

vocabulary words used, and increase in numbers of sentences and subsequent decrease in use of pictures and letters. Such a chart would come in handy at parent conferences and when evaluating a student's progress in language arts. An example of such a chart is on the previous page.

A Few Final Notes

Two Pieces of Advice

Keep it simple. Since you explain the "why" of all the corrections when you go over the *Caught'ya*, you don't want to go beyond what your students can learn. (Remember Piaget?) By using the fundamental eight parts of speech, you easily can explain all the essential grammar and usage without using the more technical terms and "turning off" students. This tool is especially useful in teaching very young, "regular," and below-level students.

For example, seven-year-olds can comprehend something as complicated as a participial phrase if you identify it as an "-ing verb" that does not have an "is" or "was" before it. Whenever students see an "-ing verb" without an "is" or "was," they can learn that commas must be used.

Similarly, second-grade teachers do not want to teach about subordinate clauses, and yet there are subordinate clauses in the *Caught'ya*s because second-grade teachers do want to model and introduce complex sentences. If the clause comes at the beginning of the complex sentence, you can explain the comma (if you choose to explain it at all) without using the term "subordinate clause." The key is to keep your explanations understandable and as simple as possible when you go over the reason behind each correction. The **Appendix** contains a suggestion for teaching this skill.

As stated above, the goal (and the end result) is not to learn English terms, but to be able to write correctly. If a second grader can write a clear paragraph of simple sentences with very few errors, you have accomplished a lot. At this point, your aim is for good, fluent writing, not complex structure. Indeed, authors like Hemingway illustrate that simple writing works just fine and can be quite beautiful.

Don't be shy. It is important to keep in mind that English rules are not always hard and fast. In fact, many of the rules of English are debatable. I, for example, always put the comma before the "and" in a series of three or more. Others do not. Some paragraphing is personal as, for example, in a long introduction to a quote. Optional commas after introductory adverbs abound. Some grammar books list "quick" as an adverb (without the "ly"). I refuse to do so.

In other words, feel free to disagree with me. I am not even the "absolute word" in my own classroom. My students and I have hot debates over paragraphing and optional comma use, for example. By the way, just so you know how far I do go in order to be comfortable with the rules — the apostrophe in *Caught'ya* is a contraction of the made-up word, "caughtchya."

A Request

Now for the request. Even though I read through each set of *Caught'ya*s at least five times (once out loud), and even though four other people, all experienced editors, also proofread them very carefully, I know that a few errors probably still lurk among the sentences and lists of skills. *Please*, if you spot one, especially an egregious mistake that is *not* debatable, write to me via the publisher, who will forward your letter to me. The errors you find will be corrected at the next printing of the book.   The address can be found on the copyright page.

What Is Included in the Following Story

There are two sets of the *Caught'ya*s for the second-grade story. The first (labeled **B** for "board") is the set to put on the board or overhead, the sentences that contain the errors to correct or the blanks to fill in. The second (labeled **C** for "corrected") is a corrected version for you.

Listed to the left of each *Caught'ya*, you will find all the grammar, mechanics, and usage skills and rules related to that particular *Caught'ya*. If the example of a skill is fairly obvious, it is not specifically identified in the **C** section. If the example is something that we teachers (with our rusty recollections of English grammar from college) might not recognize at first glance, it is listed. Check the **Appendix** for explanations.

At the second-grade level, the *Caught'ya*s do not require students to change spelling, verb tense, word usage, etc. If you think your students are ready and you wish to have your students work with any of these, simply change a word (like the spelling of a homophone, for example) or leave something out (like a comma).

Many *Caught'ya*s also include simple literary devices and a few teaching suggestions. In addition to the grammar, mechanics, and usage skills, each *Caught'ya* in the following story has at least one "$100 word" in it. Most have more. Young children love such words. They love to use them. Sometimes children will write big words more correctly than the smaller, more commonly used ones. Most of the new words are repeated many times in subsequent *Caught'ya*s. After a few repetitions, words no longer are put in bold type nor are they featured at the top of the *Caught'ya* sentences.

Four Other Very Important Notes for Using This Particular Story

1) You will have to write your name and the names of your students in the appropriate blanks when they occur. Fifty-two blanks have been left for the names of your students since you will want to use some children's names more than once.

2) Note that quotation marks have been supplied for modeling purposes in the first thirty *Caught'ya*s (in the **B** sentences). After that, most have been omitted. You need to go over them each time in the first thirty *Caught'ya*s so that your students can supply them in the last ninety if you choose to omit them as I have. All types of quotes are covered, more than are needed at the second-grade level.

Similarly, commas have been supplied in the **B** sentences for modeling purposes in the first sixty *Caught'ya*s and then omitted after that. Again, it is up to you whether to put back the commas when you write the *Caught'ya* on the board (or type it) for your students. All comma rules (see **Appendix**) but the commas in the greeting and closing of a letter are covered in *Caught'ya*s #1 through #60 for modeling and in #61–120 for practice.

In addition, paragraphs are modeled in the first eighty *Caught'ya*s. After that, there are none in the student sentences. Therefore, it is important to have a daily discussion of why there is (or is not) a paragraph when the class goes over the first eighty.

Colons, semi-colons, hyphens, and apostrophes are not eliminated from the student sentences because most second graders are not yet ready to understand the use of these.

3) Note that although I have supplied the types of sentences (simple, compound, complex) to the left of each of the third-grade *Caught'ya*s, at the second-grade level, I have not included them because the teaching of such labels is superfluous for younger students. Modeling the different types of sentences is sufficient. Of course, point them out if you feel that your students are ready to learn the names of the types of sentences.

4) Since this story is told in the past tense (with "ed"), you may want to teach that form before beginning the *Caught'ya*s.

Conclusion

Following this section is a quick-reference lesson plan (without the extra comments) to use as you teach the basic *Caught'ya* lesson. It won't be long, though, until you no longer need it. After you have read the Introduction and this chapter, relax and use the sentences in this story to forge a partnership with your students that will result in improved writing, increased vocabulary, and maybe a few laughs as you teach and correct. Enjoy!

2
Lesson Plans for the *Caught'ya*

This plan assumes that you already have completed Steps 1, 2, and 3.

- Before school, write the *Caught'ya* for the day on the board or overhead, box the vocabulary word, and beside it or on the board, list what you want your students to do with it. (For example: correct the *Caught'ya*; copy the vocabulary words; put meaning and a synonym or two for one of the vocabulary words; list parts of speech of underlined words, etc.)

- When the bell rings, read the sentence to the class with a dramatic flair, reviewing the story that went before, eliciting the meaning of the vocabulary words, and discussing the need for a capital letter and end punctuation. Debate the need for a paragraph.

- Instruct students to copy the *Caught'ya* as correctly as they can and to follow the required guidelines listed on the board. Instruct students to write in their response journals when they have completed the *Caught'ya*. You may want to suggest a topic that is related to a word or idea in the *Caught'ya*.

- Walk around the room, giving students individual feedback. Say *"Caught'ya"* or something comparable if you catch a student with an error, and praise or challenge a student who has caught all of the errors so far. Give hugs, encouragement, and mini-lessons. Quickly read response journals and write a brief comment.

- Go back to the blackboard or overhead and check the *Caught'ya* sentences out loud with your class. Elicit answers from the students. Be sure to discuss the *reason* for each correction. Using proofreading symbols and a pen of a different hue, correct the *Caught'ya* on the board or overhead as your students do the same with any error they did not catch. Refer to the **Appendix** at the back of this book for simple explanations and other examples.

- Review the vocabulary words. Discuss the literary device (a simile, for example) in the sentence and conduct a mini-lesson in whatever skill you think needs more reinforcement. *Keep it short!*

- Instruct students to be sure that they write the date and day of the week and the number of the *Caught'ya* right above the sentence, count their errors, and indicate them in the right-hand margin.

- Collect editing and response journals after one week for comments and for charting progress of your students.

3
Text to Be Read Aloud by the Teacher

At the beginning of the year, read the following story line to the class to introduce the background of the story. Vocabulary beyond a second-grade level has been bolded the first time each word is used. Since this part of the story is intended for oral reading by an adult, these words are pointed out only to highlight their level of difficulty. Words with hearts (♥) after them will be included frequently in the children's sentences.

Putrescent Petra

Finds Friends

Putrescent♥ Petra♥ waddled♥ through the grass of a big **field♥**. It was night, her favorite time to hunt food. Petra stopped briefly to eat a yummy grasshopper. Her little brown nose at the end of her pointy head twitched as she sniffed an apple core a few feet away. After she ate the grasshopper, Petra **ambled** over to the apple core and ate that as well. She was not a fussy eater.

Petra's long, thick, hairy coat was black and white. A white patch went down her pointed **snout**, right between her eyes. There was another white patch on top of her head. Two white stripes **extended** down on either side of her back to the place where her big, **plume-like** ♥tail began. From that spot, one, **double-wide** white stripe continued down the middle of her big, long, bushy tail. Petra's tail was almost as long as her body! All four of her short legs ended in little white feet with long claws at the end. She was the size of a big house cat. What was Petra? Petra was a **striped skunk♥**.

Now, the **scientific** name for a striped skunk is *Mephitis mephitis. Mephitis* means "really stinky" or "**evil** smelling." So, to repeat the word *"mephitis"* in the scientific name for a striped skunk makes it mean "double stinky." The Algonquin Indians called the skunk *Segonku*. Some Americans call skunks "polecats," but skunks are *not* polecats. Polecats are related to skunks, but they are *not* the same **species** of animal. They are not skunks. Some people call skunks "woodpussies" because they are the size of a house cat, and they often live in the woods. But, wild skunks live everywhere in **North America**. They live in the woods, on farms, in small towns, and even in big cities!

Some **domesticated** skunks (that have had their **scent♥ glands** taken away) live in houses with boys and girls like you. Skunks do not make as good a pet as a dog or a cat because they are wild and always want to be free. They sometimes bite their owners, and they are very **stubborn**. Do you know someone who is very stubborn?

There are only three types of skunks — striped skunks, spotted skunks (which do a handstand when they squirt their stink), and the hog-nosed skunks. Maybe your teacher will take you to the library to find out more about Putrescent Petra and other skunks. But, back to Petra's story.

Petra was a striped skunk, and she was still hungry, even after the yummy grasshopper and apple core. As Petra nosed through the grass for more goodies to eat, a big brown dog ran onto the field. It could smell Petra. Petra did not run. She was not afraid. She did what all skunks do. Petra turned around and put her behind toward the dog. She turned her head around to watch the dog and stamped her front feet in **warning**♥. The dog came closer. Petra **chattered**♥ her teeth and **hissed**♥ and **growled**♥ to warn the dog again. The dog came even closer and growled at Petra. The dog showed his teeth. Petra still did not move. She was not afraid. Petra had a secret **weapon**♥.

Petra then raised her tail. It went straight up in the air with the tip still hanging limp. She began to **arch**♥ her back. The big dog suddenly ran away. He ran before Petra could poke the tip of her tail up straight and spray her **musk**♥ to protect herself. That dog learned slowly, but he was smart enough to pay attention to Petra's warnings before it was too late.

Petra was glad that she did not have to use her secret weapon. She only used it in an emergency when all her warnings had failed. Petra continued across the field in search of food. She found a candy wrapper and licked the insides. There was still a **morsel** of chocolate clinging to the paper. Yummy! Petra was an **omnivore**. She ate everything.

Petra ate and ate. This field was filled with yummy **insects** and other goodies. In the darkness of the night, Petra could see the shadow of a big building. What was it? As she waddled her chubby body towards it, the building **loomed** larger and larger.

Petra crossed some hard concrete. She could smell no food there, so she hurried across to where the grass grew. She ambled and waddled closer and closer to the big building. Petra smelled more food near the building. A trash can! This was a perfect place to set up skunk **housekeeping**.

The sun's first rays peeked over the trees and began to light up the sky. Petra knew it was time to find a **burrow**♥ for the day. You see, skunks are **nocturnal** animals like cats. And, like cats, they hunt for food during the night and sleep most of the day.

Petra looked up and up, way up to the top of the building. Then she looked down at the base. She spotted a small hole to her left, a little hole right under the building. She waddled towards it. The hole became a small **tunnel** that went two feet under the big building. She went in. Petra was happy. This was perfect!

Petra's long claws dug out a place that was just big enough for a skunk to sleep in along the side of the little tunnel. Then she curled around into a black and white ball, **buried** her pointed snout in her tail, and went to sleep. Her belly was full, and Petra was content. No **predators**♥ could find her there in her little hole under the building. Petra was full and safe.

Suddenly, Petra the Putrescent woke with a start. She heard the sound of many animals making a lot of noise. She heard animals running. She heard animals walking. She heard animals making strange sounds. Not growls and hisses. Not barks. Not hoots like her enemy, the owl. What was it? The noises did not sound threatening, but they were loud.

Then, an even louder sound rang out. It rang until the building above Petra seemed to shake. Petra leapt to her feet. This was scary. She sniffed the air. She smelled food, lots of good food, lots of different kinds of food. She did not want to leave this place, but the loud ringing noise scared her for a minute. Just as she was about to **investigate** the sound, it stopped. The animal noises stopped, too. Petra curled up again and went back to sleep dreaming of big, juicy roaches and her favorite food, eggs.

Stop reading out loud here.

4

120 *Caught'ya* Sentences for Second Graders

Putrescent Petra, Finds Friends

1. putrescent, burrow

Paragraph – beginning of story
Capitalization – always begin sentences and quotes with a capital letter; always capitalize proper nouns and "I"
Punctuation – sentences always have end punctuation
Commas – subordinate clause at beginning of sentence; city, state,
Verb tense – "sat" is past tense of irregular verb "to sit"
Spelling rules – compound words
Skills – write school name; strong verb use

B – as **putrescent** petra slept, the children at _____ elementary school in (put your city, state here) sat in a classroom right above her **burrow**

C – As **Putrescent** Petra slept, a class of children at _____ Elementary School in (put your city, state here) sat in a classroom right above her **burrow.**

2. editing, journal, response, snack, gazed

No paragraph – same topic
Capitalization – always begin sentences and quotes with a capital letter
Punctuation – sentences always have end punctuation
Verb tense – add "ed" to end of regular verbs to put in past tense; "ate" is past tense of irregular verb "to eat"
Spelling rules – compound words; add "s" to most nouns to make plural
Skills – possessive of singular noun; strong verb practice

B – some students worked in their **editing journals** or their **response journals**. others ate the popcorn of that morning's **snack** and **gazed** out the window

C – Some students worked in their **editing journals** or their **response journals**. Others ate the popcorn of that morning's **snack** and **gazed** out the window.

NOTE: *Possession is a new skill for second graders. They are not ready, this early in the year, to learn how to use an apostrophe to indicate ownership. Possession is, however, used in many Caught'yas. This is for modeling purposes only. When you feel that your students are ready for a simple explanation of why and when an apostrophe is used to show possession, go for it. If you think that your students are not ready, continue modeling and hope that it will sink in eventually. Middle school students still have trouble with this concept.*

B = the sentence(s) to be put on the board or overhead   **C = the corrected sentence(s)**

3. idea, snoozed

No paragraph – same topic, same speaker
    (narrator)
Capitalization – always begin sentences and
    quotes with a capital letter
Punctuation – sentences always have end
    punctuation
Commas – extra information
Verb tense – add "ed" to end of regular verbs to
    put in past tense; "had" is past tense of
    irregular verb "to have"
Spelling rules – "no one" is 2 words; plural of
    "foot" is "feet"

Skills – "no one" is singular, thus the possessive
    pronoun and the verb must be singular.

B – no one, not even the teacher, had any **idea** what **snoozed** right beneath his or her feet

C – No one, not even the teacher, had any **idea** what **snoozed** right beneath his or her feet.

---

4. recess, alarmed, noise

Paragraph – time change and action change
Capitalization – always begin sentences
    and quotes with a capital letter; always
    capitalize proper nouns and "I"
Punctuation – sentences always have end
    punctuation; hyphens needed when many
    words act as one word
Commas – participial phrase (used to tell more
    about Petra); 2 adjectives where the 2nd is
    not color, age, or linked to the noun
Verb tense – add "ed" to end of regular verbs to
    put in past tense; "rang" is past tense of
    irregular verb "to ring"
Skills – strong verb practice
Literary device – simile

B –   the bell rang for **recess**. petra jumped up like a black and white jack-in-the-box, **alarmed** again by the loud, ringing **noise**

C –   The bell rang for **recess**. Petra jumped up like a black and white jack-in-the-box, **alarmed** again by the loud, ringing **noise**.

---

5. entrance, burrow

No paragraph – same topic
Capitalization – always begin sentences and
    quotes with a capital letter
Punctuation – sentences always have end
    punctuation
Commas – long introductory adverb (out of
    place so needs to be set apart)
Verb tense – add "ed" to end of regular verbs to
    put in past tense; "ran" is past tense of
    irregular verb "to run"; "had" is past tense
    of "to have"
Spelling rules – consonant/vowel/consonant
    (if suffix is added, double 2nd consonant)
Skills – recognizing correct homophone
    (there/their/they're)

B – she ran to the **entrance** of her **burrow.** by the time she got there, the ringing had stopped

C – She ran to the **entrance** of her **burrow.** By the time she got there, the ringing had stopped.

B = the sentence(s) to be put on the board or overhead   **C = the corrected sentence(s)**

6. dangerous, noise

Paragraph – new person speaking
Capitalization – always begin sentences and quotes with a capital letter; always capitalize proper nouns and "I"
Punctuation – sentences always have end punctuation; use of quotation marks around what is said out loud
Verb tense – "thought" is past tense of irregular verb "to think"; switch to present tense for quote
Skills – negatives; word recognition; compound verb
Literary device – simile

B – petra thought and __ __ __ __ __ __. "that ringing sound is not **dangerous.** it is just lots of **noise** like thunder "

C – Petra thought and <u>thought</u>. "That ringing sound is not **dangerous.** It is just lots of **noise** like thunder."

---

7. awake, putrescent, decided, field

Paragraph – new person speaking (narrator)
Capitalization – always begin sentences and quotes with a capital letter; always capitalize proper nouns and "I"
Punctuation – sentences always have end punctuation
Commas – subordinate clause at beginning of sentence (long adverb)
Verb tense – add "ed" to end of regular verbs to put in past tense; "was" is past tense of irregular verb "to be"; "thought" is past tense of "to think"
Skills – go over comparatives good/better/best; "good as adjective and "well" as adverb

B – since she was **awake, putrescent** petra **decided** to go find more food. she thought about the good __ __ __ __ in the big **field**

C – Since she was **awake, Putrescent** Petra **decided** to go find more food. She thought about the good <u>food</u> in the big **field.**

---

8. putrescent, peered, burrow, belonged

Paragraph – action change
Capitalization – always begin sentences and quotes with a capital letter; always capitalize proper nouns and "I"
Punctuation – sentences always have end punctuation
Commas – introductory adverb (out of place)
Verb tense – add "ed" to end of regular verbs to put in past tense; "ran" is past tense of irregular verb "to run"
Spelling rules – most nouns form plurals by adding "s"
Skills – possessive of singular noun; "who" is subject and "whom" is object; strong verb practice
Literary device – alliteration

B – suddenly, a lot of strange legs ran by right in front of petra's nose. **putrescent** petra **peered** up from her **burrow** to see to whom the legs **belonged**

C – Suddenly, a lot of strange legs ran by right in front of Petra's nose. **Putrescent** Petra **peered** up from her **burrow** to see to whom the legs **belonged.**

B = the sentence(s) to be put on the board or overhead   **C = the corrected sentence(s)**

9. belonged, plump

No paragraph – same topic, same speaker
    (narrator)
Capitalization – always begin sentences and
    quotes with a capital letter; always capitalize
    proper nouns and "I"
Punctuation – sentences always have end
    punctuation; abbreviations need a period
Commas – noun series
Verb tense – add "ed" to end of regular verbs to
    put in past tense; "were" is past tense of
    irregular verb "to be"
Spelling rules – consonant/vowel/consonant
    double 2nd consonant (ski**nn**y)
Skills – word recognition; possessive of singular
    nouns; hyphen in two words acting as one
    adjective
Literary device – repetition

B – the legs **belonged** to the boys and girls in
    _____'s second-grade class.
there were short legs and long legs, skinny
legs and **plump** ___ ___ ___ ___, girl
___ ___ ___ ___ and boy ___ ___ ___ ___

C – The legs **belonged** to the boys and girls in
    _____'s second-grade class.
There were short legs and long legs, skinny
legs and **plump** <u>legs</u>, girl <u>legs</u> and boy <u>legs</u>.

> **NOTE:** *Put your name in the blank.*

---

10. however, alarmed, noisy

No paragraph – same topic
Capitalization – always begin sentences and
    quotes with a capital letter; always capitalize
    proper nouns and "I"
Punctuation – sentences always have end
    punctuation
Commas – interrupter; adjective series
Verb tense – "was" is past tense of irregular verb
    "to be"
Spelling rules – most nouns add "s" to make
    them plural
Skills – negatives
Literary device – metaphor

B – petra, however, was not **alarmed**. she was
not afraid of anything except owls and those
noisy, big, shiny things on the hard black
path that sometimes did not stop for skunks

C – Petra, **however**, was not **alarmed**. She was
not afraid of anything except owls and those
noisy, big, shiny things on the hard black
path that sometimes did not stop for
skunks.

**11. respected, weapon, putrescent, curious,
alarmed**

No paragraph – same topic
Capitalization – always begin sentences and
    quotes with a capital letter; always capitalize
    proper nouns and "I"
Punctuation – sentences always have end
    punctuation; use of quotation marks
    around what is said out loud
Commas – extra information
Verb tense – add "ed" to end of regular verbs to
    put in past tense; "was" is past tense of
    irregular verb "to be"
Spelling rules – most nouns form plurals by
    adding "s"
Skills – plural rules
Literary device – metaphor

B – other animals, except owls, **respected** petra
and her secret **weapon**. that was why
putrescent petra was more **curious** than
alarmed

C – Other animals, except owls, **respected** Petra
and her secret **weapon**. That was why
Putrescent Petra was more **curious** than
alarmed.

B = the sentence(s) to be put on the board or overhead   **C = the corrected sentence(s)**

12. putrescent, waddled

No paragraph – same topic, same speaker

Capitalization – always begin sentences and quotes with a capital letter; always capitalize proper nouns and "I"

Punctuation – sentences always have end punctuation

Commas – compound sentence (2 sentences stuck together with a coordinating conjunction "for, and, nor, but, or, yet, so.") I call these FANBOYS

Verb tense – add "ed" to end of regular verbs to put in past tense

Skills – strong verb practice; homophone (whole/hole)

Literary device – alliteration (p,p)

B – putrescent petra **waddled** out of her hole, and then she looked around

C – Putrescent Petra **waddled** out of her hole, and then she looked around.

> **NOTE:** *It is a good idea to teach very young students the coordinating conjunctions (there are only seven of them) used to make compound sentences. Once learned, students can be taught not to capitalize them in a title, to put commas before them only if they are in a series or there is a compound sentence, and never to begin a sentence with one. Chant these conjunctions over and over again and, when needed, recall them using the mnemonic device "FANBOYS" (for, and, nor, but, or, yet, so). Memorization gives young (and, indeed, any age) students ownership of a skill. I suggest your students learn them and then chant them every time one appears in a Caught'ya. The teachers who follow you will want to kiss your toes in gratitude!*

13. tracks

No paragraph – same time, same topic

Capitalization – always begin sentences and quotes with a capital letter; always capitalize proper nouns and "I"

Punctuation – sentences always have end punctuation

Verb tense – add "ed" to end of regular verbs to put in past tense; "spoke" is past tense of irregular verb "to speak"

Spelling rules – consonant/vowel/consonant = double final consonant before suffix; "no one" is 2 words

Skills – strong verb practice; possessive of singular noun; homophone (there/their/they're)

Literary device – aphorism (overused, idiomatic expression) "stopped dead in their tracks"

B – at the same time _____'s students stopped dead in their **tracks**. no one moved. no one spoke for a whole minute

C – At the same time _____'s students stopped dead in their **tracks**. No one moved. No one spoke for a whole minute.

B = the sentence(s) to be put on the board or overhead   C = the corrected sentence(s)

14. skunk

2 Paragraphs – someone new speaking

Capitalization – always begin sentences and quotes with a capital letter; always capitalize proper nouns and "I"

Punctuation – sentences always have end punctuation; use of quotation marksaround what is said out loud

Commas – quotes

Verb tense – add "ed" to end of regular verbs to put in past tense; "said" is past tense of irregular verb "to say"

Spelling rules – consonant/vowel/consonant + suffix = double 2nd consonant

Skills – homophone (its/it's); it's = it is; common contractions

Literary device – onomatopoeia (made up word for sound)

B –   "it's a **skunk**," said _____.
"eeew," said _____
as she stepped away from petra

C –   "It's a **skunk**," said _____.
"Eeew," said _____
as she stepped away from Petra.

15. observed, sniffed, rotten

Paragraph – new person speaking

Capitalization – always begin sentences and quotes with a capital letter; always capitalize proper nouns and "I"

Punctuation – sentences always have end punctuation; use of quotation marks around what is said out loud; need question mark at end of question

Commas – quotes

Verb tense – add "ed" to end of regular verbs to put in past tense; switch to present tense for quote

Spelling rules – plurals of most nouns are formed by adding "s"

Skills – common contractions

Literary device – simile

B –   _____ **observed** as he **sniffed**, "it doesn't smell bad at all. don't all skunks smell bad like **rotten** eggs "

C –   _____ **observed** as he **sniffed**, "It doesn't smell bad at all. Don't all skunks smell bad like **rotten** eggs?"

B = the sentence(s) to be put on the board or overhead   **C = the corrected sentence(s)**

16. disgust, stink

Paragraph – new person speaking
Capitalization – always begin sentences and
   quotes with a capital letter; always capitalize
   proper nouns and "I" ("Skunk Breath" is
   being used as a name of someone)
Punctuation – sentences always have end
   punctuation; use of quotation marks around
   what is said out loud
Commas – introductory word; direct address;
   quote
Verb tense – "said" is past tense of irregular verb
   "to say"; switch to present tense for quote
Skills – word recognition
Literary device – repetition of word for effect

B –   "no, skunk breath, they don't **stink**,"
said _____ in **disgust**.
"they only ___ ___ ___ ___ ___ when they
spray you "

C –   "No, Skunk Breath, they don't **stink**,"
said _____ in **disgust**.
"They only <u>stink</u> when they spray you."

---

17. rabies

> **NOTE:** *This is a good place to discuss the real danger of skunks, the fact that they are often carriers of rabies. Warn students never to approach a wild skunk or even touch a dead one. Skunks are often carriers of the disease because they eat bats.*

Paragraph – new person speaking
Capitalization – always begin sentences and
   quotes with a capital letter; always capitalize
   proper nouns and "I"
Punctuation – sentences always have end
   punctuation; use of quotation marks around
   what is said out loud
Commas – quotes; appositive
Verb tense – "said" is past tense of irregular verb
   "to say"; switch to present tense for quote; use
   of imperative
Skills – strong verb practice; pronunciation of
   "ght"

B –   "get back," said _____,
the teacher. "move ___ ___ ___ ___ very
slowly. it might spray you. it might have
rabies "

C –   "Get back," said _____,
the teacher. "Move <u>back</u> very slowly. It might
spray you. It might have **rabies**.

B = the sentence(s) to be put on the board or overhead   C = the corrected sentence(s)

18. cautiously

Paragraph – new person speaking (narrator)

Capitalization – always begin sentences and quotes with a capital letter; always capitalize proper nouns and "I"

Punctuation – sentences always have end punctuation

Commas – 2 adjectives where 2nd is not age or color

Verb tense – add "ed" to end of regular verbs to put in past tense; "stood" is past tense of irregular verb "to stand"

Spelling rules – ad "s" to most nouns to make plural; consonant/vowel/consonant + suffix = double 2nd consonant

Skills – strong verb practice; plural rules; many adverbs end in "ly"; compound subject

B –   the boys and girls **cautiously** and slowly moved back from petra. they stopped and stood very still in a large, far circle around petra

C –   The boys and girls **cautiously** and slowly moved back from Petra. They stopped and stood very still in a large, far circle around Petra.

19. exciting, dangerous

Paragraph – narrator continues but topic changes

Capitalization – always begin sentences and quotes with a capital letter

Punctuation – sentences always have end punctuation; exclamation mark needed in a dramatic statement

Commas – compound sentence (review FANBOYS)

Verb tense – "was" is past tense of irregular verb "to be";

Skills – word recognition

Literary device – suspense building

B –   a skunk at school was **exciting**! it was
__ __ __ __ __ __ __ __, but it also was
dangerous

C –   A skunk at school was **exciting**! It was **exciting**, but it also was **dangerous**.

> **NOTE:** *Refer to the list of prepositions in the* **Appendix** *and begin to have your students memorize them at the rate of a few each week. Knowing the prepositions is a useful tool. Once young students have memorized the prepositions, it is easy to tell them not to capitalize them in a title. When the prepositions have been memorized, whenever one occurs in a subsequent Caught'ya, have your students recite them. Then you can model their use. Again, you will be very popular with the teachers who come after you.*

B = the sentence(s) to be put on the board or overhead   C = the corrected sentence(s)

20. putrescent

Paragraph – change of topic
Capitalization – always begin sentences and quotes with a capital letter; always capitalize proper nouns and "I"
Punctuation – sentences always have end punctuation
Verb tense – add "ed" to end of regular verbs to put in past tense; "saw" is past tense of irregular verb "to see"
Spelling rule – "i" before "e" except after "c," and n**ei**ghbor, w**ei**gh, and th**ei**r are w**ei**rd
Skills – word recognition
Literary device – alliteration

B – **putrescent** petra looked up at all the faces. she saw friendly faces. she saw scared
— — — — —

C – **Putrescent** Petra looked up at all the faces. She saw friendly faces. She saw scared **faces**.

---

21. chatter, hiss, growl, warning

No paragraph – same subject, same person speaking (narrator)
Capitalization – always begin sentences and quotes with a capital letter; always capitalize proper nouns and "I"
Punctuation – sentences always have end punctuation
Commas – verb series
Verb tense – "did" is past tense of irregular verb "to do"
Skills – do not begin a sentence with a coordinating conjunction (for, and, nor, but, or, yet, so); homophone (tail/tale)

B – and petra did not stamp her feet. and she did not **chatter**, **hiss,** or **growl**. and she did not turn around or lift her tail in **warning**

C – Petra did not stamp her feet. She did not **chatter**, **hiss,** or **growl**. She did not turn around or lift her tail in **warning**.

---

22. putrescent, blueberry pancakes, sniffed

No paragraph – same subject, same person speaking
Capitalization – always begin sentences and quotes with a capital letter; always capitalize proper nouns and "I"
Punctuation – sentences always have end punctuation
Commas – 2 adjectives (2nd not age or color)
Verb tense – add "ed" to end of regular verbs to put in past tense;
Spelling rules – most nouns form plural by adding "s"; breath vs. breathe
Skills – possessive of singular nouns; name recognition
Literary device – alliteration

B – **putrescent** petra liked these small humans. she could smell **blueberry pancakes** on _____'s breath. she **sniffed** fresh, hot corn in _____'s hand

C – **Putrescent** Petra liked these small humans. She could smell **blueberry pancakes** on _____'s breath. She **sniffed** fresh, hot corn in _____'s hand.

---

23. chocolate, peanut butter, grin, amiable

Paragraph – new person referred to
Capitalization – always begin sentences and
   quotes with a capital letter; always capitalize
   proper nouns and "I"
Punctuation – sentences always have end
   punctuation
Commas – compound sentence
Verb tense – add "ed" to end of regular verbs to
   put in past tense
Skills – do not begin a sentence with a coordinating conjunction (for, and, nor, but, or, yet,
   so); name recognition; strong verb use

B –   and _____ smelled of
chocolate and **peanut butter**. and
_____ smiled a friendly
grin, and _____ looked
amiable dressed in the colors of a skunk

C –   _____ smelled
of **chocolate** and **peanut butter**.
_____ smiled a friendly
grin, and _____ looked
amiable dressed in the colors of a skunk.

---

24. human, threatening, frown, wrinkled

No paragraph – same topic, same speaker
Capitalization – always begin sentences and
   quotes with a capital letter; always capitalize
   proper nouns and "I"
Punctuation – sentences always have end
   punctuation
Commas – compound sentence
Verb tense – add "ed" to end of regular verbs to
   put in past tense
Skills – strong verb use; possessive pronouns

B – the big **human** did not look **threatening** at
   all. her face___ ___ ___ ___ ___ ___ friendly
   and kind, but a **frown wrinkled** her
   forehead

C – The big **human** did not look **threatening** at
   all. Her face <u>looked</u> friendly and kind, but a
   frown wrinkled her forehead.

---

25. voice

2 Paragraphs – new persons speaking
Capitalization – always begin sentences and
   quotes with a capital letter; always capitalize
   proper nouns and "I"
Punctuation – sentences always have end
   punctuation; use of quotation marks around
   what is said out loud
Commas – direct address; quote; 2 adjectives
Verb tense – "began" is past tense of irregular
   verb "to begin"; "heard" is past tense of verb
   "to hear"; switch to present tense for quote
Spelling rules – irregular plural of "child"
Skills – possessive of singular noun; name
   recognition; abbreviation of "Mr., Ms, or
   Mrs." in your name

B –   "children, let's get out...." she (*he*)
   began.
      petra heard _____'s
   soft, kind **voice**

C –   "Children, let's get out...." she (*he*)
   began.
      Petra heard _____'s
   soft, kind **voice**.

---

26. sniffed

No paragraph – same topic, same person
    speaking
Capitalization – always begin sentences and
    quotes with a capital letter
Punctuation – sentences always have end
    punctuation
Commas – noun series
Verb tense – add "ed" to end of regular verbs to
    put in past tense
Skills – strong verb practice; word recognition;
    name recognition; compound verb

B – she **sniffed** and __ __ __ __ __ __ __. she
waddled towards _____,
_____, and _____

C – She **sniffed** and **sniffed**. She waddled
towards _____, _____,
and _____.

---

27. whispered, breathe

Paragraph – new person speaking
Capitalization – always begin sentences and
    quotes with a capital letter; always capitalize
    proper nouns and "I"
Punctuation – sentences always have end
    punctuation; use of quotation marks around
    what is said out loud
Commas – quote; appositive
Verb tense – switch to present tense for quote;
    use of imperative
Spelling rules – breathe vs. breath
Skills – abbreviation in your name; common
    contractions; word recognition
Literary device – repetition for emphasis

B –   "don't move," **whispered**
_____, the teacher. don't
talk. __ __ __ __ _ __ even **breathe** "

C –   "Don't move," **whispered**
_____, the teacher. Don't
talk. <u>Don't</u> even **breathe**!"

NOTE: *Contractions are an important second-grade skill. Add more to the following Caught'yas if your students need more practice.*

---

28. ambled, unmoving, gasped

Paragraph – new person speaking (narrator)
Capitalization – always begin sentences and
    quotes with a capital letter; always capitalize
    proper nouns and "I"
Punctuation – sentences always have end
    punctuation
Verb tense – add "ed" to end of regular verbs to
    put in past tense; "fell" is past tense of
    irregular verb "to fall";
Spelling rules – "i" before "e" except after "c,"
    and n**ei**ghbor, w**ei**gh, and th**ei**r are w**ei**rd;
    compound words (popcorn)
Skills – do not begin a sentence with a coordi-
    nating conjunction; strong verb practice;
    possessive of singular noun
Literary device – simile; aphorism (a fish out of
    water — trite expression)

B –   and petra **ambled** slowly towards the
class. and a piece of popcorn fell from
_____'s **unmoving** hand. and
everyone **gasped** like fish out of
water

C –   Petra **ambled** slowly towards the class.
A piece of popcorn fell from _____'s
unmoving hand. Everyone **gasped** like fish
out of water.

B = the sentence(s) to be put on the board or overhead   C = the corrected sentence(s)

29. sensed, plume-like

No paragraph – same topic, referring to the same person

Capitalization – always begin sentences and quotes with a capital letter; always capitalize proper nouns and "I"

Punctuation – sentences always have end punctuation

Commas – subordinate clause at beginning of sentence

Verb tense – add "ed" to end of regular verbs to put in past tense

Spelling rules – compound words

Skills – strong verb practice; possessive of singular noun; name recognition; homophone (tail/tale); hyphen in two words acting as one

B – petra smelled the warm corn. since she **sensed** no danger, she waddled over and ate the popcorn. her **plume-like** tail brushed _____'s leg as she ate

C – Petra smelled the warm corn. Since she **sensed** no danger, she waddled over and ate the popcorn. Her **plume-like** tail brushed _____'s leg as she ate.

30. finished, putrescent, amazed

Paragraph – time change

Capitalization – always begin sentences and quotes with a capital letter; always capitalize proper nouns and "I"

Punctuation – sentences always have end punctuation

Commas – subordinate clause at beginning of complex sentence; participial phrase (verb used as an adjective)

Verb tense – add "ed" to end of regular verbs to put in past tense; "saw" is past tense of irregular verb "to see"

Spelling rules – compound words

Skills – strong verb practice

Literary device – alliteration (circle of children and Putrescent Petra)

B – when she **finished** the popcorn, **putrescent** petra walked around the circle of children, sniffing legs and looking up at **amazed** faces. she liked what she saw

C – When she **finished** the popcorn, **Putrescent** Petra walked around the circle of children, sniffing legs and looking up at **amazed** faces. She liked what she saw.

NOTE: *For the next ten Caught'yas, the end quotation mark has been omitted. This was done to ease your second graders into inserting quotes appropriately by themselves. After that, all quotation marks have been eliminated. If your students are not developmentally ready to begin to insert quotation marks, put the quotes back in the student sentences and only begin eliminating them when you know your students are ready.*

B = the sentence(s) to be put on the board or overhead   **C = the corrected sentence(s)**

31. whispered, sudden

Paragraph – new person speaking
Capitalization – always begin sentences and
quotes with a capital letter; always capitalize
proper nouns and "I"
Punctuation – sentences always have end
punctuation; use of quotation marks around
what is said out loud
Commas – appositive (extra info about a noun)
Verb tense – add "ed" to end of regular verbs to
put in past tense; switch to present tense for
quote; use of imperative
Skills – strong verb use; common contractions

B – _____, the teacher, **whispered**
to the class, "slowly back off. don't make
any **sudden** move or noise to scare the
skunk

C – _____, the teacher, **whispered**
to the class, "Slowly back off. Don't make
any **sudden** move or noise to scare the
skunk."

---

32. putrescent, scent

No paragraph – same person speaking; Paragraph – new person speaking (narrator)
Capitalization – always begin sentences and
quotes with a capital letter
Punctuation – sentences always have end
punctuation; use of quotation marks around
what is said out loud
Commas – quote
Verb tense – add "ed" to end of regular verbs to
put in past tense; "went" is past tense of
irregular verb "to go"
Spelling rules – compound words
Skills – strong verb practice; review long vowels;
homophone (its/it's); it's = it is common
contractions

B – she added, "it might bite or spray you with
its **putrescent scent**.
the class backed off and went back to
the classroom

C – She added, "It might bite or spray you with
its **putrescent scent**."
The class backed off and went back to
the classroom.

---

33. awesome

No paragraph – same person speaking, similar
topic
Capitalization – always begin sentences and
quotes with a capital letter; always capitalize
proper nouns and "I"
Punctuation – sentences always have end
punctuation
Verb tense – add "ed" to end of regular verbs to
put in past tense; "did" is past tense of
irregular verb "to do"; use of pluperfect (had
eaten) to indicate action that took place
before this paragraph
Spelling rules – compound words; "no one" is 2
words
Skills – possessive of singular noun; name
recognition; abbreviation in your name

B – no one did any work for the rest of the day.
_____'s class could think
only about the **awesome** skunk that had
eaten _____'s popcorn

C – No one did any work for the rest of the day.
_____'s class could think
only about the **awesome** skunk that had
eaten _____'s popcorn.

B = the sentence(s) to be put on the board or overhead   C = the corrected sentence(s)

34. foraged, begged, officers (Your State) Game and Freshwater Fish Commission

> **NOTE:** *Look in your phone book for whatever organization you have that would come get a wild animal that is infringing on human territory. The name is slightly different in different states. In Florida it is the "Florida Game and Freshwater Fish Commission." Supply your local version wherever appropriate.*

No paragraph – same person speaking, same topic
Capitalization – always begin sentences and quotes with a capital letter; always capitalize proper nouns and "I"
Punctuation – sentences always have end punctuation
Verb tense – add "ed" to end of regular verbs to put in past tense
Spelling rules – compound words ("freshwater")
Skills – strong verb practice

B – they watched petra from the window as she **foraged** for food in the field. they **begged** their teacher not to call the **(Your State) Game and Freshwater Fish Commission officers** to take petra away

C – They watched Petra from the window as she **foraged** for food in the field. They **begged** their teacher not to call the **(Your State) Game and Freshwater Fish Commission officers** to take Petra away.

---

35. beseeched, scientists

Paragraph – new person speaking
Capitalization – always begin sentences and quotes with a capital letter; always capitalize proper nouns and "I"
Punctuation – sentences always have end punctuation; use of quotation marks around what is said out loud
Commas – direct address; quote
Verb tense – add "ed" to end of regular verbs to put in past tense; switch to present tense for quote
Skills – abbreviation in your name; name recognition; subject pronouns; "like" is used to compare nouns and pronouns ("like scientists" and "we")
Literary device – simile

B – "please, _____, let it live under our classroom, they **beseeched**. "like **scientists**, we can study skunks

C – "Please, _____, let it live under our classroom," they **beseeched**. "Like **scientists**, we can study skunks."

---

36. promised

2 Paragraphs – new persons speaking
Capitalization – always begin sentences and quotes with a capital letter; always capitalize proper nouns and "I"
Punctuation – sentences always have end punctuation; use of quotation marks around what is said out loud
Commas – quotes
Verb tense – add "ed" to end of regular verbs to put in past tense; switch to present tense for quote
Skills – name recognition

B – "we won't go near it, **promised** _____ and _____
"we just want to watch it, added
_____

C – "We won't go near it," **promised** _____ and _____.
"We just want to watch it," added
_____.

B = the sentence(s) to be put on the board or overhead   C = the corrected sentence(s)

37. notice, putrescence

Paragraph – new person speaking
Capitalization – always begin sentences and
    quotes with a capital letter; always capitalize
    proper nouns and "I"
Punctuation – sentences always have end
    punctuation; use of quotation marks around
    what is said out loud
Commas – quote
Verb tense – add "ed" to end of regular verbs to
    put in past tense; correct use of conditional
    (many incorrectly use it instead of past tense)
Spelling rules – "no one" is 2 words; compound
    words
Skills – name recognition; homophone (its/it's)

B –   "we could keep it in the bathroom. no
one would **notice** its **putrescence** in there,
laughed _____

C –   "We could keep it in the bathroom. No
one would **notice** its **putrescence** in there,"
laughed _____.

---

38. dangerous

Paragraph – new person speaking
Capitalization – always begin sentences and
    quotes with a capital letter; always capitalize
    proper nouns and "I"
Punctuation – sentences always have end
    punctuation; use of quotation marks around
    what is said out loud; need for question mark
    after question
Commas – quote
Verb tense – "said" is past tense of irregular verb
    "to say"; switch to present tense for quote
Skills – homophone (its/it's); it's = it is;
    common contractions; "too" as intensifier;
    comparatives (big, bigger, biggest)

B –   the teacher said, "it's too **dangerous**.
what if a bigger boy or girl surprised or
scared it

C –   The teacher said, "It's too **dangerous**.
What if a bigger boy or girl surprised or
scared it?"

---

39. continued, rabies, putrescent, stink

No paragraph – same person speaking, same
    subject
Capitalization – always begin sentences and
    quotes with a capital letter
Punctuation – sentences always have end
    punctuation; use of quotation marks around
    what is said out loud
Commas – quote; compound sentence
Verb tense – add "ed" to end of regular verbs to
    put in past tense; switch to present tense for
    quote; correct use of conditional
Skills – word recognition; possessive of singular
    noun; FANBOYS review
Literary device – alliteration (s,s,s,s)

B – she **continued**, "it might bite or spray. it
could have **rabies**, and the **putrescent
stink** of skunk's spray stays around for days

C – She **continued**, "It might bite or spray. It
could have **rabies**, and the **putrescent
stink** of skunk's spray stays around for
days."

NOTE: *After this Caught'ya all quotation marks have been left out in the student sentences. If your children are not ready for this, put them back in for them.*

B = the sentence(s) to be put on the board or overhead   C = the corrected sentence(s)

40. whined

Paragraph – new person speaking
Capitalization – always begin sentences and
   quotes with a capital letter; always capitalize
   proper nouns and "I"
Punctuation – sentences always have end
   punctuation; use of quotation marks around
   what is said out loud
Commas – quote
Verb tense – add "ed" to end of regular verbs to
   put in past tense; correct use of conditional
   tense (most incorrectly use it as past tense)
Skills – strong verb use
Literary device – onomatopoeia

B –   awwww, **whined** _____.
we could warn everyone. we would be
careful. please

C –   "Awwww," **whined** _____.
"We could warn everyone. We would be
careful. Please."

41. (Your State) Game and Freshwater Fish Commission, protect, humans

Paragraph – new person speaking
Capitalization – always begin sentences and
   quotes with a capital letter; always capitalize
   proper nouns and "I"
Punctuation – sentences always have end
   punctuation; use of quotation marks around
   what is said out loud
Commas – introductory word; always put
   commas around "too" if it means "also";
   compound sentence; quote
Verb tense – "said" is past tense of irregular verb
   "to see"; switch to present tense for quote
Skills – homophone (know/no); FANBOYS

B –   no, we have to call the **(Your State) Game and Freshwater Fish Commission** people. we must **protect** the skunk, and we must_ _ _ _ _ _ _ **humans**, too, said the teacher

C –   "No, we have to call the **(Your State) Game and Freshwater Fish Commission** people. We must **protect** the skunk, and we must **protect humans**, too," said the teacher.

42. thrive, captivity

No paragraph – same person speaking,
   continuation
Capitalization – always begin sentences and
   quotes with a capital letter
Punctuation – sentences always have end
   punctuation; use of quotation marks around
   what is said out loud
Verb tense – switch to present tense for quote
Spelling rules – most nouns form plural by
   adding "s"
Skills – do not split infinitives ("not to thrive"
   instead of "to not thrive"); word recognition

B – a skunk is a wild animal. wild
_ _ _ _ _ _ _ are not able to **thrive**
in **captivity**. they need to be free and wild

C – "A skunk is a wild animal. Wild <u>animals</u> are not able to **thrive** in **captivity**. They need to be free and wild."

NOTE: *The announcer on Star Trek is wrong. "To boldly go" is incorrect. It should be "to go boldly."*

B = the sentence(s) to be put on the board or overhead   C = the corrected sentence(s)

43. office

Paragraph – new person speaking (narrator)
Capitalization – always begin sentences and quotes with a capital letter; always capitalize proper nouns and "I"
Punctuation – sentences always have end punctuation
Commas – interrupter
Verb tense – add "ed" to end of regular verbs to put in past tense; "told" is past tense of "to tell"; "did" is past tense of irregular verb "to do"; "was" is past tense of verb "to be"
Skills – possessive of singular noun; negatives; homophone (know/no)
Literary device – use of parentheses for narrator aside

B – then she called the **office** and told them about the skunk. (the teacher, of course, did not know petra's name)

C – Then she called the **office** and told them about the skunk. (The teacher, of course, did not know Petra's name.)

44. (Your State) Game and Freshwater Fish Commission

Paragraph – time and place change
Capitalization – always begin sentences and quotes with a capital letter; always capitalize proper nouns and "I"
Punctuation – sentences always have end punctuation
Verb tense – add "ed" to end of regular verbs to put in past tense; "came" is past tense of irregular verb "to come"
Skills – strong verb practice; go over adverbs ending in "ly"; possessive of singular noun

B – the **(Your State) Game and Freshwater Fish Commission** people came quickly. _____'s class watched sadly out the window

C – The **(Your State) Game and Freshwater Fish Commission** people came quickly. _____'s class watched sadly out the window.

45. amble, waddle, burrow

No paragraph – same person speaking, same topic
Capitalization – always begin sentences and quotes with a capital letter; always capitalize proper nouns and "I"
Punctuation – sentences always have end punctuation
Commas – verb series
Verb tense – add "ed" to end of regular verbs to put in past tense
Skills – strong verb practice; compound verb
Literary device – alliteration

B – they watched putrescent petra **amble** into the field, eat something, and **waddle** back to her **burrow**

C – They watched Putrescent Petra **amble** into the field, eat something, and **waddle** back to her **burrow**.

B = the sentence(s) to be put on the board or overhead   **C = the corrected sentence(s)**

46. discovered

No paragraph – same person speaking, same
    topic
Capitalization – always begin sentences and
    quotes with a capital letter
Punctuation – sentences always have end
    punctuation
Verb tense – add "ed" to end of regular verbs to
    put in past tense; use of pluperfect tense for
    action taking place before this paragraph
    (had found)
Spelling rules – compound words
Skills – do not begin a sentence with a coordi-
    nating conjunction; word recognition;
    homophone (their/there/they're)
Literary device – use of italics for emphasis

B – and *they* had **discovered** the skunk. and the
skunk liked *them.* and it ___ ___ ___ ___ ___
their popcorn

C – *They* had found the skunk. The skunk liked
them. It <u>liked</u> their popcorn.

---

47. wandered, half-eaten, palmetto

Paragraph – new time, new topic
Capitalization – always begin sentences and
    quotes with a capital letter; always capitalize
    proper nouns and "I"
Punctuation – sentences always have end
    punctuation
Verb tense – use of pluperfect tense to indicate
    action that took place before this paragraph
    (had)
Spelling rules – compound words
Skills – strong verb practice; hyphen in two
    words acting as one
Literary device – alliteration

B –   now after the popcorn, putrescent petra
had **wandered** through the field. she had
found a **half-eaten** bag of chips and a
palmetto bug

C –   Now after the popcorn, Putrescent Petra
had **wandered** through the field. She had
found a **half-eaten** bag of chips and a
palmetto bug.

---

48. waddled, burrow

No paragraph – same person speaking, same
    topic
Capitalization – always begin sentences and
    quotes with a capital letter
Punctuation – sentences always have end
    punctuation
Verb tense – add "ed" to end of regular verbs to
    put in past tense; "ate" is past tense of
    irregular verb
    "to eat"
Skills – strong verb practice
Literary device – simile

B – she ate them both. then, like a black and
white duck, she **waddled** back to her
burrow to take another day nap

C – She ate them both. Then, like a black and
white duck, she **waddled** back to her
burrow to take another day nap.

---

49. burrow

No paragraph – same person speaking, same topic

Capitalization – always begin sentences and quotes with a capital letter; always capitalize proper nouns and "I"

Punctuation – sentences always have end punctuation

Verb tense – add "ed" to end of regular verbs to put in past tense; "saw" is past tense of irregular verb "to see";

Spelling rules – "i" before "e" except after "c," and n**ei**ghbor, w**ei**gh, and th**ei**r are w**ei**rd

Skills – do not begin a sentence with a coordinating conjunction; homophone (there/their/they're)

B – and petra looked up at the windows above her **burrow**. and she saw the friendly faces there

C – Petra looked up at the windows above her **burrow**. She saw the friendly faces there.

NOTE: *After this Caught'ya there are no more sentences that begin incorrectly with "and." If your students have problems eliminating this practice, simply add "and," "but," or "so" to any Caught'ya to keep making your point.*

---

50. voice

No paragraph – same person narrating, continuation of topic

Capitalization – always begin sentences and quotes with a capital letter; always capitalize proper nouns and "I"

Punctuation – sentences always have end punctuation

Verb tense – add "ed" to end of regular verbs to put in past tense; "said" is past tense of irregular verb "to say"

Spelling rules – "i" before "e"...; compound words

Skills – strong verb use

B – _____ said something to her in a friendly **voice**. _____ waved at petra

C – _____ said something to her in a friendly **voice**. _____ waved at Petra.

---

51. elated

No paragraph – same person narrating, same topic

Capitalization – always begin sentences and quotes with a capital letter; always capitalize proper nouns and "I"

Punctuation – sentences always have end punctuation

Commas – compound sentence

Verb tense – add "ed" to end of regular verbs to put in past tense; "was" and "were" are past tense of irregular verb "to be"

Skills – review coordinating conjunctions (FANBOYS)

Literary device – alliteration

B – putrescent petra was **elated** that the children were nearby. she liked having friends, and she wanted more popcorn

C – Putrescent Petra was **elated** that the children were nearby. She liked having friends, and she wanted more popcorn.

B = the sentence(s) to be put on the board or overhead   C = the corrected sentence(s)

52. burrow, odor

Paragraph – new place
Capitalization – always begin sentences and
    quotes with a capital letter; always capitalize
    proper nouns and "I"
Punctuation – sentences always have end
    punctuation
Commas – noun series
Verb tense – add "ed" to end of regular verbs to
    put in past tense; "woke" is past tense of
    irregular verb "to wake"
Spelling rules – the use of prefix "un"
Skills – strong verb practice; compound verbs;
    use of dash to separate

B –   petra curled up in her **burrow** and took a nap. she woke up to an unfriendly stench, a clanking noise, and the **odor** of her favorite food—eggs

C –   Petra curled up in her **burrow** and took a nap. She woke up to an unfriendly stench, a clanking noise, and the **odor** of her favorite food—eggs.

53. burrow, answer

Paragraph – narrator aside
Capitalization – always begin sentences and
    quotes with a capital letter; always capitalize
    proper nouns and "I"
Punctuation – sentences always have end
    punctuation; need for question marks in
    questions
Verb tense – "was" is past tense of irregular verb
    "to be"; "did" is past tense of verb "to do";
    imperative in last sentence
Skills – end punctuation
Literary device – narrator aside

B –   what did petra smell. what did petra hear. ___ ___ ___ ___ was in front of her new **burrow**. write the **answer** here

C –   What did Petra smell? What did Petra hear? <u>What</u> was in front of her new **burrow**? Write the **answer** here.

54. (Your State) Game and Freshwater Fish Commission. propped, metal

Paragraph – new topic
Capitalization – always begin sentences and
    quotes with a capital letter; always capitalize
    proper nouns and "I"
Punctuation – sentences always have end
    punctuation
Verb tense – add "ed" to end of regular verbs to
    put in past tense; "put" is past tense of
    irregular verb "to put"; use of pluperfect tense
    to indicate action that took place previous to
    this paragraph
Skills – strong verb practice; possessive of
    singular noun; compound verb

B –   the **(Your State) Game and Freshwater Fish Commission** lady had come. she put a cage on the ground in front of petra's hole and **propped** open the door with a **metal** stick

C –   The **(Your State) Game and Freshwater Fish Commission** lady had come. She put a cage on the ground in front of Petra's hole and **propped** open the door with a **metal** stick.

B = the sentence(s) to be put on the board or overhead   C = the corrected sentence(s)

55. placed, scent

No paragraph – same topic
Capitalization – always begin sentences and quotes with a capital letter; always capitalize proper nouns and "I"
Punctuation – sentences always have end punctuation
Verb tense – add "ed" to end of regular verbs to put in past tense; correct use of conditional (not to be used instead of past tense)
Skills – strong verb use; homophone (scent/sent)
Literary device – alliteration

B – she **placed** an egg inside the cage. then she walked away so that petra would not smell her **scent**

C – She **placed** an egg inside the cage. Then she walked away so that Petra would not smell her **scent**.

---

56. hung, dejected

Paragraph – change of topic
Capitalization – always begin sentences and quotes with a capital letter; always capitalize proper nouns and "I"
Punctuation – sentences always have end punctuation; use of quotation marksaround what is said out loud
Verb tense – add "ed" to end of regular verbs to put in past tense; "was" and "were" are past tense of irregular verb "to be"; "hung" is past tense of verb "to hang"
Skills – possessive of singular noun; compound verb; abbreviation in your name

B – _____'s class **hung** out the window and watched. they were **dejected**

C – _____'s class **hung** out the window and watched. They were **dejected**.

---

57. burrow

No paragraph – same topic
Capitalization – always begin sentences and quotes with a capital letter
Punctuation – sentences always have end punctuation
Verb tense – add "ed" to end of regular verbs to put in past tense
Skills – homophone (their/they're/there); homophone (it's/its); it's = it is; common contractions; word recognition

B – they watched the cage with the egg in it. they looked for their skunk to come out of its ___ ___ ___ ___ ___ ___

C – They watched the cage with the egg in it. They looked for their skunk to come out of its **burrow**.

B = the sentence(s) to be put on the board or overhead   C = the corrected sentence(s)

58. burrow, gasped, old-fashioned steam engines, approached

No paragraph – same topic, same speaker
Capitalization – always begin sentences and quotes with a capital letter
Punctuation – sentences always have end punctuation
Verb tense – add "ed" to end of regular verbs to put in past tense; "saw" is past tense of irregular verb "to see"
Skills – strong verb practice; use of hyphen between 2 words acting as one; review pronoun use (subject and possessive)
Literary device – simile

B – they saw the skunk come out of her **burrow** under the school. they **gasped** like **old-fashioned steam engines** as she **approached** the cage

C – They saw the skunk come out of her **burrow** under the school. They **gasped** like **old-fashioned steam engines** as she **approached** the cage.

---

59. musk

Paragraph – narrator aside
Capitalization – always begin sentences and quotes with a capital letter
Punctuation – sentences always have end punctuation; need for question marks in questions
Verb tense – correct use of conditional tense (not as past tense)
Skills – strong verb practice; homophone (tail/tale)
Literary device – narrator aside

B – would she go in the cage. would she lift her tail and spray her putrescent **musk** on the cage

C – Would she go in the cage? Would she lift her tail and spray her putrescent **musk** on the cage?

---

60. favorite, propped

Paragraph – new topic
Capitalization – always begin sentences and quotes with a capital letter; always capitalize proper nouns and "I"
Punctuation – sentences always have end punctuation
Commas – extra information
Verb tense – add "ed" to end of regular verbs to put in past tense; "did" is past tense of irregular verb "to do"
Spelling rules – consonant/vowel/consonant + suffix – double 2nd consonant
Skills – negatives; go over sense verbs (to smell, to see, to hear, to taste, to touch)

B – putrescent petra smelled the egg, her **favorite** food. she did not see the stick that **propped** up the door of the cage

C – Putrescent Petra smelled the egg, her **favorite** food. She did not see the stick that **propped** up the door of the cage.

NOTE: *After this point all commas have been left out, but I suggest that if you think your students are ready for this, leave an extra space or two to hint that something is missing. If you believe your students are not ready for this (and many will not be), simply add them yourself before you put the sentence on the board or overhead and continue to discuss them until students are ready to insert commas by themselves.*

B = the sentence(s) to be put on the board or overhead   C = the corrected sentence(s)

61. waddled

No paragraph – same topic; Paragraph – time change
Capitalization – always begin sentences and quotes with a capital letter
Punctuation – sentences always have end punctuation; need for exclamation mark to denote enthusiasm
Commas – introductory adverb (optional)
Verb tense – add "ed" to end of regular verbs to put in past tense
Skills – strong verb practice; go over adverbs that end in "ly"
Literary device – onomatopoeia

B – she **waddled** into the cage and slowly ate the egg. yumm
    suddenly the door to the cage closed very quickly

C – She **waddled** into the cage and slowly ate the egg. Yumm!
    Suddenly, the door to the cage closed very quickly.

---

62. trapped

No paragraph – continuation of same topic
Capitalization – always begin sentences and quotes with a capital letter; always capitalize proper nouns and "I"
Punctuation – sentences always have end punctuation; exclamation mark needed in alarming statement
Verb tense – "was" is past tense of irregular verb "to be"; "ate" is past tense of verb "to eat"
Skills – go over past tense of irregular verbs so far
Literary device – alliteration; made-up word

B – putrescent petra was **trapped**! she ate the rest of the yummy egg

C – Putrescent Petra was **trapped**! She ate the rest of the yummy egg.

---

63. messed, except

No paragraph – same topic, same speaker
Capitalization – always begin sentences and quotes with a capital letter; always capitalize proper nouns and "I"
Punctuation – sentences always have end punctuation
Commas – adjective series
Verb tense – "was" is past tense of irregular verb "to be"; "did" is past tense of verb "to do"
Spelling rules – most nouns form plurals by adding "s"
Skills – negative
Literary device – metaphor; idiom (messed with)

B – petra was not scared. nobody **messed** with skunks **except** owls and those noisy big shiny things on the hard black path that sometimes did not stop for skunks

C – Petra was not scared. Nobody **messed** with skunks **except** owls and those noisy, big, shiny things on the hard black path that sometimes did not stop for skunks.

---

64. (Your State) Game and Freshwater Fish Commission

2 Paragraphs – new topic; new person speaking
Capitalization – always begin sentences and
    quotes with a capital letter; always capitalize
    proper nouns and "I"
Punctuation – sentences always have end
    punctuation; use of quotation marksaround
    what is said out loud
Commas – direct address; quote; noun series
Verb tense – add "ed" to end of regular verbs to
    put in past tense; "said" is past tense of
    irregular verb "to say"; "took" is past tense of
    verb "to take"
Skills – strong verb practice; name recognition

B – the **(your state) Game and Freshwater Fish Commission** lady covered the cage with a cloth and took petra to her truck
    bye bye petra said _____

_____ _____

and _____

C – The **(Your State) Game and Freshwater Fish Commission** lady covered the cage with a cloth and took Petra to her truck.
    "Bye bye, Petra," said _____,

_____, _____,

and _____.

---

65. remember

2 Paragraphs – new persons speaking
Capitalization – always begin sentences and
    quotes with a capital letter; always capitalize
    proper nouns and "I"
Punctuation – sentences always have end
    punctuation; use of quotation marks around
    what is said
    out loud
Commas – quotes
Verb tense – "said" is past tense of irregular verb
    "to say"; switch to present tense for quote
Skills – common contractions; negatives;
    punctuating a quote

B – we'll never see our skunk again cried

_____.
    let's give the skunk a name said the teacher so that we can **remember** it

C – "We'll never see our skunk again," cried

_____.
    "Let's give the skunk a name," said the teacher, "so that we can **remember** it."

---

66. voted, decided, company

Paragraph – new person speaking (narrator)
Capitalization – always begin sentences and
    quotes with a capital letter
Punctuation – sentences always have end
    punctuation
Verb tense – add "ed" to end of regular verbs to
    put in past tense
Skills – strong verb practice; collective nouns
    (class); comparatives (good/better/best);
    must have (*not* "must of" as is so often used
    by students)

B – the class **voted** on names the rest of the day. they **decided** it must have been a girl skunk because girl skunks like **company** better than boy skunks

C – The class **voted** on names the rest of the day. They **decided** it must have been a girl skunk because girl skunks like **company** better than boy skunks.

B = the sentence(s) to be put on the board or overhead   **C = the corrected sentence(s)**

67. putrescence (the noun), foulness

NOTE: *Warn that some periods might have to be changed to question marks.*

Paragraph – narrator aside
Capitalization – always begin sentences and
    quotes with a capital letter
Punctuation – sentences always have end
    punctuation; question mark needed for
    question
Verb tense – switch to present tense for narrator
    aside
Spelling rules – turn a verb into an adjective by
    adding "y"
Skills – deliberate use of fragment (but
    elementary and middle-school students
    should avoid them)
Literary device – narrator aside; fragments for
    effect

B –   what should they name their skunk.
susie? mary. stinky? **putrescence**. smelly?
foulness. can you suggest some good
names

C –   What should they name their skunk?
Susie? Mary? Stinky? **Putrescence**? Smelly?
Foulness? Can you suggest some good
names?

---

68. suggested

2 Paragraphs – new persons speaking
Capitalization – always begin sentences and
    quotes with a capital letter; always capitalize
    proper nouns and "I"
Punctuation – sentences always have end
    punctuation; use of quotation marks around
    what is said out loud and when something is
    referred to; need for question mark after
    question
Commas – introductory adverb (optional)
Verb tense – add "ed" to end of regular verbs to
    put in past tense
Spelling rules – 2 "l's" in "finally"
Skills – name recognition; strong verb practice;
    deliberate use of fragment; periods and
    commas *always* go inside quotes
Literary device – alliteration (P P)

B –   finally _____ **suggested** the name
"putrescent petra   "
    why asked _____

C –   Finally, _____ **suggested** the
name "Putrescent Petra."
    "Why?" asked _____.

---

69. sense

2 Paragraph – new persons speaking

Capitalization – always begin sentences and quotes with a capital letter; always capitalize proper nouns and "I"

Punctuation – sentences always have end punctuation; use of quotation marks around what is said out loud and around what is referred to

Commas – compound sentence; quotes; compound sentence

Verb tense – "said" is past tense of irregular verb "to say"; switch to present tense for quote

Skills – never start a sentence with "because" unless the subordinate clause is followed by an independent clause; word recognition; homophone (sense/cents); review subject pronouns; review FANBOYS

Literary device – alliteration

B – because we know what putrescent means and petra starts with a "p" like

— — — — — — — — — —

said _____

that doesn't make **sense** said

_____ but i like the name petra

C – "Because we know what putrescent means, we want to name her that, and Petra starts with a "P" like <u>putrescent</u>," said

_____.

"That doesn't make **sense**," said

_____, "but I like the name Putrescent Petra."

---

70. (Your State) Game and Freshwater Fish Commission, happened

Paragraph – new person speaking (narrator)

Capitalization – always begin sentences and quotes with a capital letter; always capitalize proper nouns and "I"

Punctuation – sentences always have end punctuation

Verb tense – add "ed" to end of regular verbs to put in past tense (first change end "i" to "y"); "wrote" is past tense of irregular verb "to write"; use of pluperfect tense to denote action previous to this paragraph

Spelling rules – most nouns form plurals by adding "s"

Skills – possessive of singular noun; strong verb practice

B – _____'s class studied skunks. they even wrote letters to the **(your state) game and freshwater fish commission** to find out what had **happened** to petra

C – _____'s class studied skunks. They even wrote letters to the **(Your State) Game and Freshwater Fish Commission** to find out what had **happened** to Petra.

> **NOTE:** *Caught'ya #71 and Caught'ya #73 are much longer than usual because they are letters. Plan to spend more time completing them. I did not want to split up the letters as the children might find that confusing. Put your school's name and address in the heading and look up the address of your local Game and Freshwater Fish Commission in the phone book. I've given a fake address for an example. You might want to follow #71 (the one the children write) and #73 (the one the children receive in return) with a letter-writing unit, business and friendly. Children can write to each other, to friends, to parents, to you, and to various local businesses. They might even want to write to your state's Game and Freshwater Fish commission for information about skunks.*

---

71. (Your State) Game and Freshwater Fish Commission, rabies

> **NOTE:** *Warn your students that some of the periods need to be changed to question marks. Note, too, the correct indentations (greeting flush with the margin, beginning indented). This is important. I would wait until at least the fifth grade to teach the other forms of business letters.*

Paragraph – new person speaking in body of letter

Capitalization – always begin sentences and quotes with a capital letter; always capitalize proper nouns, "I," words in greeting, first word only in closing, signature

Punctuation – sentences always have end punctuation; need for question marks after questions; colon needed after greeting in business letter

Commas – city, state; greeting; closing

Verb tense – switch to present tense for letter; use of future tense with "will"

Spelling rules – in a letter, use the postal code for the state; "truly" does not have an "e"

Skills – letter writing format; abbreviations; possessive of singular noun; name recognition; "whom" is object of preposition; hyphen needed in two words acting as one adjective (when capitalized, second word remains lower case)

Literary device – letter within a story; alliteration

B – _____'s second-grade class
_____ elementary school

(put your address here)
city state zip
(put the correct date here)

(your state) game and freshwater fish commission
1234 save a skunk st
gainesville fl 32608

to whom it may concern**:**

we want to know what you did with the skunk you found at _____ elementary school this week. is it a boy or a girl? does it have **rabies**. will you kill it? will you keep it. will you set it free? may we come see our skunk. we named her putrescent petra. we call her petra for short. putrescent means stinky

yours truly
_____'s second-grade class

C – _____'s Second-grade Class
_____ Elementary School

(Put your address here)
City, State Zip
(Put the correct date here)

(Your State) Game and Freshwater Fish Commission
1234 Save a Skunk St.
Gainesville, FL 32608

To Whom It May Concern**:**

We want to know what you did with the skunk you found at _____ Elementary School this week. Is it a boy or a girl? Does it have **rabies**? Will you to kill it? Will you keep it? Will you set it free? Can it still spray? May we come see our skunk? We named her Putrescent Petra. We call her Petra for short. Putrescent means stinky.

Yours truly,
_____'s Second-grade Class

B = the sentence(s) to be put on the board or overhead   **C = the corrected sentence(s)**

72. received, (Your State) Game and Fresh water Fish Commission

Paragraph – narrator speaking, time change

Capitalization – always begin sentences and quotes with a capital letter; always capitalize proper nouns and "I"

Punctuation – sentences always have end punctuation

Commas – introductory adverb (optional as it is short)

Verb tense – add "ed" to end of regular verbs to put in past tense; "was" is past tense of irregular verb "to be"

Spelling rules – "i" before "e".....

B –   three days later the class received a letter in return. it was from the **(your state) game and freshwater fish commission**

C –   Three days later, the class **received** a letter in return. It was from the **(Your State) Game and Freshwater Fish Commission**.

73. (Your State) Game and Freshwater Fish commission, rabies, scent glands, weapon, release, wildlife officer

> **NOTE:** *This Caught'ya necessarily has a lot of vocabulary. You might want to have an added lesson to make sure that your students understand and can use these words.*

Paragraph – new person speaking in body of letter

Capitalization – always begin sentences and quotes with a capital letter; always capitalize proper nouns, "I," words in greeting, only first word in closing, signature

Punctuation – sentences always have end punctuation; need for question marks after questions; colon needed after greeting in business letter; use of semicolon in compound sentence that is closely linked

Commas – city, state; greeting; compound sentence; closing;

Verb tense – switch to present tense for letter; use of future tense with "will"; correct use of conditional tense (not yet happened but may happen)

Spelling rules – in a letter, include the postal code for your state

Skills – letter writing format; abbreviations; possessive of singular noun; name recognition; review FANBOYS; hyphen needed between two words acting as one adjective (when capitalized, second word remains lower case)

Literary device – letter within a story; alliteration

B –   **(your state) game and freshwater fish commission**
1234 save a skunk st
gainesville fl 32608

(put the correct date here)

_____'s second-grade class
_____elementary school

(put your address here)
city state zip

dear children:

thank you for your letter. we still have petra. you are right; she is a girl. we are watching her for signs of **rabies** and she does not show any yet. we usually kill animals to check for rabies but your skunk did not bite anyone and is very friendly. We are watching her for three weeks instead. we will not take away petra's **scent glands** because then she would have no secret **weapon** to defend herself. we will set her free in a local woods next week. you may come see her before we **release** her into the wild. ask your teacher to bring you

sincerely yours
mary brown, **wildlife officer**

C –   **(Your State) Game and Freshwater Fish Commission**
1234 Save a Skunk St.
Gainesville, FL 32608

(Put the correct date here)

_____'s Second-grade Class
_____Elementary School

(Put your address here)
City, State Zip

Dear Children:

Thank you for your letter. We still have Petra. You are right; she is a girl. We are watching her for signs of **rabies**, and she does not show any yet. We usually kill

---

B = the sentence(s) to be put on the board or overhead   C = the corrected sentence(s)

animals to check for rabies, but your skunk did not bite anyone and is very friendly. We are watching her for three weeks instead. We will not take away Petra's **scent glands** because then she would have no secret **weapon** to defend herself. We will set her free in a local woods next week. You may come see her before we **release** her into the wild. Ask your teacher to bring you.

Sincerely yours,
Mary Brown, **Wildlife Officer**

---

74. begged, pleaded, voice

2 Paragraphs – new person speaking, 1st is narrator

Capitalization – always begin sentences and quotes with a capital letter; always capitalize proper nouns and "I"

Punctuation – sentences always have end punctuation; use of quotation marks around what is said out loud

Commas – appositive; quote

Verb tense – add "ed" to end of regular verbs to put in past tense; switch to present tense for quote

Spelling rules – consonant/vowel/consonant + suffix = double 2nd consonant

Skills – strong verb practice; homophone (their/there/they're); object pronouns (her, them); abbreviation in your name

Literary device – use of synonyms

B – the class **begged** their teacher _____ to take them to see petra please take us to see her **pleaded** _____ in a very nice **voice**

C – The class **begged** their teacher, _____, to take them to see Petra. "Please take us to see her," **pleaded** _____ in a very nice **voice**.

---

75. pleaded, beseeched

Paragraph – new person speaking (narrator)

Capitalization – always begin sentences and quotes with a capital letter

Punctuation – sentences always have end punctuation

Verb tense – add "ed" to end of regular verbs to put in past tense; "wrote" is past tense of irregular verb "to write"

Skills – strong verb practice; object pronouns vs. subject pronouns; homophone (their/there/they're)

Literary device – repeat of synonyms

B – they **pleaded** with their teacher. they **beseeched** her. they even wrote her letters

C – They **pleaded** with their teacher. They **beseeched** her. They even wrote her letters.

NOTE: *Have students write you a few letters to beg you to do something they want to do.*

B = the sentence(s) to be put on the board or overhead   C = the corrected sentence(s)

76. compound, (Your State) Game and Freshwater Fish Commission

Paragraph – new subject
Capitalization – always begin sentences and quotes with a capital letter; always capitalize proper nouns and "I"
Punctuation – sentences always have end punctuation
Commas – appositive
Verb tense – add "ed" to end of regular verbs to put in past tense
Skills – strong verb practice; review prepositions

B – _____ their teacher agreed to take the class to the **compound** of the **(your state) game and freshwater fish commission**

C – _____, their teacher, agreed to take the class to the **compound** of the **(Your State) Game and Freshwater Fish Commission**.

---

77. compound

Paragraph – change of time and place
Capitalization – always begin sentences and quotes with a capital letter
Punctuation – sentences always have end punctuation
Verb tense – "were" is past tense of irregular verb "to be"; "took" is past tense of verb "to take"
Skills – collective nouns take singular verbs (everyone "was," not "were")

B – all the students were excited. they took a school bus to the **compound**

C – All the students were excited. They took a school bus to the **compound**.

---

78. promised

Paragraph – time and place change
Capitalization – always begin sentences and quotes with a capital letter; always capitalize proper nouns and "I"
Punctuation – sentences always have end punctuation
Commas – subordinate clause at beginning of complex sentence
Verb tense – add "ed" to end of regular verbs to put in past tense; "got" is past tense of irregular verb "to get"
Spelling rules – "no one" is 2 words
Skills – strong verb practice

B – when they got there everyone even _____ and _____
(Teachers, put the names of two of your talkers here.) **promised** not to say a word. no one wanted to scare petra

C – When they got there, everyone, even _____ and _____ **promised** not to say a word. No one wanted to scare Petra.

B = the sentence(s) to be put on the board or overhead   C = the corrected sentence(s)

79. tiptoed, peered

No paragraph – same time, same place, same speaker, same topic

Capitalization – always begin sentences and quotes with a capital letter; always capitalize proper nouns and "I"

Punctuation – sentences always have end punctuation

Verb tense – add "ed" to end of regular verbs to put in past tense; "did" is past tense of irregular verb "to do"

Spelling rules – compound words

Skills – strong verb practice; negatives

B – the class **tiptoed** to the cage. they **peered** in at petra. she did not look happy

C – The class **tiptoed** to the cage. They **peered** in at Petra. She did not look happy.

NOTE: *After this point, paragraphs no longer are indicated in the student sentence. If your students still are not ready to indent on their own, you can do so before you put the sentence on the board. If they are ready to indent, you can omit any indention in the Caught'yas and have the class as a group discuss whether or not there should be a paragraph. When students are comfortable indenting as a group, try leaving out all indentations and see if they can begin to paragraph on their own. If students at an early age can get used to the paragraphing rule that a writer must indent every time someone new speaks, it circumvents later problems. Point out the indentations in the books that you read with them. Make your students aware.*

---

80. confined

2 Paragraphs – 2 persons speaking (2nd is narrator)

Capitalization – always begin sentences and quotes with a capital letter; always capitalize proper nouns and "I"

Punctuation – sentences always have end punctuation; use of quotation marks around what is said out loud; need for question mark in question

Commas – quote

Verb tense – add "ed" to end of regular verbs to put in past tense; switch to present tense for quote; correct use of conditional tense

Skills – word recognition and practice; compound verb

Literary device – narrator aside

B – skunks are wild animals officer brown explained. they need to run free and do not like being **confined** in a cage. would you like to be _____ in a cage

C –   "Skunks are wild animals," Officer Brown explained. "They need to run free and do not like being **confined** in a cage."
   Would you like to be **confined** in a cage?

B = the sentence(s) to be put on the board or overhead   C = the corrected sentence(s)

81. waddles, fuzzy

Paragraph – new person speaking
Capitalization – always begin sentences and
  quotes with a capital letter; always capitalize
  proper nouns and "I"
Punctuation – sentences always have end
  punctuation; use of quotation marks around
  what is said out loud
Commas – quote; 2 adjectives where 2nd is not
  age or color
Verb tense – "said" is past tense of verb "to say";
  switch to present tense for quote
Skills – strong verb use; negatives
Literary device – simile

B – putrescent petra does not run said
_____. she **waddles** like a
big **fuzzy** duck

C –   "Putrescent Petra does not run," said
_____. "She **waddles** like a
big, **fuzzy** duck."

---

82. voices, familiar

Paragraph – new person speaking (narrator)
Capitalization – always begin sentences and
  quotes with a capital letter; always capitalize
  proper nouns and "I"
Punctuation – sentences always have end
  punctuation
Commas – 2 adjectives (2nd not age or color)
Verb tense – "were" is past tense of irregular verb
  "to be"; "heard" is past tense of verb "to hear"
Spelling rules – "i" before "e"...

B – petra heard the soft friendly **voices**. they
were **familiar**

C –   Petra heard the soft, friendly **voices**.
They were **familiar**.

---

83. sniffed, reeked, blueberry pancakes

No paragraph – same topic, same speaker
Capitalization – always begin sentences and
  quotes with a capital letter
Punctuation – sentences always have end
  punctuation
Verb tense – add "ed" to end of regular verbs to
  put in past tense
Spelling rules – compound words
Skills – strong verb practice; vocabulary learning;
  compound verb

B – she **sniffed** and __ __ __ __ __ __ __.
_____ **reeked** of **blueberry**
pancakes again

C – She **sniffed** and <u>**sniffed**</u>. _____
reeked of **blueberry pancakes** again.

B = the sentence(s) to be put on the board or overhead   **C** = the corrected sentence(s)

84. chocolate, peanut butter, reeked

No paragraph – same speaker, same topic
Capitalization – always begin sentences and quotes with a capital letter; always capitalize proper nouns and "I"
Punctuation – sentences always have end punctuation
Commas – compound sentence; 2 adjectives
Verb tense – add "ed" to end of regular verbs to put in past tense
Skills – strong verb practice; homophone (hole/whole); review FANBOYS

B – _____ still smelled of **chocolate** and **peanut butter** and the whole class **reeked** of yummy warm corn. petra squeaked with joy

C – _____ still smelled of **chocolate** and **peanut butter**, and the whole class **reeked** of yummy, warm corn. Petra squeaked with joy.

85. waddled

Paragraph – new action
Capitalization – always begin sentences and quotes with a capital letter; always capitalize proper nouns and "I"
Punctuation – sentences always have end punctuation; exclamation mark needed to show emphasis
No comma (2nd adjective is color)
Verb tense – add "ed" to end of regular verbs to put in past tense; "stuck" is past tense of irregular verb "to stick"
Spelling rules – "i" before "e"...
Skills – strong verb practice; homophone (through/threw); homophone (hole/whole); compound verb

B – her friends had come! petra **waddled** to the edge of the cage and stuck her little brown nose through the small holes

C – Her friends had come! Petra **waddled** to the edge of the cage and stuck her little brown nose through the small holes.

86. warned, rabies, mites

Paragraph – new person speaking
Capitalization – always begin sentences and quotes with a capital letter; always capitalize proper nouns and "I"
Punctuation – sentences always have end punctuation; use of quotation marks around what is said out loud
Commas – quote; compound sentence
Verb tense – add "ed" to end of regular verbs to put in past tense; switch to present tense for quote; use of imperative
Skills – common contractions; do not split verbs ("still can bite" rather than "can still bite"); homophones (might/mite); review FANBOYS
Literary devices – alliteration ("might have mites")

B – dont touch her **warned** Officer Brown. she doesn't have **rabies** but she still can bite and might have **mites**

C – "Don't touch her," **warned** Officer Brown. "She doesn't have **rabies**, but she still can bite and might have **mites**."

B = the sentence(s) to be put on the board or overhead   C = the corrected sentence(s)

87. threaten

Paragraph – new person speaking (narrator)

Capitalization – always begin sentences and quotes with a capital letter; always capitalize proper nouns and "I"

Punctuation – sentences always have end punctuation

Verb tense – add "ed" to end of regular verbs to put in past tense; "did" is past tense of irregular verb "to do"; switch to present tense for quote and narrator aside; use of future tense

Spelling rules – "i" before "e"...; "no one" and "a lot" are 2 words

Skills – spelling rules; negatives; "who" is subject and used with a person (never use "that" to refer to a person; use "as" instead of "like" if followed by a subject and verb ("like" is only used in a direct comparison of two nouns or pronouns)

Literary device – use of parentheses and present tense for narrator aside; simile

B – petra did not mind that no one touched her. (skunks don't need a lot of hugs as people do. they just need friends who will not **threaten** them)

C – Petra did not mind that no one touched her. (Skunks don't need a lot of hugs as people do. They just need friends who will not **threaten** them.)

88. content, escape, nasty, field

Paragraph – new subject

Capitalization – always begin sentences and quotes with a capital letter; always capitalize proper nouns and "I"

Punctuation – sentences always have end punctuation

Commas – introductory adverb (optional); adjective series

Verb tense – "was" is past tense of irregular verb "to be"; correct use of conditional

Skills – comparatives (good/better/best)

B – petra was **content**. Now if only she could **escape** this **nasty** cage and go back to her nice new warm burrow near the **field** with the good food

C – Petra was **content**. Now, if only she could **escape** this **nasty** cage and go back to her nice, new, warm burrow near the **field** with the good food.

89. melancholy, curled, dreamed

No paragraph – same topic

Capitalization – always begin sentences and quotes with a capital letter; always capitalize proper nouns and "I"

Punctuation – sentences always have end punctuation

Verb tense – add "ed" to end of regular verbs to put in past tense; "was" is past tense of irregular verb "to be"

Spelling rules – compound words

Skills – strong verb practice; compound verb; possessive of singular noun

B – petra was **melancholy** when _____'s second-grade class left. she **curled** up in a corner of the cage and **dreamed** of popcorn

C – Petra was **melancholy** when _____'s second-grade class left. She **curled** up in a corner of the cage and **dreamed** of popcorn.

B = the sentence(s) to be put on the board or overhead   **C = the corrected sentence(s)**

90. officer

Paragraph – new person speaking
Capitalization – always begin sentences and quotes with a capital letter; always capitalize proper nouns and "I"
Punctuation – sentences always have end punctuation; use of quotation marks around what is said out loud
Commas – quote
Verb tense – "told" is past tense of irregular verb "to tell"; switch to present tense for quote
Spelling rules – most nouns form plurals by adding "s"
Skills – strong verb practice

B – **officer** brown told the class we plan to put petra into a woods near here. wild skunks need to be free

C – **Officer** Brown told the class, "We plan to put Petra into a woods near here. Wild skunks need to be free."

91. melancholy

> **NOTE:** *Warn students that one word needs to be changed ("never").*

Paragraph – new person speaking (narrator)
Capitalization – always begin sentences and quotes with a capital letter; always capitalize proper nouns and "I"
Punctuation – sentences always have end punctuation
Verb tense – "was" is past tense of irregular verb "to be"; "rode" is past tense of verb "to ride"; correct use of conditional tense (referring to future)
Skills – never use a double negative; collective nouns and pronouns (class, group, team, everyone, none, etc.) are singular
Literary device – simile

B – the class rode back to school in silence. everyone was **melancholy** like petra because none of them would never see her again

C – The class rode back to school in silence. Everyone was **melancholy** like Petra because none of them would ever see her again.

92. secret, rabies

No paragraph – same topic
Capitalization – always begin sentences and quotes with a capital letter; always capitalize proper nouns and "I"
Punctuation – sentences always have end punctuation
Commas – interrupter; compound sentence
Verb tense – "was" is past tense of irregular verb "to be"; "did" is past tense of verb "to do"; correct use of conditional tense (has not yet happened
Skills – collective pronouns (everyone, everybody, no one) are singular; review FANBOYS

B – in **secret** however everyone was happy for petra. she would be wild and free again and she did not have **rabies**

C – In **secret**, however, everyone was happy for Petra. She would be wild and free again, and she did not have **rabies**.

B = the sentence(s) to be put on the board or overhead   C = the corrected sentence(s)

93. dragged

Paragraph – time change
Capitalization – always begin sentences and quotes with a capital letter; always capitalize proper nouns and "I"
Punctuation – sentences always have end punctuation
Verb tense – add "ed" to end of regular verbs to put in past tense; "thought" is past tense of irregular verb "to think"
Skills – name recognition; strong verb practice; abbreviation in your name; possessive of singular noun; articles (a/an)
Literary device – simile

B – the next few weeks **dragged** by like slow turtles on a road. everyone in _____'s class thought about petra

C –   The next few weeks **dragged** by like slow turtles on a road. Everyone in _____'s class thought about Petra.

94. studied, library

No paragraph – same topic
Capitalization – always begin sentences and quotes with a capital letter
Punctuation – sentences always have end punctuation
Verb tense – add "ed" to end of regular verbs to put in past tense (but if end is "y," change "y" to "i"; "went" is past tense of irregular verb "to go"; "read' is past tense of verb "to read" with same spelling but different pronunciation
Spelling rules – "library" needs 2 "r's"
Skills – strong verb practice; compound verb

B – they **studied** skunks. they went to the **library** and read about skunks

C – They **studied** skunks. They went to the **library** and read about skunks.

95. heroine

No paragraph – same speaker, same topic
Capitalization – always begin sentences and quotes with a capital letter; always capitalize proper nouns and "I"
Punctuation – sentences always have end punctuation
Verb tense – "wrote" is past tense of irregular verb "to write"; "made" is past tense of verb "to make"
Spelling rules – form plural of nouns ending in "y" by changing the "y" to "i" and adding "es" (stories)
Skills – strong verb practice

B – they wrote about skunks. they made up skunk stories with petra as the **heroine**

C – They wrote about skunks. They made up skunk stories with Petra as the **heroine**.

NOTE: *This is a good time to practice narrative writing.*

B = the sentence(s) to be put on the board or overhead   C = the corrected sentence(s)

96. peered

Paragraph –time change
Capitalization –always begin sentences and quotes with a capital letter; always capitalize proper nouns and "I"
Punctuation –sentences always have end punctuation
Commas –long introductory adverb (not optional); noun series
Verb tense –add "ed" to end of regular verbs to put in past tense
Spelling rules –compound words
Skills –name recognition; compound subject; strong verb practice; homophone (hole/whole); preposition practice

B – every morning before school _____
_____ and _____
peered in the hole under the school below their classroom

C –   Every morning before school,
_____, _____,
and _____ **peered** in the hole under the school below their class-room.

---

97. guess, pessimist

NOTE: *Be careful whom you name in this one. You might even want to make up a name of a hypothetical pessimist. It might be unwise to label a child negatively (no matter how accurately).*

No paragraph – same topic; Paragraph – new person speaking
Capitalization – always begin sentences and quotes with a capital letter; always capitalize proper nouns and "I"
Punctuation – sentences always have end punctuation; use of quotation marks around what is said out loud
Commas – quote; appositive
Verb tense – "was" is past tense of irregular verb "to be"; "said" is past tense of verb "to say"; switch to present tense for quote
Skills – contraction with "is" (it's, she's, he's); homophone (there/their/they're); name recognition

B – petra was never there.
i **guess** she's gone for good said _____ a **pessimist**

C – Petra was never there.
        "I **guess** she's gone for good," said _____, a **pessimist**.

---

98. suggested, optimist

Paragraph – new person speaking
Capitalization – always begin sentences and
    quotes with a capital letter; always capitalize
    proper nouns and "I"
Punctuation – sentences always have end
    punctuation; use of quotation marks around
    what is said out loud
Commas – quote; appositive
Verb tense – add "ed" to end of regular verbs to
    put in past tense; switch to present tense for
    quote
Spelling rules – compound words
Skills – common contractions; strong verb
    practice
Literary device – alliteration

B – lets put popcorn inside her burrow every day
    suggested _____ an **optimist**.
    putrescent petra loves popcorn

C – "Let's put popcorn inside her burrow every
    day," **suggested** _____, an
    optimist. "Putrescent Petra loves popcorn."

99. idea

Paragraph – new person speaking
Capitalization – always begin sentences and
    quotes with a capital letter; always capitalize
    proper nouns and "I"
Punctuation – sentences always have end
    punctuation; use of quotation marks around
    what is said out loud; need for exclamation
    mark after exclamation
Commas – appositive (you can only have one
    best friend so name is not needed)
Verb tense – "said" is past tense of irregular verb
    "to say" switch to present tense for quote
Spelling rules – "i" before "e".....; compound
    words
Skills – strong verb practice; deliberate use of
    fragment

B – good **idea**! said his best friend _____.
    we can take turns bringing eggs and
    popcorn

C – "Good **idea**!" said his best friend,
    _____. "We can take turns bringing
    eggs and popcorn."

B = the sentence(s) to be put on the board or overhead   **C = the corrected sentence(s)**

100. edibles

Paragraph – new person speaking (narrator) and time change

Capitalization – always begin sentences and quotes with a capital letter; always capitalize proper nouns and "I"

Punctuation – sentences always have end punctuation; use of quotation marks around what is said out loud

Commas – compound sentence

Verb tense – "went" is past tense of irregular verb "to go"; "left" is past tense of verb "to leave"; "came" is past tense of "to come"

Spelling rules – most nouns form plural by adding "s"

Skills – strong verb practice; possessive of singular noun; introduce the difference between plurals and possessives (Teachers who follow will love you.); review FANBOYS

B – days went by. every day someone left a little bit of skunk **edibles** in putrescent petra's burrow but petra never came

C –   Days went by. Every day someone left a little bit of skunk **edibles** in Putrescent Petra's burrow, but Petra never came.

101. dashed

Paragraph – time change

Capitalization – always begin sentences and quotes with a capital letter; always capitalize proper nouns and "I"

Punctuation – sentences always have end punctuation

Commas – introductory adverb (optional)

Verb tense – add "ed" to end of regular verbs to put in past tense; "were" is past tense of irregular verb "to be"

Skills – compound subject; name recognition; possessive of singular noun

Literary device – building of suspense

B – one morning _____ and _____ were almost at petra's burrow. suddenly a big dog **dashed** out of the nearby woods

C –   One morning, _____ and _____ were almost at Petra's burrow. Suddenly, a big dog **dashed** out of the nearby woods.

B = the sentence(s) to be put on the board or overhead   C = the corrected sentence(s)

102. growled, menacingly

No paragraph – same topic
Capitalization – always begin sentences and quotes with a capital letter
Punctuation – sentences always have end punctuation
Comma – extra information
Verb tense – add "ed" to end of regular verbs to put in past tense; "ran" is past tense of irregular verb "to run"
Skills – strong verb practice; review adverbs (those ending in "ly" and those that do not like "one"
morning" in the previous *Caught'ya*); homophone (its/it's); it's = it is; common contractions with "is" (it's, he's, she's); possessive pronoun "its"
Literary device – building suspense

B – the dog ran up to them. it **growled menacingly** low in its throat

C – The dog ran up to them. It **growled menacingly**, low in its throat.

103. fierce

Paragraph – similar topic, but change of perspective
Capitalization – always begin sentences and quotes with a capital letter; always capitalize proper nouns and "I"
Punctuation – sentences always have end punctuation
Verb tense – add "ed" to end of regular verbs to put in past tense; "was" and "were" are past tense of irregular verb "to be"
Spelling rules – "i" before "e"...
Skills – compound subject; name recognition
Literary device – still building suspense

B – _____ and _____ were scared. the dog was big and **fierce**. it looked mean

C – _____ and _____ were scared. The dog was big and **fierce**. It looked mean.

104. fangs

No paragraph – same topic and perspective
Capitalization – always begin sentences and quotes with a capital letter; always capitalize proper nouns and "I"
Punctuation – sentences always have end punctuation
Verb tense – add "ed" to end of regular verbs to put in past tense; "felt" is past tense of irregular verb "to feel"
Skills – strong verb practice; comparatives (good, worse, worst) homophone (its/it's); it's = it is; common contractions with "is" (it's, he's, she's); possessive pronouns (his, its); sense verbs (to feel, see, hear, taste, smell)
Literary device – building of suspense

B – _____ felt something soft brush his leg. the dog growled even worse. it showed its **fangs**

C – _____ felt something soft brush his leg. The dog growled even worse. It showed its **fangs**.

B = the sentence(s) to be put on the board or overhead   **C = the corrected sentence(s)**

105. peed, trepidation

NOTE: *Be sure to pick a student for this one who is secure in his ego and would take this in the spirit in which it is intended.*

No paragraph – same topic, same person being discussed

Capitalization – always begin sentences and quotes with a capital letter; always capitalize proper nouns and "I"

Punctuation – sentences always have end punctuation

Verb tense – add "ed to end of regular verbs to put in past tense; "felt" is past tense of irregular verb "to feel"; use of pluperfect to suggest action previous to this paragraph

Skills – name recognition; sense verbs

Literary device – humor

B – _____ felt something on his leg again. Maybe he had **peed** in his pants in fear and **trepidation**. he looked down

C – _____ felt something on his leg again. Maybe he had **peed** in his pants in fear and **trepidation**. He looked down.

---

106. brushed, approached, growling

No paragraph – same topic

Capitalization – always begin sentences and quotes with a capital letter; always capitalize proper nouns and "I"

Punctuation – sentences always have end punctuation

Comma – introductory word

Verb tense – add "ed" to end of regular verbs to put in past tense; "stood" is past tense of irregular verb "to stand"

Spelling rules – turn a verb into an adjective by adding "ing"

Skills – strong verb practice; homophone (there/their/they're); homophone (tail/tale)

B – no there between his legs stood putrescent petra! her tail **brushed** his leg again as she **approached** the **growling** dog

C – No, there between his legs stood Putrescent Petra! Her tail **brushed** his leg again as she **approached** the **growling** dog.

---

107. ferocious, canine

Paragraph – new movement and action

Capitalization – always begin sentences and quotes with a capital letter; always capitalize proper nouns and "I"

Punctuation – sentences always have end punctuation

Verb tense – add "ed" to end of regular verbs to put in past tense; "went" is past tense of irregular verb "to go"

Spelling rules – consonant/vowel/consonant + suffix = double 2nd consonant

Skills – strong verb practice

B – the two boys stepped back. petra went up to the **ferocious canine**

C – The two boys stepped back. Petra went up to the **ferocious canine**.

B = the sentence(s) to be put on the board or overhead   C = the corrected sentence(s)

108. brutish, limp

No paragraph – same topic, same perspective

Capitalization – always begin sentences and quotes with a capital letter; always capitalize proper nouns and "I"

Punctuation – sentences always have end punctuation

Commas – extra information

Verb tense – add "ed" to end of regular verbs to put in past tense; "hung" is past tense of irregular verb "to hang"

Skills – strong verb practice; homophone (straight/strait)

Literary device – building suspense

B – petra turned around so that her back end faced the **brutish** dog. she stamped her feet and raised her tail up straight all except the tip which hung **limp**

C – Petra turned around so that her back end faced the **brutish** dog. She stamped her feet and raised her tail up straight, all except the tip which hung **limp**.

---

109. chattered, growled, hissed

No paragraph – same topic, same action

Capitalization – always begin sentences and quotes with a capital letter; always capitalize proper nouns and "I"

Punctuation – sentences always have end punctuation

Commas – verb series

Verb tense – add "ed" to end of regular verbs to put in past tense; "did" is past tense of irregular verb "to do"

Skills – strong verb practice; compound verb

Literary device – building of suspense

B – petra **chattered** her teeth **growled** and **hissed**. the dog did not back away

C – Petra **chattered** her teeth, **growled**, and **hissed**. The dog did not back away.

---

110. arched, putrid

No paragraph – same subject, same action

Capitalization – always begin sentences and quotes with a capital letter; always capitalize proper nouns and "I"

Punctuation – sentences always have end punctuation

Commas – verb series; extra information

Verb tense – add "ed" to end of regular verbs to put in past tense; "let" is past tense of irregular verb "to let"

Skills – strong verb practice; homophone (hole/whole); good place to review prepositions

Literary device – alliteration

B – putrescent petra then looked around her back at the dog. she **arched** her back raised her whole tail even the tip and let fly with her **putrid** scent

C – Putrescent Petra then looked around her back at the dog. She **arched** her back, raised her whole tail, even the tip, and let fly with her **putrid** scent.

B = the sentence(s) to be put on the board or overhead   C = the corrected sentence(s)

111. noxious, musk, yelped

No paragraph – same action
Capitalization – always begin sentences and quotes with a capital letter; always capitalize proper nouns and "I"
Punctuation – sentences always have end punctuation; need for exclamation mark after dramatic statement
Commas – introductory adverb; adjective series
Verb tense – add "ed" to end of regular verbs to put in past tense; "fired" is past tense of irregular verb "to fire"
Skills – strong verb practice; adverbs that end in "ly"; possessive of singular noun

B – very quickly petra fired two streams of **noxious** putrescent oily **musk** right into the dog's face. the dog **yelped**

C – Very quickly, Petra fired two streams of **noxious**, putrescent, oily **musk** right into the dog's face. The dog **yelped**!

112. cheetah, odoriferous, musk

No paragraph – continuation and conclusion of action
Capitalization – always begin sentences and quotes with a capital letter; always capitalize proper nouns and "I"
Punctuation – sentences always have end punctuation
Commas – extra information
Verb tense – "put" is past tense of irregular verb "to put"; "ran" is past tense of verb "to run"
Skills – strong verb practice; comparative (fast/faster/fastest); possessive of singular noun; negatives; homophone (its/it's); it's = it is; common contractions with "is" (it's, he's, she's); possessive pronouns; homophone (tail/tale)
Literary device – simile

B – then it put its tail between its legs and ran as fast as it could faster than a **cheetah**. it could not get away from petra's **odoriferous musk**

C – Then it put its tail between its legs and ran as fast as it could, faster than a **cheetah**. It could not get away from Petra's **odoriferous musk**.

113. proud

Paragraph – new person speaking
Capitalization – always begin sentences and quotes with a capital letter; always capitalize proper nouns and "I"
Punctuation – sentences always have end punctuation; use of quotation marks around what is said out loud
Commas – quotes; participial phrase
Verb tense – "said" is past tense of irregular verb "to say"; switch to present tense for quote; use of pluperfect to denote previous action
Skills – word recognition
Literary device – made-up word for sound made; alliteration

B – pheew said _____.
putrescent petra really can be

__ __ __ __ __ __ __ __ __ __

when she wants to be he said **proud** that he had used such a big word

C –   "Pheew," said _____.
"Putrescent Petra really can be <u>putrescent</u> when she wants to be," he said, **proud** that he had used such a big word.

B = the sentence(s) to be put on the board or overhead　　　　**C = the corrected sentence(s)**

114. reek, juice

Paragraph – new person speaking
Capitalization – always begin sentences and
   quotes with a capital letter
Punctuation – sentences always have end
   punctuation; use of quotation marks around
   what is said out loud; need for exclamation
   mark in dramatic statement
Commas – quote
Verb tense – "said" is past tense of irregular verb
   "to say"; "held" is past tense of "to hold";
   switch to future tense for quote
Skills – possessive of plural noun
Literary device – humor

B – that dog will **reek** for the next few weeks
said the boys' teacher as she held her nose
and came up to the boys. it needs a bath in
tomato **juice**

C –   "That dog will **reek** for the next few
weeks," said the boys' teacher as she held
her nose and came up to the boys. It needs a
bath in tomato **juice**!

115. proud, waddled

Paragraph – new person speaking (narrator) and
   new topic
Capitalization – always begin sentences and
   quotes with a capital letter; always capitalize
   proper nouns and "I"
Punctuation – sentences always have end
   punctuation
Commas – participial phrase
Verb tense – add "ed" to end of regular verbs to
   put in past tense
Skills – strong verb practice
Literary device – alliteration

B – putrescent petra **proud** of herself for
saving some of her friends **waddled** back
to her burrow

C –   Putrescent Petra, **proud** of herself for
saving some of her friends, **waddled** back
to her burrow.

116. musk, sprayed

No paragraph – same topic, same speaker
Capitalization – always begin sentences and
   quotes with a capital letter
Punctuation – sentences always have end
   punctuation
Verb tense – use of pluperfect tense to denote
   previous action; correct use of conditional
   tense (possible future action)
Spelling rules – compound word
Skills – homophone (there/their/they're);
   possessive pronouns

B – none of her putrescent **musk** had **sprayed**
on her fur. maybe there would be popcorn
waiting for her in her burrow

C – None of her putrescent **musk** had **sprayed**
on her fur. Maybe there would be popcorn
waiting for her in her burrow.

B = the sentence(s) to be put on the board or overhead   **C** = the corrected sentence(s)

117. stench, lingered

Paragraph – time change, subject change

Capitalization – always begin sentences and quotes with a capital letter; always capitalize proper nouns and "I"

Punctuation – sentences always have end punctuation

Verb tense – add "ed" to end of regular verbs to put in past tense; "was" is past tense of irregular verb "to be"; "wore" is past tense of "to wear"; "went" is past tense of verb "to go"

Spelling rules – most nouns form plurals by adding "s"

Skills – irregular verbs; homophone (to/two/too); use of slang ("went off")

B – the **stench lingered** for days. it was hard to work. some students wore nose clips to school. even petra went off her food

C –   The **stench lingered** for days. It was hard to work. Some students wore nose clips to school. Even Petra went off her food.

---

118. ferocious, canine, despite, stench, musk

Paragraph – subject change

Capitalization – always begin sentences and quotes with a capital letter; always capitalize proper nouns and "I"

Punctuation – sentences always have end punctuation

Commas – subordinate clause at the beginning (complex sentence); extra information

Verb tense – add "ed" to end of regular verbs to put in past tense; use of pluperfect tense to denote past action

Skills – strong verb practice; name recognition; homophone (whole/hole)

Literary device – dénouement (bringing action to a logical conclusion)

B – after petra had saved _____ and _____ from the **ferocious canine** the whole school wanted to let petra live in her burrow **despite** the **stench** of her **musk**

C –   After Petra had saved _____ and _____ from the **ferocious canine**, the whole school wanted to let Petra live in her burrow, **despite** the **stench** of her **musk**.

---

119. officers, (Your State) Game and Freshwater Fish Commission, rabies, symptoms, disease

No paragraph – continuation
Capitalization – always begin sentences and quotes with a capital letter; always capitalize proper nouns and "I"
Punctuation – sentences always have end punctuation
Commas – series of verbs; compound sentence
Verb tense – add "ed" to end of regular verbs to put in past tense
Skills – strong verb practice; never split infinitives (unlike the narrator on *Star Trek*); review FANBOYS
Literary device – dénouement; alliteration ("dread disease")

B – all the students signed a pledge never to approach touch or tease petra. the **officers** at the **(your state) game and freshwater fish commission** checked petra for **symptoms** of **rabies** every month and the students were alerted to watch petra for signs of the dread **disease**

C – All the students signed a pledge never to approach, touch, or tease Petra. The **Officers** at the **(Your State) Game and Freshwater Fish Commission** checked Petra for **symptoms** of **rabies** every month, and students were alerted to watch Petra for signs of the dread **disease**.

NOTE #1: *FYI. Signs of rabies vary with each animal, but they include aggression, lunging at anything, drooling, constant growling, circling behavior, pressing head against something, being overly responsive or overly listless, becoming overly agitated or a non-responsive lump, water phobic. This is a disease that affects the brain tissue, and the only way to be sure that an animal has or does not have rabies is to kill it and check its brain. In many states, vets are required to kill any animal suspected of rabies and send the head to an official state agency for checking. Wild skunks also carry parasites like lice and mites. These are also dangerous to children. Probably, Petra would have been killed, despite the complete lack of symptoms, simply because she hung around children. But, then there would be no story.*

NOTE #2: *This last Caught'ya is rather long since it wraps up the story. You might want to do it together as a class. I also suggest that you ask your students to write further adventures of Petra.*

120. hibernation, predators

Paragraph – new action
Capitalization – always begin sentences and quotes with a capital letter; always capitalize proper nouns and "I"
Punctuation – sentences always have end punctuation; need for question mark after question
Commas – compound sentence; introductory phrase
Verb tense – "had" is past tense of irregular verb "to have"; "was" is past tense of irregular verb "to be"; "did" is past tense of verb "to do"
Spelling rules – compound words; "i" before "e"....
Skills – comparatives (happy, happier, happiest); review FANBOYS
Literary device – alliteration; dénouement

B – what about petra. petra was the happiest of them all. she had a safe warm burrow. she had plenty of food. she had her freedom and she had eggs and popcorn every day. she did not have to worry about winter **hibernation** or **predators**. best of all putrescent petra had friends

C – What about Petra? Petra was the happiest of them all. She had a safe, warm burrow. She had plenty of food. She had her freedom, and she had eggs and popcorn every day. She did not have to worry about winter **hibernation** or **predators**. Best of all, Putrescent Petra had friends.

B = the sentence(s) to be put on the board or overhead   C = the corrected sentence(s)

⑪   2/28/97

The   estuary   is   protected
from   all   around. Mangroves
forests   and   barrier
islands   can   be   found.
⑫   2/28/97
Now, little   creatures,
we   will   leave   you   alone.
In   your   estuary   the
place   you   call   home.
There   three
Their   are   3   types
of   mangrove   trees —
red, black, and   white.

Example of 2ND Grader's
Caught'yas. These are
from a thematic unit on
estuaries.

3

THIRD-GRADE STORY

Willem (pronounced Villemm)

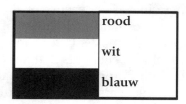

and

Marie (gargle the "R")

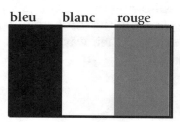

Join The Class

rouge & rood = red
blanc & wit = white
bleu & blauw = blue

What Is Included in This Chapter

1) A how-to section which will detail how to implement the *Caught'ya* method in your classroom. This includes some general, final notes.

2) An explanation of the three steps necessary to evaluate your students' *Caught'ya*s.

3) One-page, quick lesson plans for teaching the *Caught'ya*s.

4) The part of Willem's and Marie's story to be read aloud by the teacher.

5) One-hundred twenty five *Caught'ya* sentences for Willem's and Marie's story. These include the sentences to be put on the board or overhead for the students **(B)**, the corrected sentences **(C)**, a list of skills included in each *Caught'ya*, and some teaching suggestions.

1

How to Implement *Caught'yas* in Your Third-grade Classroom

Third graders can begin to understand the more complicated rules of English. They should be able to write simple paragraphs, vary sentence structure, employ good vocabulary, and punctuate sentences correctly. To aid them in this endeavor, the *Caught'ya* story in this chapter has been written exclusively to appeal to the expanding interests of third graders' worlds and to give them practice in the skills that they should master before going on to the next grade.

Willem and Marie Join the Class includes elements that appeal to eight-year-olds: bathroom humor, threatened fights, children finding solutions, learning to insult someone in two other languages, and world culture. While learning English skills and vocabulary, your students also will learn a bit of French and Dutch (the fun stuff only). At this age, children are beginning to be fascinated by foreign places and languages, and the story should dovetail with most third-grade social studies curricula in which the children explore the different countries of the world.

Following the next page, which is an encapsulated version of the ten steps to implement *Caught'yas* in the third grade, you will find the detailed information you need to begin your students on their way to fluent writing and use of good vocabulary. Each of the ten steps is fully detailed.

Ten Easy Steps for Third-grade *Caught'yas*

1. Write your own plot or choose the story in this chapter that was written especially for third graders. Buy a prop that has to do with France and/or Holland.

2. Decide on skills and vocabulary words you want to be sure to include and A) Compose your own sentences; B) Use the *Caught'yas* as written in Willem's and Marie's story; or C) Change the sentences in this story to fit your students' needs.

3. Teach your students about editing journals and response journals. Construct them so that every student has one of each. Read to your class the introduction to the story included in this chapter.

4. Write the day's *Caught'ya* incorrectly **Sentence B** on the board or overhead. Read the sentences dramatically, going over the vocabulary words, and reviewing paragraphing, capitalization and end punctuation.

5. Students write the *Caught'ya* as correctly as they can, and then with as many sentences as they can, write in their response journals on something related to the *Caught'ya*.

6. Walk around the room, helping students with the *Caught'ya*, giving individual mini-lessons, commenting on each student's effort, giving hugs, and aiding with response journals by offering suggestions and writing a few comments or questions of your own.

7. Return to the board or overhead and check the *Caught'ya* with the class, eliciting answers from students and reviewing the vocabulary words.

8. Students mark mistakes with proofreading symbols and take notes on the reasons for some of the corrections (if possible).

9. Students count and indicate the number of errors in the margin.

10. Collect the editing journals and make some positive, individual comments in each student's journal. Collect response journals. For further instruction at a later time, note errors your students make.

The *Ten Easy Steps* Explained More Fully

STEP 1

Write your own plot or choose the story in this chapter that was written especially for third graders. Buy a prop that has to do with France and/or Holland.

What Caught'yas to Use

If you have never used *Caught'yas* before, I recommend that you use Willem's and Marie's story for the first year to get the feel of the method. Then, after you have finished this *Caught'ya* story, you might want to branch out. Write your own story to suit your own students and their environment. You can brainstorm with fellow third-grade teachers. You could also write a story with other colleagues. I know of a school where teachers wrote a story that is continued in each grade level throughout the school, somewhat like a funny, ongoing soap opera.

Before Using Willem's and Marie's Story

If you use the *Caught'ya* story in this chapter, involve students in the plot so that it is familiar to them before they begin editing it. First, before school starts, buy some French and Dutch items such as dolls, flags, wooden shoes, etc. There are catalogues galore that sell the stuff to foreign language teachers. Look for an international store or try antique shops near you. You might want to buy several of each item to have a backup in case the first one "walks off" or disappears. Place these items in a prominent place in your classroom. This will generate interest. A trip to the library to find out a little about France and Holland before beginning the story might be a good idea.

If You Finish Willem's and Marie's Story Early

After the introduction (to be read by the teacher to the class), the rest of the story will unfold bit by bit in the daily *Caught'ya* sentences. There are 125, enough for one per day for the first twenty-five weeks of school. If you do one a day, which gives consistent practice to ensure better skills mastery, you'll need approximately thirty more of them (figuring ten days of field trips, assemblies, standardized tests, etc.).

Having to come up with some of your own *Caught'yas* gives you the flexibility to add sentences anywhere you wish, extra sentences that incorporate words and skills you wish to reinforce. You have an automatic diagnostic tool in your students' response journals! **(Explanation in Step 3.)** From reading these journals, you will know what skills need more emphasis, and you easily can give more detail to the basic story line to add more practice in these skills (See the **Appendix** for an alphabetized list of skills.) There are plenty of places in Willem's and Marie's story where more detail or conversation can be added without changing the story line.

On the other hand, if you have not added sentences, and you run out of *Caught'yas* at the end of April, you might ask your students to write additional adventures for Willem and Marie and their friends. These stories can be used as *Caught'yas* for the rest of the year. Using students' writing for actual *Caught'yas* can be very effective since it automatically programs in the errors they still are making.

For Your Plans — Time Necessary to Complete the Caught'yas

Many third-grade teachers who already use the *Caught'ya* stories in my other books tell me that it takes approximately fifteen to twenty minutes to complete a *Caught'ya*. If you require them to write in response journals as well (a good idea for daily writing practice), you need to add another ten minutes or so for a total of thirty minutes.

Teachers tell me that they need five minutes to read the *Caught'ya* aloud and introduce the vocabulary. Students consume another fifteen to twenty minutes to copy and correct the *Caught'ya* in their editing journals and to write a paragraph or two in their response journals.

You will use those same fifteen minutes to walk around the room looking over students' work, giving mini-lessons, and interacting with them. With you at the blackboard or overhead, the whole class spends a final five minutes reviewing vocabulary, going over some skills, and correcting the *Caught'ya*. This amount of time is needed no matter which *Caught'ya* story you use.

STEP 2

Decide on skills and vocabulary words you want to be sure to include and A) Compose your own sentences; B) Use the *Caught'yas* as written in Willem's and Marie's story; or C) Change the sentences in this story to fit your students' needs.

Skills to Be Included

By the third grade, students should be developmentally ready to master most of the comma rules, basic punctuation (including quotations), paragraphing, and a few more difficult skills including learning the four types of sentences, how to form them, and varying sentence structure. All the required third-grade skills and many more have been included in the story in this chapter. If you write your own story, make sure to include in your sentences all the skills that are required for third-grade English in your state.

Although most skills and many "big juicy" vocabulary words are repeated many times in the 125 *Caught'ya*s of this story, you might want to check for any basic skills your students may need repeated even more often. These *Caught'ya*s are generic and are designed for the "average" (if there is such a thing) third-grade student. If you teach gifted classes or classes in which more than half of your students are educationally below level, you may want to make the sentences more or less difficult according to the needs of your particular students.

Vocabulary

Remember that if you write your own sentences, you will want to insert at least one "big juicy" vocabulary word in each *Caught'ya* that you write. The difficulty of the word doesn't matter. Just write the sentences and then find a good place in each sentence to substitute a more sophisticated word. One of those little electronic spell checkers and thesauruses is perfect for finding delicious synonyms. Young children *love* to use these words, the bigger the better!!

Changing the Caught'yas

Changing the existing sentences or composing a few more of your own is easy. Check your students' writing efforts to see which skills need to be taught and which skills need more practice. For example, let's say in March, your students need more practice writing complex sentences. Keeping loosely to the plot of the story you chose, simply add a few more complex sentences for your students to punctuate.

On the other hand, below-level students in need of basic skills may have to keep working only on putting a capital letter at the beginning of a sentence and punctuation at the end of it. You can simplify the existing sentences to use with your students before you put them on the board or overhead, or you can put in missing commas, etc. on the papers of those weaker students as you stop by to see if you "caught" them.

In a nutshell, if you wish to add or take away something, you can do either in several ways. This is the hallmark of the *Caught'ya* method — each teacher can modify the sentences for his or her classes. You can do any or all of the following:

- Go over as an entire class the skills you decide are too difficult for your students to do individually and have students make the changes with you as you write on the board or overhead.

- Pick only one of the sentences in each *Caught'ya* for your weaker students to copy. Since you go over the *Caught'ya* as a class, they will hear the rest and feel as if they have accomplished something since they wrote at least one sentence.

- Add or delete punctuation from a *Caught'ya* before you put it on the board or overhead, depending on your students' developmental level.

- Rewrite the *Caught'ya* sentences in Willem's and Marie's story in order to include fewer or more skills.

- As your students' writing fluency increases, add another short sentence to each *Caught'ya*.

STEP 3

Teach your students about editing journals and response journals. Construct them so that every student has one of each. Read to your class the introduction to the story.

Use of Editing and Response Journals

At the third-grade level, students may no longer need to use editing journals (journals in which they keep their *Caught'ya*s) and can begin using (and not losing) regular, lined paper instead. Some teachers find it convenient to have a student copy, correct, and keep the *Caught'ya*s in a separate little notebook they call an editing journal. The choice is yours. While it is more convenient for a student to have a separate journal just for *Caught'ya*s, it makes a heavier load for you to carry when you collect them all for grading.

The response journals are for use after a student finishes copying and correcting the *Caught'ya*. These response journals are for free writing about any subject the student desires. You can suggest a topic for those children who cannot think of a subject, but it should be just that, a suggestion. It is a good idea to link the suggestion to the action or vocabulary in the day's *Caught'ya* (more later in **STEP 5**).

Periodically, you may want to ask your students to search in one of their already filled response journals for capital letters and end punctuation that need to be applied, for sentences in which to substitute strong, active verbs, and for places to insert some really "big, juicy" vocabulary words.

Making Editing and Response Journals

You can construct the editing and response journals from unlined newsprint (although it tears easily), 8 1/2" by 11" greenbar computer paper (without carbons), or large-lined primary paper. Old, still usable computer paper often is given away by businesses who are delighted to donate their unused, fading, outdated paper instead of throwing it out. Make construction paper covers and staple the paper inside the covers or, if you have one, use the machine that perforates the left edge and buy those big, curling-edge claw binders that hold a booklet together.

The students then can decorate their folders or booklets. Your students will need to make several editing and response journals during the course of the year. Another idea for both journals — if you can find them and your budget can afford it, buy spiral notebooks with big spaces between lines for the response journals and paste a piece of white construction paper over the cover so that each student can decorate his or her own notebook.

Preparing Your Students for Willem's and Marie's Story

When you are ready to begin doing *Caught'ya*s, introduce some of the more difficult words (the "big juicy words") that will appear in the first few *Caught'ya*s. Post them on the board. Sound them out daily. Display the French and Dutch materials prominently.

Then, after your students' interest is titillated, read the beginning of the story of **Willem and Marie Join the Class**, the part that is meant to be read aloud by the teacher. This introductory story (that leaves the listener hanging) primes your students to do the *Caught'ya*s and also introduces a few of the vocabulary words that will be repeated in the *Caught'ya*s that follow.

Read this introduction aloud several times until students are hooked and want to know more about Will (pronounced "Vill") and Marie (pronounced "Mahreee" with the accent on the last syllable). A trip to the library to find out about the Netherlands and France might be a good idea. Teaching a thematic unit on these two countries also might be in order. Third graders love mystery, action, and foreign things.

STEP 4

Write the day's *Caught'ya* incorrectly (Sentence B) on the board or overhead. Read the sentences dramatically, going over the vocabulary words, and reviewing paragraphing, capitalization, and end punctuation.

Overhead vs. Blackboard

Personally, I dislike using audio-visual devices of any kind, even one as simple as an overhead. The cord trips you, the bulb burns out just as your most difficult students enter the room, and the squirt bottle (or else you have to use spit) is a tempting weapon for students to use on each other.

Another problem with the use of an overhead is that the uncorrected sentence needs to be written on the transparency in permanent marker so that you can use an erasable overhead marker when you correct the sentence without erasing the uncorrected sentence. Once written in permanent marker, the incorrect sentences cannot be changed in order to play with quotations or to add another phrase with a comma or two.

On the other hand, with the use of the overhead, you do have the sentences already copied for subsequent years. It also affords you time for a few more sips of coffee and deep breaths before beginning the next subject or ushering in your class. At the primary level, you do not usually change classes and the skills to be included are basic. This, too, makes the overhead more practical. The choice (and dilemma) is yours.

Introducing Each Day's Caught'ya

Whichever mode of presentation you choose, copy the day's *Caught'ya*, box the vocabulary words and leave out the punctuation you want your students to insert on their own.

When you put the sentence on the board or overhead (the sentence marked "**B**" for board), list beside it, or on the board somewhere, what you want your students to do with the *Caught'ya*. At first you may ask students only to add capital letters and end punctuation. Children could be asked to write a synonym or two for one or more of the words or to define the vocabulary word. You can require them to identify the part of speech of an underlined word. What do *your* students need to practice?

This is where it is especially important to challenge your students to correct the sentences. Dare them. Make funny bets with them. Do whatever it takes to intrigue your students enough to work hard to correct the sentence, to find any literary device (mostly similes), and to learn the vocabulary words well enough to recall them when writing their own compositions.

What to Include in the Introduction to a Day's Caught'ya

It is a good idea to do the following:

- Read the *Caught'ya* dramatically.

- Review what happened previously in the story (for those who have been absent).

- Elicit the meaning of the vocabulary words in a way that will make your students remember them for more than five minutes (or make someone look it up for the class).

- Have a discussion of "to paragraph or not to paragraph," especially the use of a new paragraph every time someone new speaks.

- Point out any literary device like similes or alliteration and elicit other examples.

- Warn of any difficult skill that is included (like a comma in a compound sentence).

STEP 5

Students write the *Caught'ya* as correctly as they can, and then with as many paragraphs as they can, write in their response journals on something related to the *Caught'ya*.

Editing Journal Work

After you instruct your students to write the sentence in their editing journals as correctly as they can, you should see them hard at work. First, students should write their name, the day of the week (to practice spelling), the date (copied from the board) and the number of the *Caught'ya* above the line where they began to write. Encourage students to read and reread the sentence to try to catch all the errors. This is good practice for what will be asked of them in the fourth grade, when most students in this country take a state writing test and need to write a complete essay or story with a minimum of errors.

During the second half of the year, third-grade students should be capable of identifying the reason behind each correction. These reasons could be added in the margin of the paper, beside the *Caught'ya*. This extra requirement helps cement a skill. For example, if students know *why* they need to put a comma in a compound sentence and write the rule that applies, there is a better chance that they will remember that rule as they write their own compositions.

Response Journal Work

After copying and correcting the *Caught'ya*, students focus on writing several sentences or a paragraph in their response journals. This free writing may be about any subject a student wishes, but, some third graders still need a suggestion for a topic. Use a word or action from the day's *Caught'ya* for this purpose. For example, *Caught'ya* #9 reads: "Luckily, Willem did not comprehend his classmate, or he would have been embarrassed like a little boy." Topics for response journals that day could be any one of the following:

- Write about a time you did not understand something someone said.
- Write about a time you have been embarrassed.
- Write about a time you were lucky.
- When have you acted like a little boy or little girl? Why?
- Write about one of your classmates.

Each *Caught'ya* contains enough information to generate topics for the response journals. You might even want to ask your class, after they have read the *Caught'ya*, to suggest a topic for the day's entry in the response journal.

STEP 6

Walk around the room, helping students with the *Caught'ya*, providing individual mini-lessons, commenting on each student's effort, giving hugs, and aiding with response journals by offering suggestions and writing a few comments or questions of your own.

What to Do as You Go around the Classroom

As your students attempt to write the *Caught'ya* sentences as correctly as they can (or just one of them if they are not yet capable of more), you walk around to each student and do some of the following:

- Give a hug of encouragement to each student on task;
- Tease those students you know are being lazy;
- Issue a challenge to your top students;
- Goad good-naturedly those who are slow starters but could work faster;
- Offer individual encouragement to your weaker writers;
- Provide a ten-second mini-lesson to those who are not up-to-level on skills;
- Skim that day's entry in the response journals of those who have finished the *Caught'ya*, and write a brief comment as well.

Tricks to Time Management

Time yourself very carefully. After practice, you will find it takes fewer than ten minutes to circulate around a class of thirty students. There is, however, a trick to this — several tricks in fact.

If your classes are large, as happens all too frequently, you will see only part of a *Caught'ya* sentence in the first papers you examine. If you wait to circulate around the many desks until all your students have completed the *Caught'ya* in their editing journals and have begun writing in their response journals, you could have pandemonium and boredom on your hands. (More suggestions to avoid this problem can be found later in this section.) Instead, simply glance at the first few words of the *Caught'ya* and praise those who have not yet made errors. Then, as students' sentences are more and more complete, look for only *one* thing such as the capitalization of a proper noun.

As you amble around the room glancing at your students' *Caught'ya*s, choose the most difficult correction in the *Caught'ya* because many of your students probably will miss it at first glance. If that error still exists in a student's paper, tease quickly (I say, "*Caught'ya*") and move on. If, on the other hand, a student has found and corrected the error, take a few more seconds to check the rest of the sentences in the *Caught'ya*. In this way, you can move very quickly around the room. I sometimes hum a tune (one at least thirty years old) as I circulate, stopping only occasionally to praise a student whose *Caught'ya* has no errors. My students hate my hummed rendition of "She'll Be Coming 'Round the Mountain" the most.

Keeping It Fair and Keeping Students Occupied

Remember to vary the place where you begin checking the papers. I start at the right side of the room for even-numbered and the left side of the room for odd-numbered *Caught'ya*s. This keeps me straight and the feedback fair since the first few that I check never have the *Caught'ya* and the response journals completed.

It is a good idea, of course, to have the day's reading or math assignment already posted on the board so that if a few of your top students finish correcting the *Caught'ya* and finish writing in their response journals, they can put their journals aside for a few minutes and begin working math problems or read until you make it around the entire classroom. It is also wise to have your students become accustomed to the routine of switching immediately to the next activity when they finish the *Caught'ya* and response journal. You can establish this routine at the beginning of the year. Harry Wong, in his tapes and books, offers some wonderfully practical ideas for establishing classroom routines.

The reality of today's classroom, assignment on board or not, practiced routine or not, is that most students do not like to switch to a new activity before bringing closure to the previous one. They will wait for you to finish going around the room and will jabber when finished with the *Caught'ya* and response journal. Read on, though. I offer one more solution.

If you have a particularly rowdy class, give feedback to only half of the class each day, again varying the side of the room, so that each student gets the feedback once every two days. In my experience, however, students dislike this practice and will look at the board to find something constructive to do so that I can complete my rounds of the entire class daily. Of course, third graders are still young enough to fall into line with the old ploy: "I like the way John is working so quietly..."

A Student Chain of Checkers

Another trick to successful *Caught'ya*s that works especially well with third graders is to ask students on whose papers you find no errors to join you in checking their peers' work (after they finish writing in their response journals).

Assign each superlative student a row or a table, depending on how your room is arranged. In this way, the number of checkers increases as you move around the room, sort of like a chain letter. Third graders especially enjoy this activity because they are at the stage where they want to be in charge and have more autonomy in their learning. Be careful, though, if you choose to do this. Some students will rush through their writing in the response journals just to go check other's *Caught'ya*s.

STEP 7

Return to the board or overhead and check the *Caught'ya* with the class, eliciting answers from students and again reviewing the vocabulary words.

After the students have written the *Caught'ya* sentences as correctly as they can and noted any part of speech or synonym you asked for, and after you have circulated around the room giving feedback to each child, return to the blackboard or overhead and have the class tell you how to correct the sentences.

As your students point out each correction, you supply the appropriate proofreading symbols on the board or overhead and go over the *why* of each correction. If a mini-lesson is in order, give one. In this book, to the left of each sentence in the story, you will find the "why" listed for each correction. If a plethora of your students missed a certain skill (punctuating a quote, for example), you can launch into a brief explanation and elicit other examples.

Teaching Suggestions

It is always a good idea to use something different (especially humor) in your explanations. For example, when I teach the difference between the intransitive verb "to rise" (does not take an object) and the transitive verb "to raise" (always takes an object), I use props, including myself, and rise from unusual places like the trash can. I ask the students to rise and to raise various objects. They laugh and think that I must be crazy, but the next time in their writing, they might use the correct form of the verb and even smile as they do it.

I use mnemonic devices because they work. I find that students learn difficult material much faster with the use of mnemonics (like **FANBOYS** to learn the seven coordinating conjunctions and songs to learn the helping verbs). Suggestions like this are salted throughout the *Caught'ya* sentences for you to use if you wish.

From a primary teacher, I borrowed a way to teach students capital letters and end punctuation right from the start. I still use this method with middle-school students, so third graders are not too old for this. Ask students to nod or stamp their feet at a capital letter in the *Caught'ya* and clap their hands for a period. Your students should do this twice daily — once when you initially go over the *Caught'ya* and the second time when you go over it with the class.

It is also very effective to ask students to "stand up and move it over" whenever a new paragraph is needed in a *Caught'ya*. I like to use a "raspberry" (tongue only slightly out—no spit) for commas and a "click" sound accompanied by appropriate hand signals for a quote. By using their bodies in these very effective kinesthetic-learning exercises, students recall the rules better and usually remember to include end punctuation and capital letters when they write their own compositions. The more advanced students even may learn to indent, to use commas in the appropriate places, or to punctuate a quote correctly in their own writing before the end of the year.

The **Appendix** of this book offers a few suggestions on how to teach some of the hard-to-teach points with humor, simple-to-understand explanations, and humorous examples that you can use to supplement your own. For example: Sally Larson, a wonderfully inventive eighth-grade English teacher, pointed out to me that the main subordinating conjunctions can fit into the mnemonic "A White Bus." Students as early as third grade can memorize them that way, and once memorized, the conjunctions can be more easily remembered, used, and punctuated correctly in papers. Think about it — **A** after, although, as; **W** when, while, where; **H** how; **I** if; **T** than; **E** even though; **B** because, before; **U** until, unless; **S** since, so that.

I am sure that you already use all kinds of similar techniques to wrest your students' attention from their friends and the latest computer games in order to teach them English. (I was told by one fifth-grade teacher that he has his students sing an opera of the irregular verbs!) This is the step where you put such innovative ideas to good use. Because of the *Caught'ya*, you already should have their attention.

Vital Advice

My only advice (which comes from painful experience) is to keep your explanations bizarre, funny, and *short*. Teach no more than one point a day and keep it to fewer than three to five minutes, even with a class of gifted students. Absorbing correct English usage, mechanics, and grammar must be done in short, but intense, bursts if retention and carry-over are to take place. This is especially true in the third grade.

Repetition is the key. Keep on plugging a little bit each day, and keep on repeating *ad nauseam* until your students get the point and, most importantly, begin to use it correctly in their writing. I think that the much used quote about "All's fair in love and war" should be amended to say, "All's fair in love, war, and the teaching of correct English to young children."

STEP 8

Students mark mistakes with proofreading symbols and take notes on the reasons for some of the corrections.

As you go over the *Caught'ya* sentence at the board or overhead, students should use simple proofreading symbols to correct any error they did not catch when they corrected the *Caught'ya* on their own. Third graders have finally reached the stage of writing development where they are capable of understanding editing. Many can even take a few notes such as to denote a type of sentence or put the "why" of a comma rule. They can do this in the margins around the *Caught'ya*. You, of course, model the "notes" on the board. In this manner, you not only are teaching them how to edit, you are teaching them how to take notes.

Encourage your students to indicate corrections with a colored pencil, pen, or marker in a hue different from the one with which they wrote the sentences. You may want to make sure that there is one in each child's desk just for this purpose. Use the students' work in their response journals as a barometer on improvement in writing. I think you will be pleasantly surprised at the unconscious carry-over from *Caught'ya*s to free writing.

Proofreading Symbols

Listed below are a few of the most commonly used proofreading symbols. These are the simplest ones. Ease your young students into using them by introducing them one at a time over a period of a few weeks. If you feel that your students are not developmentally ready to handle the use of proofreading symbols at the beginning of the year, then wait a month or so and introduce them even more slowly.

Symbol	Meaning	Symbol	Meaning
¶	Indent	¶̶	Take out indent
^	Add words here	e̶	Take out, delete
≜	Capitalize	A̶	Make a small letter
→	Move word	(the and)	Reverse order
◯	Add punctuation (whatever is inside circle)		

Using Caught'yas as Tests

By marking errors in another color and using proofreading symbols, students easily can study the errors they did not catch. In this way, they do not miss the same errors in future *Caught'ya*s, in their writing, or on *Caught'ya* tests. While I do not recommend giving tests at below third-grade level, which might discourage budding learners, third graders should be able to handle infrequent, simple quizzes on the skills they have learned. Since teachers in the upper elementary grades and in middle school give *Caught'ya* tests, you want your children to be prepared and relaxed when they approach one.

Occasionally (like once a month or whenever you come upon an appropriate *Caught'ya*), give students *one* of the *Caught'ya*s as an informal quiz. Use a *Caught'ya* that contains many of the skills you have been teaching. Simply have students complete the *Caught'ya* in the usual way, but instead of putting it in their editing journal, they put it on a separate piece of paper. You still may walk around the room and tell students that you "caught" them, but do not tell them where. This routine procedure takes away most of the "sting" of the quiz, gets students accustomed to taking tests without stress, and relieves their anxiety.

Delay going over and correcting the *Caught'ya* together until *after* you have graded the *Caught'ya* as a quiz. In this way, you have a short, pop quiz, completed under relaxed conditions, that gives you a picture of your students' progress. As for grading it, if you choose to do so, count the number of errors in the *Caught'ya* and divide into one hundred to get the number you take off for each error. You could, if there are very few errors, take off only five or ten points each so that you do not discourage your students. I suggest that you go no lower than a "C."

Another testing suggestion: if you wish to give a quick test, write a new sentence (not yet corrected, of course) that includes many of the skills that you and the *Caught'ya*s have taught up to that point. Make it funny. Follow the procedure in the previous paragraphs to implement the test.

In the third-grade story in this chapter, all nine comma rules (except those in a letter) are covered within the first twenty *Caught'ya* sentences. A quickie quiz (oral or written) of most of the comma rules might be appropriate after you have completed those *Caught'ya*s. (The comma rules, by the way, are repeated constantly in subsequent sentences to ensure mastery.) See the **Appendix** for a list of them.

STEP 9

Students count and indicate the number of errors in the margin.

Students count the number of errors they did not catch when they attempted to correct the sentence on their own. They indicate the number in the right-hand margin. This process has two advantages. It makes students leave a good, healthy, right-hand margin, and it provides them with immediate feedback. Remind your students to make all corrections, notations, and notes in a color different from the one they used to write the *Caught'ya* itself. Again, this is a study technique that makes it easier for students to see where they need to concentrate.

Keep Students Honest

Encourage, cajole, forbid, threaten, do anything you can think of to keep your students honest. Since the grade the students receive from you on the *Caught'ya* (if you give them a grade) has nothing to do with the number of errors they made when they attempted to write the sentence on their own, it would be pointless to try to hide errors and correct them surreptitiously as the answers are divulged. Moreover, cheating would only hinder a student from learning from his/her mistakes.

STEP 10

Collect the editing journals, and make some positive, individual comments in each student's journal. Collect response journals. For further instruction at a later time, note errors your students made.

Collecting the Journals and Dealing with Absentees

Keeping an editing journal and a response journal helps your students organize themselves and learn to hang onto booklets they use daily. This trains them for later grades when they have to keep notebooks as well as one piece of paper with a week's worth of *Caught'ya*s on it. It also helps you keep track of students' writing progress. Collect these journals as often as you wish. I suggest once a week.

Students who have been absent should write the day(s) of the week they missed and write the word "absent" underneath. Since there are no student texts for the *Caught'ya* method, it is difficult for students to make up missed *Caught'ya*s.

One teacher I know, however, does require that students make up missed *Caught'ya*s by copying from a peer's paper. She exhorts her students to be careful. Any error the peer missed also counts against the copying student. I would not suggest doing this until January of the third-grade year. I require absent students to obtain from a peer or from me the vocabulary words taught during their absence, but they do not have to make up the *Caught'ya*s themselves.

Grading the Caught'yas

Grade the *Caught'ya*s using the quick three-step method that follows this step. I think you will be pleased at how little time it takes.

Using Response Journals to Chart Progress

After grading the *Caught'ya*s and making positive comments, take a look at each child's response journal. These are the real indicators of progress and improvement in writing fluency. You might want to keep a chart for each child to indicate skills mastered (capitalization and end punctuation, for example), number of more sophisticated vocabulary words used, and increase in numbers of sentences and subsequent decrease in use of pictures and letters. Such a chart would come in handy at parent conferences and when evaluating a student's progress in language arts. Below is an example of such a chart.

Student's Name _____

Week	Basic Skills Mastered and Used	Extra Skills Mastered and Used	Vocabulary Used	Number of Sentences and x's per Entry	Comments
Sept.13-17					
Sept. 20-24					
9/27-10/2					
Oct. 5-9					
etc.....					

A Few Final Notes

Two Pieces of Advice

Keep it simple. Since you explain the "why" of all the corrections when you go over the *Caught'ya*, you don't want to go beyond what your particular students can learn. (Remember Piaget?) By using the fundamental eight parts of speech, you easily can explain all the essential grammar and usage without using the more technical terms and "turning off" students. This tool is especially useful in teaching very young, "regular," and below-level students.

For example, an eight-year-old can comprehend a concept as complicated as a participial phrase by identifying it as an "-ing verb" that does not have an "is" or "was" before it. Whenever students see an "-ing verb" without an "is" or "was," they can learn that commas must be used. Keep in mind that the end result is not to learn the terms, but to write correctly.

Similarly, third-grade teachers do not want to teach about subordinate clauses, and yet there are subordinate clauses in the *Caught'ya*s because third-grade students do need to learn how to write and correctly punctuate complex sentences. If the clause comes at the beginning of the complex sentence, you can explain the comma without using the term "subordinate clause." The **Appendix** contains a suggestion for teaching this. The key is to keep your explanations understandable and as simple as possible as you go over the reason behind each correction.

After all, the goal (and the end result) is not to learn English terms but to write fluently with a minimum of egregious errors (like forgetting to capitalize the beginning of a sentence). If a third grader can write a clear, simple, short essay or story with a beginning, middle (elaboration), and an end that includes a few good vocabulary words, a few strong verbs, maybe a simple simile, a compound sentence or two, and a minimum of errors, you have accomplished a lot. At this point, your aim is for good, fluent writing, not complex structure. Indeed, authors like Hemingway have demonstrated that simple writing works just fine and can be quite beautiful!

Don't be shy. It is important to keep in mind that English rules are not always hard and fast! In fact, many of the rules of English are debatable. I, for example, always put the comma before the "and" in a series of three or more. Others do not. Sometimes paragraphing is a personal matter as, for example, in a long introduction to a quote — some paragraph the quote, some don't. Optional commas after introductory adverbs abound. Some grammar books list "quick" as an adverb (without the "ly"). I refuse to do so.

In other words, feel free to disagree with me. I am not even the "absolute word" in my own classroom. My students and I have hot debates over paragraphing and optional comma use. By the way, just so you know how far I do go in order to be comfortable with the rules — the apostrophe in *Caught'ya* is a contraction of the made-up word, "caughtchya." That is why the "y" in the word "*Caught'ya*" should not be capitalized.

A Request

Now for the request. Even though I have read through each set of *Caught'ya*s at least five times (once out loud), and even though four other people, all experienced editors, also proof-read them very carefully, I know that a few errors probably still lurk among the sentences and lists of skills. *Please*, if you spot one, especially an egregious mistake that is *not* debatable, write to me via the publisher, who will forward your letter to me. The errors you find will be corrected at the next printing of the book. The address for Maupin House Publishing is printed on the copyright page.

What Is Included in the Following Story and in the Appendix

There are two sets of the *Caught'ya*s for the third-grade story. The first (labeled **B** for "board") is the *Caught'ya* I suggest putting on the board or overhead, the sentences that contain the errors to correct or the blanks to fill in. The second (labeled **C** for "corrected") is a corrected version for you.

Listed to the left of each *Caught'ya*, you will find all the grammar, mechanics, and usage skills and rules related to that particular *Caught'ya*. If the example of a skill is fairly obvious, it is not specifically identified in the section to the left of the *Caught'ya*. If, however, the example is something that we teachers (with our rusty recollections of English grammar from college days) might not recognize at first glance, it *is* listed. I suggest that you peruse the **"Other skills"** part of each list on the left for the skills that you want to teach. By no means are you expected to teach them all. All are offered so that you may pick and choose. You, alone, know what your students are ready to learn.

At the third-grade level, the *Caught'ya*s begin to require students to change spelling, verb tense, word usage, etc. If you think your students are not ready to do this, simply change an incorrect word to the correct one when you put the *Caught'ya* on the board or overhead.

Many *Caught'ya*s also include simple literary devices and a few teaching suggestions. All the skills or rules that are referred to at the left of each *Caught'ya* are listed, annotated, and explained with examples in the **Appendix**. The explanations in the **Appendix** are for you, not for your students. Obviously, at the third-grade level, you will not teach all the grammar, mechanics, and usage listed there.

Nine Other Very Important Notes for Using This Particular Story

1) As noted before, you may want to purchase something that represents France and Holland (dolls, wooden shoes, flags, a model of the Eiffel Tower, etc.). These objects can accompany you as you walk around the room checking your students' *Caught'ya*s and reading their response journals. The object can do the teasing with you. It can sit on the desk of a particularly good child. It can go to the hospital for a temporary stay with a sick one. This involves students even more in the story. If you use a doll, it can become the class mascot. And, learning a bit of French and Dutch will be fun. (Don't worry, I'll give

you helpful hints for pronunciation.) You may want to post, on a bulletin board, the foreign words students have learned.

You can stress the importance of learning another language. Hopefully, this story will serve a dual purpose: teach correct English and give students impetus and desire to pursue the study of a foreign language. Some schools offer rudimentary Spanish at the third-grade level. There are private French academies throughout the United States at which everything is taught in French!

2) You will have to write your name and the names of your students in the appropriate blanks when they occur. Fifty-six blanks have been left for the names of your students in the preliminary story and in the subsequent *Caught'ya*s since you will want to use some children's names more than once.

3) All punctuation and paragraphing have been left out of the student *Caught'ya*s. You have three choices: **A)** Leave the sentences as they are when you put them on the board or overhead and have your students attempt to supply that punctuation; **B)** Leave the *Caught'ya*s as they are when you put them on the board or overhead and have the class as a group decide the paragraphing and punctuation with you *before* students attempt to write the sentences correctly; or **C)** Provide some (or most) of the paragraphs, quotation marks, commas, and end punctuation when you write the *Caught'ya* on the board for your students. *You* alone know what your students can handle. You want them to learn, not get frustrated.

For your information, all nine comma rules are covered in the first twenty *Caught'ya*s (go over the rules—see **Appendix**). All types of quotes also are addressed as well as reasons for indenting. When the class goes over the *Caught'ya*s, it is important to have a daily discussion of why there is or is not a paragraph, especially if a quote is involved.

Third graders need to learn the simple paragraphing rule that one indents every time someone new speaks. Point it out to your students in the books they read as well as in the *Caught'ya*s. If your students can master this, subsequent teachers will sing your praises, and your school's State Writing Assessment average will rise a tad.

Hyphens and apostrophes have been left out in some *Caught'ya*s, but you may wish to restore these if you find your students have trouble understanding the concept. Colons and semi-colons are never taken out of the student sentences since third graders are not yet ready to understand the use of them.

4) Since this story is told in the past tense (with "ed"), you may want to teach that form before beginning the *Caught'ya*s.

5) Young children love to use big words. To this end, there are one or two "big, juicy" vocabulary words in each *Caught'ya*. Use them all week long in *your* speech. Encourage your students to use them in their writing and when they talk. Make a bulletin board of your students' favorites. Comfortably using superior vocabulary can really help your students when it comes time to take your state's Writing Assessment Test in the fourth grade, especially if that good vocabulary comes in the form of strong verbs **(See Chapter 4)**.

6) Since varied sentence structure is an important component of most (if not all) state writing tests, and third grade is only one year away from that test, you may want to pay particular attention to the four main types of sentences. In each *Caught'ya*, the sentence type has been identified in order to help you in teaching the four different types. The second half of the year you may want to ask your students to write under each *Caught'ya* a

simple, a compound, a complex, or a compound/complex sentence of their own. In this manner, they really are practicing this vital skill.

7) Since the first few sentences are difficult, and because you want your students to experience success, it might be a good idea (especially if your students never have experienced *Caught'ya*s before) to do them together as a class. I always walk my students through the first few for modeling purposes. After that, if there are two sentences, and/or the *Caught'ya* is too long for your students, break it up into two and do the second half the next day.

8) It is a good idea to make your students copy or write the day of the week and the date above each *Caught'ya*. This serves two purposes. You easily can see a child's progress, and the children practice and learn to write the days of the week.

9) One final note about the teaching of these *Caught'ya*s. If your students have poor English skills or below-average attention spans, they may not be able to copy an entire *Caught'ya* and correct it. If this is the case, then, if a *Caught'ya* is comprised of more than one sentence, do the first sentence aloud with your students, eliciting the answers, and make students copy and correct only one sentence on their own. This practice may save time as well. You want to adapt the *Caught'ya*s to fit the needs and capabilities of your particular students.

Enjoy this "grammatical expedition" with your students. I wish you much good writing, new vocabulary, and many hugs and giggles as you share and correct this story of Marie, Willem, and their new friends!

2

Three Steps to Evaluate the *Caught'yas*

STEP 1 — Check the format
STEP 2 — Check the content of one *Caught'ya*.
STEP 3 — Take notes and reward students

Introduction

Evaluating the *Caught'ya*s for third-grade students is just as important as the process of doing one. The *Caught'ya* is designed to eliminate the feeling of failure and to foster success in language arts for "regular" and below-level students and to challenge gifted students to new heights. We English teachers need to improve the image of English classes. The evaluation of the *Caught'ya*s can help!

The most important thing to remember about evaluating the *Caught'ya*s is that the sentences are *not* graded on how well a student initially grasps the rules of the English language when he/she corrects the sentence on his/her own, but on how carefully that student corrects the sentence when you and the class go over the *Caught'ya* at the blackboard or overhead.

A student can make one or twenty errors in any *Caught'ya* and still earn an "A" *if* that student has caught all of those errors and corrected them, complete with notes as to the reason or rule for each correction. This is the secret. You are grading the *Caught'ya*s only to spark your students to pay close attention when you go over the *Caught'ya*s and to keep them honest when they count their errors. Evaluation of students' progress can be made through the short *Caught'ya* tests mentioned above in **STEP 8**.

The title of this book promises you "grammar with a giggle." Well, get ready to have a giggle yourself! A week's worth of *Caught'ya*s takes only fifteen minutes a week to grade for a class of thirty students. This grading requires that your students follow a certain format. When you collect the editing journals, insist that your students put a marker on the page of the last *Caught'ya* completed. This will reduce your page shuffling time. *You* have to decide on the format that you like and really insist on it. You probably will want to include the following:

- Full date and day written out above each *Caught'ya* for subtle spelling practice, e.g., Wednesday, February 23, 2000;

- A two- or three-word title written at least once a week for capitalization practice;

- A fairly even margin on the left and a margin that leaves space on the right where the number of errors missed should be indicated;

- Use of different colored ink for corrections and for errors so that you (and the student when he/she studies it) can tell at a glance what has been missed and then corrected by the student.

Now get out your green and purple pens. You are ready to grade the *Caught'ya*s. The following detailed three steps assume that you have a paper in front of you. If you do not, look at the sample paper at the end of this section and use it for clarification as you note the steps.

Three Steps to Evaluate the *Caught'ya* in More Detail

STEP 1

Check the format

Glance at the paper to see if the student faithfully has followed the format you require. Except for the failure to use a different color, which should not count against a student, each error in the format, including uneven margins, is worth five points. This may seem harsh, but it encourages students to be careful.

- Date written out correctly with month spelled out correctly.

- Title correctly spelled and capitalized.

- Number of uncaught errors indicated and circled to the right of each *Caught'ya* sentence. (**Hint** — Don't count, just see if a number is there.)

- Margins large enough and an even left margin.

Mark all errors clearly in a pen that is a different color from the two hues that your student used. It always is helpful to keep an array of colors handy as you grade. Because of arthritis, I like to use those big Crayola markers.

STEP 2

Check the content of one *Caught'ya*

Choose *one* of the week's *Caught'ya* sentences. This is what really saves you time. I assure you that if you read all of the sentences each week for each of your students, the final grade would be about the same (if you take off fewer points per error).

For six years I graded every sentence of every student every week, but it got to be such a bore and a chore that I grew to dread the weekends. I struggled to keep positive about the *Caught'ya*s because my students really were learning. Then I noticed that if I increased the number of points per error and graded only one *Caught'ya* per student per week, the grade almost always came out the same. The careless students were careless, and the careful students continued to be careful. In fact, some of the careless students (perhaps because I was taking off more points per error) became more careful.

When a colleague of mine who also used *Caught'ya*s, independently came to the same conclusion, we talked it over, pooled our collective guilt at not reading every sentence, and chucked it out our classroom doors with glee at the extra hour per week we were giving ourselves.

Do not tell students which *Caught'ya* sentence you plan to grade. This makes them careful with all of the sentences. Do not always choose the most difficult sentence. In this way you will always keep your students honest.

Another important point is that you can individualize the evaluation of the *Caught'ya*s, grading an easier one for your weaker students or classes. Remember, you want to *encourage* your students to like editing and to think of it as a fun game rather than an onerous, teacher-imposed chore only to be done when pressed. You *want* your students to receive high grades on the *Caught'ya*s. By the way, you will find that the test scores on the mini-*Caught'ya* tests also go up and up as students feel better and better about English and about editing.

After you choose the *Caught'ya* you wish to grade for the week, focus on it. Ask yourself the questions that follow. Each "No" answer deducts five points from the score. Again, I suggest the lowest grade be a "C." To go lower is pointless and does not help the self-esteem of a young student on whom you probably want to work to raise self-concept.

- Did the student clearly mark the errors with the proofreading symbols you want him/her to use?

- If required, did the student take notes as to the reasons for the corrections?

- Did the student catch *every* error either the first or the second time?

- Is the number of errors indicated in the right-hand margin?

- Are all the words (including vocabulary word) spelled correctly? Take five points off per misspelled word.

- Is the sentence copied correctly from the board or overhead?

- Have any words been left out?

- Are there any extraneous capital letters?

In addition, take five points off for each error you find that has not been marked by the student or does not have the correction written above it. After all, you gave them all the answers! You will be pleasantly surprised at the results. Even your poorest student can earn an "A+." In fact, I find that my "regular" and below-level students often earn higher grades than my gifted students. Although they may miss more the first time around, "regular" and below-level students are more careful about checking each sentence. They tend to be less cocksure than the gifted students (for whom learning is easy) and the chance to earn an "A+" on a paper in language arts is exciting to them.

After you have added the number of points lost for errors in the format of the entire paper to the points lost for errors not caught in the one *Caught'ya* you checked, subtract the total from one hundred down to a "C." In other words, if a student misses more than five errors, stop grading. (Although you may want to use the grade of "C-" to indicate to yourself that a lower grade was warranted.)

Put the grade at the bottom of the last page with the most recent *Caught'ya*. Be sure to include an encouraging or positive comment. Since you grade only one *Caught'ya* per week per student, you have the luxury of making that brief, private comment on each paper. This is especially important in primary classes where encouragement is the key to success.

STEP 3

Take notes and reward students

Note frequently missed errors, and keep the list near you. I like to use the big calendar blotter on my desk as it is always handy, and I never lose it as I do a piece of paper. A small spiral notebook also works well. In this way, you can concentrate on the errors students still make and not harp on already mastered skills.

Each year different errors repeat themselves. Two years ago I struggled all year with improper verb tenses. (They kept switching back and forth between present and past.) Last year my students rarely made verb-tense errors after November, but they had a terrible time using the correct pronoun! I wonder what the error-of-the-year will be in the next class.

One of the reasons that the *Caught'ya* system is so successful and popular with students is that it makes them feel good about themselves. There is always *something* positive you can say (no student will miss *every* error). Public displays of success are most important at the primary levels, although even high-school students adore rewards.

Teachers of special-education students with learning or behavioral problems have repeatedly told me how well the *Caught'ya* technique works with their students because this is one of the few areas in which they can experience success. These teachers play the reward system to the hilt to capitalize on that feeling.

After trying other less successful methods of publicizing student achievement, I experimented with a *Caught'ya* lottery in my classroom. This did the trick. It was easy and little work for me, and my students loved it. The lottery is simple. When you pass back the *Caught'ya* papers, give 1/4 of a 3 x 5" card to each student who earned an "A+" in his/her editing journal or on the weekly *Caught'ya* paper. Announce the names of the excellent students publicly and make a big deal over the accomplishment.

The students who receive cards write their names, date, and class period on the card. Rather than just collecting the cards, make each student being rewarded walk to the front of the classroom in full view of the rest of the class. Relishing the moment of public recognition, the students each deposit the card in a box. Once a month (or each week if your prefer) open the box and draw out one card. The winning student receives a prize: a lollipop, a lunch period in your room with three friends, a coupon for something, a pencil, etc.

An example of a corrected student paper follows. *My* marks and comments are inside the dark black lines. The *Caught'ya*s are from the second-grade story in **Chapter 2**. The student is a beginning third grader. Note that there is one format error. If you wish to see more examples of student *Caught'ya*s, look in the book *Caught'ya! Grammar with a Giggle* (Kiester, 1990).

(85) **Good work, Kelly!**

Caught'ya ~~Sentences~~ #20 to 25   -5

#20 Monday, October 12, 1998
Putrescent Petra ~~looked~~ up at all
the faces. She saw (freindly) faces.
She saw scared faces.   -2   le

♡ Try to remember to use capital letters
to begin sentences and in titles!

#21 Tuesday, October 13, 1998
~~And~~ Petra did not stamp her feet.
~~And~~ she did not chatter, hiss(,)or
growl. ~~And~~ She did not turn around   -5
or lift her tail in warning.

                              Wednesday
#22 ~~#225?~~ (Wendsday) October 14, 1998
Putrescent Petra liked these small
humans she could smell blue berry   -3   -5
pan cakes on Mary's breath. She
smelled fresh hot corn in John's hand.   -5

#23 Thursday, October 15, 1998
~~And~~ Wendy smelled of chocolate and
peanut butter. ~~And~~ Kelly smiled, a   -3
friendly grin, and Rashad looked
amiable dressed in the colors of a
←skunk.

> Kelly missed only one format error in the title.
> Although she misspelled "friendly" in #22, that is not the
  Caught'ya I graded, so it does not count against her.
> I graded Caught'ya #22. Heavy marks are mine.

3
Lesson Plans for the *Caught'ya*

This plan assumes that you already have completed Steps 1, 2, and 3 of "Ten Easy Steps for Third-grade *Caught'yas*".

- Before school, write the *Caught'ya* for the day on the board or overhead, box the vocabulary word, and beside it or on the board, list what you want your students to do with it. (For example: correct the *Caught'ya*; copy the vocabulary words; put meaning and a synonym or two for one of the vocabulary words; list parts of speech of underlined words; etc.)

- When the bell rings, read the sentence to the class with a dramatic flair, reviewing the story that went before, eliciting the meaning of the vocabulary words, and discussing the need for capital letters and end punctuation. Debate the need for a paragraph.

- Instruct students to copy the *Caught'ya* as correctly as they can and follow the required guidelines listed on the board. Instruct students to write in their response journals when they have completed the *Caught'ya*. You may want to suggest a topic that is related to a word or idea in the *Caught'ya*.

- Walk around the room, giving students individual feedback. Say *"Caught'ya"* or something comparable if you catch a student with an error and praise or challenge a student who has caught all of the errors so far. Give hugs, encouragement, and mini-lessons. Quickly read response journals and write a brief comment.

- Go back to the blackboard or overhead and check the *Caught'ya* sentence out loud with your class. Elicit answers from the students. Be sure to discuss the *reason* for each correction. Use the **Appendix** at the back of this book for simple explanations and other examples. Using proofreading symbols and a pen of a different hue, correct the *Caught'ya* on the board or overhead as your students do the same with any error they did not catch.

- Go over the vocabulary words again. Discuss the literary device (a simile, for example) in the sentence and conduct a mini-lesson in whatever skill you think needs more reinforce-ment. *Keep it short!*

- Instruct students to be sure that they write the date, day of the week, and the number of the *Caught'ya* right above the sentence, count their errors, and indicate them in the right-hand margin.

- Collect editing and response journals after one week for grading, for comments, and for charting progress of your students.

4

Text to Be Read Aloud by the Teacher

This text is to be read to the class by the teacher at the beginning of the year to introduce the background of the story. Vocabulary that is beyond a third-grade level has been bolded the first time each challenging word appears. Since this part of the story is intended to be read orally by an adult, these words are pointed out only to highlight their level of difficulty. You might want to change the idioms to the ones your current students use. I think "dork," for example, is already outdated. Insert the names of your students in the blanks to personalize the story.

FYI: rouge & rood (pronounced *rouge* like what you put on your cheeks and *rude*)= red;
blanc & wit (pronounced *blahunh* without saying the "n" or "c" and *vit*) = white;
bleu & blauw (pronounced *bleuh* and *blough* which rhymes with *plow*)= blue.

Willem   and   Marie
(pronounced Villemm)   **(pronounced mahreee but gargle the "R")**

Join The Class

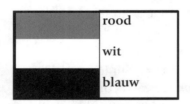

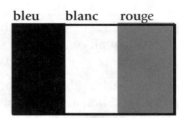

bleu   blanc   rouge

Nederland (Holland)   **La France (France)**
(pronounced *neighderlant*)   **(pronounced *laah frahnce* — do not pronounce the "n")**

   As they approached the now-familiar buildings of _____ Elementary School, _____, _____, and _____ chattered merrily about the upcoming year. Their new teacher, _____, was popular. Many of their friends were going to be in their class, and it was a bright and sunny August morning. The three were soon joined by two others, _____ and _____ who joined the **animated conversation**. All five third-graders were eager to begin the new year.
   "I sure hope _____ is as nice as my sister says," said _____.
   "Yeah, she's (he's) supposed to be cool even when you have to work and such," said _____. "My brother says she laughs all the time and almost never yells unless you're *really, really* bad."
   "Maybe we'll go on some 'neato' field trips," added _____.
   "And maybe my dog will fly," **retorted** _____.
   Still chattering the five friends approached the door of their new classroom. The teacher, _____, greeted them at the door with a big smile. She *looked* cool. Maybe they would like her as _____'s and _____'s sister and brother had said they would.

"Welcome to the third grade," greeted the teacher. "You are the last five to arrive. Come on in and join the other students."

The five entered the classroom. Bright and cheerful posters hung from the walls. Fun-looking bulletin boards **advertised** subjects and skills. The alphabet in cursive **snaked** around the wall, high up near the ceiling. Even the windows **displayed** colorful signs. *(Teachers, add more description of your room. Use strong verbs like those above.)* The desks seemed a lot bigger than last year's desks. This was going to be an awesome year.

Right in the middle of the room all the other kids **clustered** around something. What was it? _____ and _____ tried to get through the crush of kids, but _____ and _____ **blocked** their way.

_____ tried to jump up to see what was in the middle of the circle of third graders, but she couldn't jump high enough to see anything. What was in the middle of the crowd?

"OK," said their new teacher as she clapped her hands once for attention. "Let's sit down. Find your name on a desk and sit there. I have a surprise for you."

Suddenly the tight circle of kids **dispersed**. Each student found a desk with his or her name on it and sat down. The bell rang and all eyes turned to the place that had been the center of the circle of children. There, looking a little lost and afraid, were a boy and a girl — strangers. They looked like third graders but their clothes were kind of "dorkish" and definitely uncool. Who were they?

"Welcome to the third grade," _____ , the teacher, repeated. "Some of you already have discovered the surprise, but let me introduce you to two new students at our school, Marie *(Teachers, gargle the "R")* and Willem *(Teachers, pronounce all "W's" in Dutch as a "V.")* not only are new to our school, they also are new to our country.

"Marie is from France, and Willem is from the Netherlands. Most of you call Willem's country Holland," the teacher continued. "Their English is not too good, but I know you can help them learn. That is why they are here. Try to understand that they don't understand much right now. Pretend it is you in a strange classroom in a strange country where you don't understand what is going on. Be kind. Be patient with them."

"Wow," said _____ , "where are Willem's wooden shoes? Why isn't Marie dressed in a white apron and a tall hat like we saw in the pictures of France last year? Why do they look like us only like 'dorks' in uncool clothes?"

"Well," answered the teacher, "you will have to help teach Marie and Willem English first, and then you can ask them yourselves. I know that Willem is not wearing wooden shoes because no one in the Netherlands wears them anymore except to do work in the garden or the farm. They wear boots to school because of the mud. They call these boots *laarsje* (pronounced *"laarsyah"*). The people from the Netherlands prefer to call their country "The Netherlands" (Nederland — pronounced *"neighderlaunt"*) rather than Holland because Netherlands means "lowland" which does describe the fact that most of the country we call Holland is below sea level.

"The aprons and hats were worn hundreds of years ago in France," she continued. "Now some people wear them on special days for special ceremonies only in certain parts of France. They pronounce the name of their country *Frahnce* not "France" as we pronounce it. As for the 'dork' part, I'm sure you can introduce them to the styles third-grade students consider 'cool' to wear."

Marie raised her hand, "Madame," she asked. "Où est le WC?" (Pronounced *"Maah daahm, ooo eh le doobleh vay say?"* Raise your voice at the end. It means, "Where is the bathroom.")

Everyone in the class looked puzzled. What was Marie trying to ask? She obviously was talking to the teacher since she said, "Madame." But, what did the rest mean? Marie was looking more and more uncomfortable. She squirmed in her seat. She crossed her legs.

"La toilette (Pronounced *lah toahlett*)," Marie added. _____ **blurted** out, "She has to go potty! 'Toilette' means 'toilet.' The words are almost the same!" He raised his hand to slap the hand of _____ to **celebrate** his smartness.

"I'll take her," said _____. "I can show her where it is. May _____ come too?"

As the three girls **traipsed** off to the bathroom, the rest of the class wondered what Marie and Willem would say next. Would they understand? Would they be able to help? They didn't know French or Dutch, so how were they going to teach the new students English? This was certainly going to be an interesting year! No one knew what would happen next. No one had any idea of the trouble not speaking English would cause...

Stop reading out loud here.

5

125 *Caught'ya* Sentences for Third Graders

"Willem and Marie Join the Class"

Teachers Please Note:

- Since all the sentences need capital letters at the beginning and some sort of punctuation at the end, these skills are not repeated in the list of skills to the left of each *Caught'ya*. Similarly, capitalization of proper nouns and the pronoun "I" also are not listed, since these, too, are completely regular. (There are no exceptions.)

- You need to go over the above four skills every day without fail, even after all your students consistently put capital letters where they belong and always use end punctuation. Ask your weakest students to identify these points when you go over the *Caught'ya* with the class. They will be thrilled to supply information they know. These skills cannot be taught enough. I still need to go over them daily in the eighth grade!

- None of the student *Caught'yas* are indented. You will need to have a daily discussion of "to paragraph or not to paragraph."

- The phonetic pronunciations for the French and Dutch words are given in the corrected sentence in bold, italicized type. They are for your eyes only so that you can pronounce the words correctly and teach them to your students. Third grade is the perfect time to begin learning other languages.

- In preparation for your state's writing assessment test, your students *must* be able to vary sentence structure before they leave the third grade. They need to be able to write a simple, a compound, a complex, and possibly a compound/complex sentence. To this end, in the notes to the left of each *Caught'ya*, I have indicated the types of sentences in that *Caught'ya*. Go over this skill daily. Ask your student to produce their own example of whatever type of sentence is included in the day's *Caught'ya*. Target varying sentence types in your students' writing.

125 *Caught'ya* Sentences for Third Graders

"Willem and Marie Join the Class"

1. serenely

Paragraph – beginning of story; time change
Types of sentences – 1) simple; 2) simple
    (compound subject)
Commas – noun series
Verb tense – add "ed" to end of regular verbs to
    put in past tense; "went" is past tense of verb
    "to go"
Spelling rules – "i" before "e" except after "c,"
    and n**ei**ghbor, w**ei**gh, and th**ei**r are
    w**ei**rd; form most plurals by adding "s;"
    homophone (their/there/they're)
Other skills – strong verb practice; teach
    homophones "their/there/they're"

B – the rest of the morning went **serenely**.

_____.
_____ and _____
helped marie and willem learn the names of
their classmates

C –   The rest of the morning went **serenely**.

_____,
_____, and _____
helped Marie and Willem learn the names
of their classmates.

2. tranquilly

No paragraph – same person speaking (narra-
    tor), same topic
Type of sentence – complex (subordinate clause
    at the end)
Commas – interrupter
Verb tense – add "ed" to end of regular verbs to
    put in past tense; "had" is past tense of
    irregular verb "to have"
Spelling rules – "until" has one "l"
Other skills – difference between "past" and
    "passed"

B – the morning passed **tranquilly** that is until
    willem had to go to the restroom.

C – The morning passed **tranquilly**, that is,
    until Willem had to go to the restroom.

3. located

No paragraph – same person speaking
    (narrator), same topic
Type of sentence – compound
Commas – compound sentence; extra info
Verb tense – add "ed" to end of regular verbs to
    put in past tense; "did" is past tense of
    irregular verb "to do"; "were" is past tense of
    verb "to be"; "knew" is past tense of verb "to
    know"
Spelling rules – compound words (restroom,
    classroom); homophone (new/knew/gnu)
Other skills – go over compound words
    (restroom, classroom); coordinating
    conjunctions (**see note after *Caught'ya* #9**)

B – he knew where the restrooms were **located**
    and he raised his hand to be excused just as
    he always did in his classroom in the
    netherlands

C – He knew where the restrooms were **located**,
    and he raised his hand to be excused, just as
    he always did in his classroom in the
    Netherlands.

B = the sentence(s) to be put on the board or overhead   **C = the corrected sentence(s)**

4. comprehend

No paragraph – same person speaking, same subject

Types of sentences – 1) complex (subordinate clause at beginning); 2) simple

Punctuation – use of quotation marks around what is said out loud; use quotation marks around isolated words that are referred to

Capitalization – always capitalize the first letter of a quote unless it is a continuation; always capitalize the names of languages

Commas – appositive; subordinate clause at beginning (long introductory adverb); quote

Verb tense – add "ed" to end of regular verbs to put in past tense; "said" is past tense of irregular verb "to say"

Spelling rules – difference between accept/except; most plurals formed with "s"

Other skills – strong verb practice; negatives; *note* that periods and commas *always* go inside quotation marks; words out of context of a sentence must be put in quotes; abbreviations of titles (Mr., Ms., Miss, Mrs. before teacher's name)

B – when the teacher _____ called his name willem said toilet? he did not **comprehend** any english words except yes and no

C – When the teacher, _____, called his name, Willem said, "Toilet?" (*toahlett*) He did not **comprehend** any English words except "yes" and "no."

5. comprehend

No paragraph – same subject

Type of sentence – complex (subordinate clause at the end = no comma)

Capitalization – always capitalize the names of languages

Verb tense – add "ed" to end of regular verbs to put in past tense; "was" is past tense of irregular verb "to be"

Spelling rules – difference between "hoped" and "hopped"

B – willem hoped that the word was close enough to the english so that the teacher could **comprehend** what he was saying

C – Willem hoped that the word was close enough to the English so that the teacher could **comprehend** what he was saying.

6. pronounced

Paragraph – new subject

Type of sentence – complex (subordinate clause at beginning = comma) with compound verb

Capitalization – always capitalize the names of languages

Commas – subordinate clause at beginning (long introductory adverb)

Verb tense – add "ed" to end of regular verbs to put in past tense; "was" is past tense of irregular verb "to be"

Spelling rules – "i" before "e" except after "c," and n**ei**ghbor, w**ei**gh, and th**ei**r are w**ei**rd

Literary device – simile

B – since the word was **pronounced** the same in french and in dutch marie looked at willem and smiled like a true freind

C – Since the word was **pronounced** the same in French and in Dutch, Marie looked at Willem and smiled like a true friend.

B = the sentence(s) to be put on the board or overhead

C = the corrected sentence(s)

7. comprehend

No paragraph – same subject
Types of sentences – 1) compound; 2) simple
Capitalization – always capitalize the names of
languages
Commas – compound sentence
Verb tense – add "ed" to end of regular verbs to
put in past tense; "knew" is past tense of verb
"to know"
Spelling rules – homophone (new/knew/gnu)
Other skills – strong verb practice; negatives;
subject vs. object pronouns (she/her and he/
him); coordinating conjunctions (**f**or, **a**nd,
nor, **b**ut, **o**r, yet, **s**o — **see note after**
Caught'ya #9)

B – marie knew what willem wanted but
she could not help him. she did not
comprehend any english either

C – Marie knew what Willem wanted, but
she could not help him. She did not
comprehend any English either.

8. fortunately

Paragraph – new person speaking
Type of sentence – simple (compound verb)
Capitalization – first letter in quote
Punctuation – use of quotation marks around
what is said out loud
Commas – introductory adverb (optional);
appositive; quote
Verb tense – "understood" is past tense of
irregular verb "to understand"; "said" is past
tense of verb "to say"; switch to present tense
for quote
Spelling rules – compound words
Other skills – punctuation of quotes

B – **fortunately** _____ a fellow
classmate understood willem and said in a
loud voice willem wants to go to the
bathroom

C –   **Fortunately**, _____, a
fellow classmate, understood Willem and
said in a loud voice, "Willem wants to go to
the bathroom."

B = the sentence(s) to be put on the board or overhead   C = the corrected sentence(s)

9. comprehend, embarrassed

Paragraphs – new person speaking (narrator)
Type of sentence – compound
Commas – introductory adverb (optional); compound sentence
Verb tense – add "ed" to end of regular verbs to put in past tense; correct use of conditional tense to indicate possible situation
Other skills – begin teaching coordinating conjunctions
Literary device – simile

B – luckily willem did not **comprehend** _____ or he would have been **embarrassed** like a little boy

C –   Luckily, Willem did not **comprehend** _____, or he would have been **embarrassed** like a little boy.

> **NOTE:** _It is a good idea to teach very young students the coordinating conjunctions (there are only seven of them) used to make compound sentences. Once learned, students can be taught not to capitalize them in a title, to put commas before them only if they are in a series or there is a compound sentence, to recognize a compound sentence, and never, never to begin a sentence with one. I tell my students that they can do two things at age sixteen: drive, and begin an occasional sentence with a coordinating conjunction. Chant these conjunctions over and over again with your students. You can recall them using the mnemonic device "FANBOYS" (for, and, nor, but, or, yet, so). Memorization gives young (and, indeed, any age) students ownership of a skill. I suggest your students learn them and then chant them every time one appears in a Caught'ya. The teachers who follow you will want to kiss your toes in gratitude!_

10. queried

2 Paragraphs – new persons speaking
Types of sentences – 1) simple question (quote); 2) compound
Capitalization – first letter in quote
Punctuation – use of quotation marks around what is said out loud
Commas – appositive; quote; direct address; compound sentence; compound sentence; quote
Verb tense – add "ed" to end of regular verbs to put in past tense; "heard" is past tense of irregular verb "to hear"; switch to present tense for quote
Spelling rules – compound words; homophone (know/no)
Other skills – strong verb practice; silent "e" making previous vowel long; review coordinating conjunctions; note punctuation marks inside quotation marks; abbreviations of titles (Mr., Ms., Miss, Mrs. before the teacher's name)

B – the teacher _____ **queried** willem.
do you know the way to the restroom willem.
willem did not understand her but he heard his name so he said yes

C –   The teacher, _____, **queried** Willem, "Do you know the way to the restroom, Willem?"
    Willem did not understand her, but he heard his name, so he said, "Yes."

B = the sentence(s) to be put on the board or overhead   C = the corrected sentence(s)

11. flaunt, haughty, hyena

Paragraph – new person speaking (narrator)

Type of sentence – simple

Capitalization – always capitalize names of languages and countries

Commas – introductory phrase; adjective clause with relative pronoun (who); 2 adjectives not separated by "and" where the second is not color, age, or linked to the noun

Verb tense – add "ed" to end of regular verbs to put in past tense; "spoke" is past tense of irregular verb "to speak"

Spelling rules – homophones (two/to/too and new/knew/gnu); most words form plural by adding "s"; "i" before "e" except after "c," and n**ei**ghbor, w**ei**gh, and th**ei**r are w**ei**rd

Other skills – do not begin a sentence with a coordinating conjunction (FANBOYS); possessive pronouns (his); "who" is used as the subject of a verb and "whom" is used as the object of a verb ("that" is used as subject or object but not to refer to people); write out numbers up to 121

Literary device – simile; alliteration

B – and like a **haughty hyena** willem who spoke only dutch wanted to **flaunt** one of his 2 words of english to his new american friends

C – Like a **haughty hyena,** Willem, who spoke only Dutch, wanted to **flaunt** one of his two words of English to his new, American friends.

12. portal

No paragraph – same speaker, same topic

Type of sentence – compound (with compound verb in 2nd half)

Commas – compound sentence

Verb tense – add "ed" to end of regular verbs to put in past tense; "got" is past tense of irregular verb "to get"; "left" is past tense of verb "to leave"

Spelling rules – compound words

Other skills – do not begin a sentence with a coordinating conjunction (FANBOYS); review coordinating conjunctions; strong verb practice; towards vs. toward (interchangeable); possessive pronouns (his)

B – so the teacher pointed towards the **portal** of the classroom and willem got out of his desk and left the room

C – The teacher pointed towards the **portal** of the classroom, and Willem got out of his desk and left the room.

B = the sentence(s) to be put on the board or overhead   C = the corrected sentence(s)

13. located

Paragraph – new topic

Types of sentences – 1) simple; 2) simple

Commas – introductory adverb used as interjection; interrupter (however)

Verb tense – "was" is past tense of irregular verb "to be"; "knew" is past tense of verb "to know"

Spelling rules – homophones (new/knew/gnu and know/no); most words form plurals by adding "s"; compound words

Other skills – subject/verb agreement ("which one *was*" since "one" is singular)

B – now willem knew where the restrooms were **located**. he did not know however which room was for the girls and which one were for the boys

C – Now, Willem knew where the restrooms were **located**. He did not know, however, which room was for the girls and which one was for the boys.

---

14. portal, commenced

Paragraph – narrator aside

Types of sentences – 1) simple; 2) compound

Capitalization – single letters are always capitalized; languages

Punctuation – use of quotation marks around single letters; note commas and periods *always* go inside quotation marks

Commas – introductory adverb; compound sentence

Verb tense – add "ed" to end of regular verbs to put in past tense; "began" is past tense of irregular verb "to begin"

Spelling rules – compound words; homophones (hear/here)

Other skills – review coordinating conjunctions (FANBOYS); point out need for "an" with single letter "m"; use of demonstrative pronouns "this," "that," "these," "those"

Literary device – use of synonyms

B – in dutch the word for the restroom for the boys began with an m. hear the word on one of these doors started with a b and the word on the other **portal commenced** with a g

C – In Dutch the word for the restroom for the boys began with an "M." Here, the word on one of these doors started with a "B," and the word on the other **portal commenced** with a "G."

B = the sentence(s) to be put on the board or overhead   C = the corrected sentence(s)

15. perplexed

Paragraph – back to Williem

Types of sentences – 1) simple; 2) simple;
   3) simple

Punctuation – question mark needed in
   question

Verb tense – "was" is past tense of irregular verb
   "to be"; "did" is past tense of verb "to do"

Spelling rules – homophones (there/their/
   they're and know/no); teach the spelling of
   "there/their/they're"

Other skills – use of negative (never use a
   double negative)

B – willem was **perplexed**. he did not know
   which door to enter. there werent no
   pictures under the words to help him. what
   could he do

C –   Willem was **perplexed**. He did not
   know which door to enter. There were no
   (or "weren't any") pictures under the words
   to help him. What could he do?

> **NOTE:** *Teaching the dread "there/their/they're" to students requires much repetition and ingenuity. My students never know when I have misspelled them (and other common homophones) in the Caught'yas. They get almost indignant when I occasionally spell them correctly! I like to tell students that "their" has the little word "heir" in it. We look up that word. It means that someone will own something. "Their" is possessive. It means that "they" own something. "There" has the little word "here" in it. I stress to students that if they can substitute "here" for "there" in a sentence, then they are using the correct form. As for "they're," I simply insist that the apostrophe stands for an "a." If students put in the "a," it reads "they are" which is the correct definition of the word. Be inventive. I'm sure you can think of a better way to teach these difficult-to-understand homophones.*

16. glancing, apprehensive, aardvark

No paragraph – same topic

Types of sentences – simple (compound verb)

Commas – participial phrase

Verb tense – add "ed" to end of regular verbs to
   put in past tense

Spelling rules – compound words

Pronouns – go over possessive pronouns (his)

Other skills – use the article "an" before a noun
   that begins with a vowel; introduce the idea
   of prepositions and prepositional phrases

Literary device – simile; alliteration

B – he waited and waited to see if someone
   would come **glancing** every once in a while
   down the hall toward his classroom like a
   apprehensive aardvark

C – He waited and waited to see if someone
   would come, **glancing** every once in a while
   down the hall toward his classroom like an
   apprehensive aardvark.

17. linger, portal

Paragraph – narrator aside

Types of sentences – 1) simple (question);
   2) simple with compound objects

Punctuation – need for a question mark in a
   question

Verb tense – add "ed" to end of regular verbs to
   put in past tense; use of conditional tense to
   denote possible future action (would)

Other skills – homophones (to/two/too; see/
   sea; which/witch)

Literary device – questioning to involve reader
   in story

B – why did willem **linger** in front of the two
   doors. he waited to see which **portal** a boy
   would enter and which **portal** a girl would
   enter

C –   Why did Willem **linger** in front of the
   two doors? He waited to see which **portal** a
   boy would enter and which **portal** a girl
   would enter.

B = the sentence(s) to be put on the board or overhead   C = the corrected sentence(s)

18. lavatory

No paragraph – same topic
Types of sentences – 1) simple; 2) compound with compound object
Punctuation – use of quotation marks around what is said out loud
Commas – compound sentence
Verb tense – irregular past tense of verb "to think"
Possessives vs. plurals – go over rules for possessive of plural nouns
Other skills – never begin a sentence with a conjunction (but), they are meant to join; "no one" is two words; review FANBOYS

B – but no one came. willem thought and thought but he could not find any clue that would tell him which was the boys **lavatory** and which was the girls **lavatory**

C – No one came. Willem thought and thought, but he could not find any clue that would tell him which was the boys' **lavatory** and which was the girls' **lavatory**.

19. desperate, frantic

No paragraph – same topic, narrator still speaking
Types of sentences – 1) simple; 2) complex
Commas – introductory adverb; none needed after "badly" (subordinate clause "that he no...." at end)
Verb tense – "was" is past tense of irregular verb "to be"; "had" is past tense of verb "to have;" note use of infinitive (to use)
Spelling rules – compound word (restroom); homophone (which/witch)
Other skills – adverb vs. adjective (badly/bad); go over adverbs (finally, badly)

B – finally willem was **desperate** and **frantic**. he had to use the restroom so bad that he no longer cared which door was which

C – Finally, Willem was **desperate** and **frantic**. He had to use the restroom so badly that he no longer cared which door was which.

20. lavatory

Paragraph – narrator aside questioning the reader
Types of sentences – 1) simple; 2) simple; 3) simple
Punctuation – need for question mark at end of question
Commas – introductory word "yes"
Verb tense – add "ed" to end of regular verbs to put in past tense; switch to present tense for narrator aside then back to past for continuation of story; "went" is the past tense of the verb "to go"
Spelling rules – homophone (right/rite/write)
Other skills – possessive of plural noun; wrong verb tense (story in past)
Literary device – narrator aside

B – can you guess which door willem entered. yes you are right. he goes into the girls **lavatory**

C – Can you guess which door Willem entered? Yes, you are right. He went into the girls' **lavatory**.

---

21. strides

Paragraph – new person speaking

Type of sentence – complex (subordinate clause at beginning)

Commas – subordinate clause at beginning of sentence; adjective clause with relative pronoun "who" (extra information about noun "girls")

Verb tense – add "ed" to end of regular verbs to put in past tense; "was" is past tense of irregular verb "to be"; switch to present tense for quote

Spelling rules – consonant/vowel/consonant = double 2nd consonant when suffix is added; "i" before "e" except after "c," and "n**ei**ghbor" and "w**ei**gh" are "w**ei**rd;" compound word; add "s" to make most plurals (girls, friends)

Other skills – write out numbers to 121; strong verb practice; note hyphen in two words acting as one

B – before willem even stepped 2 **strides** into the room some fifth-grade girls who were close freinds opened the door of the bathroom

C –   Before Willem even stepped two **strides** into the room, some fifth-grade girls, who were close friends, opened the door of the bathroom.

22. espied, shrieked

No paragraph – same topic; new paragraph – new persons speaking

Types of sentences – 1) compound 2) simple quote

Capitalization – always capitalize the beginning of a quote

Punctuation – use of quotation marks around what is said out loud; need for exclamation mark after obvious shout

Commas – compound sentence; before quote; after interjection

Verb tense – add "ed" to end of regular verbs to put in past tense

Spelling rules – consonant/vowel/consonant = double 2nd consonant when suffix is added; most nouns form plural by adding "s;" homophone (their/there/they're)

Other skills – strong verb practice; note deliberate use of fragment in quote; review FANBOYS

Literary device – onomatopoeia (putting a sound into words)

B – they **espied** willem and they stopped dead in their tracks. the girls **shrieked** as one person ahhhhhhhhh a boy

C – They **espied** Willem, and they stopped dead in their tracks.
     The girls **shrieked** as one person, "Ahhhhhhhhhh, a boy!"

B = the sentence(s) to be put on the board or overhead   **C = the corrected sentence(s)**

23. muttered

Paragraph – new person speaking

Types of sentences – 1) compound; 2) compound

Capitalization – capitalize at beginning of quote (even in Dutch — this is a universal rule in languages that use our alphabet); in English, always capitalize the name of a language

Punctuation – use of quotation marks around what is said out loud (same in Dutch)

Commas – adjective clause with relative pronoun "who" (extra information about a noun;) direct address (meisjes) and compound sentence; before quote; direct address (girls); compound sentence

Verb tense – add "ed" to end of regular verbs to put in past tense; "did" is past tense of verb "to do"

Spelling rules – hard-to-spell word "embarrassed"

Other skills – strong verb practice; review FANBOYS

B – willem who was very embarrassed **muttered** het spijt me, meisjes, and he quickly exited the room. he wanted to say sorry girls in english but he did not know the words

C –   Willem, who was very embarrassed, **muttered**, "Het spijt me, meisjes," ("*het spayt meh, mīce yahs*") and he quickly exited the room. He wanted to say, "Sorry, girls," in English, but he did not know the words.

24. queried, disgust

3 Paragraphs – 3 persons speaking

Types of sentences – all simple quotations

Capitalization – always capitalize first letter of a quote

Punctuation – use of quotation marks around what is said out loud; question marks needed at the end of question

Commas – direct address; direct address; quote

Verb tense – add "ed" to end of regular verbs to put in past tense; "said" is past tense of verb "to say;" switch to present tense for quote

Spelling rules – homophone (it's/its); consonant/vowel/consonant = double second consonant if suffix added (dripped); compound word

Contraction – "can't" means "cannot"

Plurals vs. possessives – plural possessive here (girls) — teach that possessives always have to have something to possess

Other skills – teach "it's" as "it is;" comparatives (old/older/oldest); possessive of plural noun; teach ordinal numbers (first, second, third, etc.)

Literary device – alliteration (d, d); Anadiplosis (repeating a word or phrase for emphasis)

B – who are you you creep. asked one of the older girls. cant you read **queried** another in a voice that dripped with **disgust**. its the girls bathroom you dummy said the third girl

C –   "Who are you, you creep?" asked one of the older girls.
  "Can't you read?" **queried** another in a voice that dripped with **disgust**.
  "It's the girls' bathroom, you dummy," said the third girl.

B = the sentence(s) to be put on the board or overhead   C = the corrected sentence(s)

25. lavatory

Paragraph – narrator speaking instead of girl

Types of sentences – 1) simple (compound object); 2) simple; 3) simple

Capitalization – always capitalize the names of countries whether noun or adjective

Punctuation – use of quotation marks around word out of context of sentence; note periods and commas *always* go inside quotes, even in one-word quotes

Commas – *no* comma before "and" when not a compound sentence nor a list

Verb tense – "ran" is past tense of verb "to run"; "could" is past tense of verb "can"; "was" is past tense of irregular verb "to be"

Plural vs. possessive – "boys'" is plural possessive not to be confused with the plural "boys" since the lavatory is "owned" (possessed) by the boys

B – willem ran out to the hall and into the boys **lavatory**. he could translate the word creep. it was close enough to the dutch word kruip

C – Willem ran out to the hall and into the boys' **lavatory**. He could translate the word "creep." It was close enough to the Dutch word "kruip." ("*krowp*")

26. odoriferous

No paragraph – same subject, narrator still speaking

Types of sentences – complex (subordinate clause at the end)

Commas – three adverbs together (there/in bathroom/before lunch); noun series

Verb tense – "hid" is past tense of verb "to hide"; "came" is past tense of "to come"; and "took" is past tense of "to take"

Spelling rules – homophone (there/their/they're); compound word

Other skills – strong verb practice; possessive of plural noun

B – he hid their in the **odoriferous** boys bathroom until just before lunch when

_____ _____

and _____ came in and took him back to the classroom

C – He hid there, in the **odoriferous** boys' bathroom, until just before lunch when

_____, _____,

and _____ came in and took him back to the classroom.

B = the sentence(s) to be put on the board or overhead   C = the corrected sentence(s)

27. concealed, lavatory, faced, dire, dilemmas

Paragraph – new subject (note transition — the subordinate clause)
Types of sentences – complex (subordinate clause at beginning)
Punctuation – use of quotation marks around what is said out loud
Commas – subordinate clause at beginning
Verb tense – add "ed" to end of regular verbs to put in past tense
Spelling rules – compound word (himself)
Other skills – reflexive pronoun incorrectly spelled (very common); possessive of plural noun; possessive pronoun (her)
Literary device – alliteration (d, d)

B – while willem **concealed** hisself in the boys **lavatory** marie **faced** some **dire dilemmas** of her own

C –   While Willem **concealed** himself in the boys' **lavatory**, Marie **faced** some **dire dilemmas** of her own.

28. comprehend

No paragraph – same topic, narrator still speaking
Types of sentences – simple
Punctuation – exclamation mark needed after exclamation
Commas – repeating word ("kids, kids"); appositive (extra information about a noun)
Verb tense – switch to present tense for narrator aside to the reader; correct use of conditional tense (would) as something that has not yet happened;
Other skills – who/whom/that ("who" is subject; "whom" is object of verb; "that" can be either but *never* should refer to people); negative
Literary device – narrator aside; Anadiplosis (repeating a word for emphasis)

B – imagine what it would be like in a room full of kids kids whom you could not **comprehend**

C – Imagine what it would be like in a room full of kids, kids whom you could not **comprehend**!

NOTE #1: *Students use the conditional tense as a substitute for the past ("When I was younger, I would play with my brother"). This is wrong. You either played (past tense) with your brother or not. "Would play" means that it has not happened yet. Please stop this practice early in your students' writing.*

NOTE #2: *At the third-grade level, students are not yet ready to learn the difference between "who" and "whom." Thus, I have always written them correctly in the* **"B"** *version. They can, however, learn that you* never *use "that" to refer to a person even though they hear people use it all the time.*

B = the sentence(s) to be put on the board or overhead   C = the corrected sentence(s)

29. apprehensive

No paragraph – narrator still speaking, same
  subject
Types of sentences – 1) simple (compound
  object); 2) simple question
Punctuation – need for exclamation mark; need
  for question mark in question
Commas – noun series
Verb tense – switch to present tense for narrator
  aside; correct use of conditional tense **(see
  note after *Caught'ya* #28)**; note use of
  infinitive "to read"
Other skills – negatives (do not use double
  negative)
Literary device – narrator aside

B – imagine what it would be like not even to
be able to read no signs books or posters on
the walls. would you be **apprehensive**

C – Imagine what it would be like not even to
be able to read any signs, books, or posters
on the walls! Would you be **apprehensive**?

30. apprehensive, comprehend

Paragraph – same topic (Marie's apprehension)
  but now about Marie
Types of sentences – 1) simple; 2) simple
  (compound subject); 3) compound
Commas – noun series; compound sentence;
  repeated word
Verb tense – add "ed" to end of regular verbs to
  put in past tense; "was" is past tense of
  irregular verb "to be"
Spelling rules – "a lot" is two words
Other skills – strong verb practice; do not begin
  a sentence with a conjunction (FANBOYS);
  review FANBOYS
Literary device – repeating a word for effect

B – marie was **apprehensive**.

_____ _____
_____ _____

and all the others looked like nice girls and
boys. and they smiled at her but they asked
marie a lot of questions questions marie
could not **comprehend**

C –   Marie was **apprehensive**.

_____, _____,
_____, _____,

and all the others looked like nice girls and
boys. They smiled at her, but they asked
Marie a lot of questions, questions Marie
could not **comprehend**.

> **NOTE:** *After this point, a subordinate clause at the beginning or end of a complex sentence will not be noted. You, however, might want to look for the subordinating conjunctions and insist to your students that they NEVER put a comma before one. (See **Appendix**.)*

B = the sentence(s) to be put on the board or overhead   **C = the corrected sentence(s)**

31. peers, comprehend

No paragraph – same subject, same speaker

Types of sentences – compound/complex

Commas – compound part of compound/complex sentence

Verb tense – add "ed" to end of regular verbs to put in past tense; "knew" is past tense of irregular verb "to know"; "rose" is past tense of verb "to rise"

Spelling rules – homophone (gnu/new/knew)

Plurals vs. possessives – all plurals here, nothing owned

Contractions – "couldn't" means "could not"

Other skills – strong verb practice; negative (no double negatives – "could not not"); review FANBOYS

B – marie knew her **peers** were asking questions because there voices rose at the end of each sentence but she couldnt not **comprehend** what they asked

C – Marie knew her **peers** were asking questions because their voices rose at the end of each sentence, but she couldn't **comprehend** what they asked.

> **NOTE:** *Third graders are not yet ready to learn about transitive and intransitive verbs (rise vs. raise, sit vs. set, lie vs. lay), but they do need to know when to use each correctly. Just model them correctly and gently correct your students when they make an error. You could try to illustrate using kinesthetic means (raise the chair and rise up yourself, etc.). Leave the more complicated explanations for middle-school teachers to struggle with.*

32. exasperation

Paragraph – new person speaking

Types of sentences – 1) simple; 2) simple (in French); 3) simple

Capitalization – always capitalize "I" since each person is important; always capitalize the first letter in a quote unless it is a continued quote; always capitalize the names of countries (adjectives and nouns)

Punctuation – use of quotation marks around what is said out loud; question mark needed after question (even in French)

Commas – introductory adverb; before quote; before and after quote

Verb tense – add "ed" to end of regular verbs to put in past tense; "said" is past tense of irregular verb "to say"; "meant" is past tense of verb "to mean"; switch to present tense for quote

Spelling rules – common error (double the "l" in "finally")

Other skills – strong verb practice

B – finally she said in **exasperation** quoi? je ne vous comprends pas. in french this meant what i do not understand you

C –   Finally, she said in **exasperation**, "Quoi? Je ne vous comprends pas." In French this meant, "What? I do not understand you." *("kwoah? juh nuh voo caw(nt)praw(nt) pah" Do not pronounce the "nt." It is a nasal sound in French.)*

B = the sentence(s) to be put on the board or overhead   **C = the corrected sentence(s)**

33. perplexed, apprehensive

3 Paragraphs – new persons speaking

Types of sentences – 1) simple; 2) compound; 3) simple

Capitalization – always capitalize "I"

Punctuation – use of quotation marks around what is said out loud

Commas – quote; compound sentence; quote; quote

Verb tense – "said" is past tense of irregular verb "to say"; switch to present tense for quote

Spelling rules – homophone (know/no)

Contraction – "we've" = we have; don't = do not

Other skills – negative; review FANBOYS

Literary device – conversation

B – i think weve **perplexed** her said
_____. i dont know what marie said but she looks **apprehensive** said
_____. i agree said
_____

C – "I think we've **perplexed** her," said
_____.
"I don't know what Marie said, but she looks **apprehensive**," said _____.
"I agree," said _____.

34. queried

Paragraph – new person speaking

Types of sentences – simple quote

Punctuation – use of quotation marks around what is said out loud; question mark needed after question

Comma – relative pronoun clause (who)

Verb tense – add "ed" to most verbs to form past tense; "was" is past tense of irregular verb "to be"; switch to present tense for quote

Other skills – relative pronouns (who = subject; whom = object; that = both, but never for a person)

B – what can we do **queried** _____
who always was concerned about the feelings of others

C – "What can we do?" **queried**
_____, who always was concerned about the feelings of others.

35. queries, agreed

2 Paragraphs – two persons speaking
Types of sentences – 1) simple;
   2) deliberate fragment; 3) simple question
Capitalization – always capitalize the beginning
   of quotes except in a continued quote (one
   interrupted by the information about who
   said it); always capitalize the names of
   languages
Punctuation – use of quotation marks around
   what is said out loud; question mark after
   question
Commas – end of quote; after interjection and
   quote; after interrupter of quote before quote
   picks up again
Verb tense – add "ed" to end of regular verbs to
   put in past tense; switch to present tense for
   quote
Contractions – "let's" = let us
Other skills – strong verb practice
Literary device – use of slang word ("yeah")

B – lets stop making **queries** suggested
_____. yeah **agreed**
_____ why don't we teach her
some words in english

C –   "Let's stop making **queries**," suggested
_____.
      "Yeah," **agreed** _____.
"Why don't we teach her some words in
English?"

---

36. lectern

Paragraph – new person speaking (narrator)
Types of sentences – 1) simple; 2) simple
   (compound objects)
Capitalization – always capitalize the names of
   languages; do not capitalize the names of
   subjects unless it is a language (English)
Commas – introductory word; interrupter (extra
   information); noun list
Verb tense – "taught" is past tense of irregular
   verb "to teach"
Spelling rules – compound word; commonly
   misspelled word "a lot" is two words; difficult
   word "taught"
Other skills – strong verb practice; use of colon
   before a long list (please note that a colon
   never follows a verb)

B – well for the rest of the morning instead of
language arts the class taught marie a lot
of english nouns. they taught her the
following words: girl boy teacher desk
lectern blackboard chalk window paper
pencil book and eraser

C –   Well, for the rest of the morning,
instead of language arts, the class taught
Marie a lot of English nouns. They taught
her the following words: girl, boy, teacher,
desk, **lectern**, blackboard, chalk, window,
paper, pencil, book, and eraser.

NOTE: *Third graders are not yet ready to be able to use colons on their own. Therefore, I would suggest leaving it in when you put this Caught'ya on the board, but point it out so that they can eventually learn the concept. Also you will want to point out that a colon never follows a verb. This might sink in for later retrieval in fifth grade.*

B = the sentence(s) to be put on the board or overhead   C = the corrected sentence(s)

37. renowned

> **NOTE:** *I'm sure that you are familiar with the French song, "Frère Jacques" ("Brother John"). If not, chances are someone at your school knows the tune. Here are the words, first in French, then in English, then in phonetic spelling. There are many recordings of this in record shops. You may find that most of your children already know the song (sort of).*

Frère Jacques

Frère Jacques, Frère Jacques
Dormez-vous? Dormez-vous?
Sonnez les matines. Sonnez les matines.
Din, Din, Don

Brother John

Brother John, Brother John
Are you sleeping? Are you sleeping?
Ring the morning bells. Ring the morning bells.
Ding, ding dong

Pronunciation

frayreh jah-keh, frayreh jah-keh
dormay-voo, dormay-voo (as in "boo")
sonnay lay mateeneh, sonnay lay mateeneh
dahn, dahn, dohn (Make it nasal sounding)

Paragraph – new subject
Types of sentences – 1) simple; 2) simple question
Capitalization – capitalize names of songs and languages
Punctuation – use of quotation marks around name of song (album would be underlined)
Commas – introductory adverb; 2 adjectives without "and" in between
Verb tense – "taught" is past tense of verb "to teach"; switch to present tense for narrator aside
Spelling rules – difficult word "taught"
Other skills – strong verb practice; use of parentheses for narrator aside when you step out of the story; note use of hyphen for two words acting as one
Literary device – narrator aside in parentheses

B – in return marie taught her new class to sing the old well-known song frère jacques. (can you sing that **renowned** french song)

C –   In return, Marie taught her new class to sing the old, well-known song "Frère Jacques." (*frayreh jah-keh*) (Can you sing that **renowned** French song?)

> **NOTE #1:** *I suggest that you leave in the parentheses for modeling. This is a powerful tool, but young children can overuse it. Point them out, and the reason for them, but I wouldn't dwell on them. Personally, I overuse parentheses (just love them) all the time. You do not want your students to develop this bad habit.*
>
> **NOTE #2:** *Point out the accent in the French word "frère." You simply can tell your students how lucky they are to be speaking and writing English where there are no accents. Most other languages have them, and they count in spelling tests!*

B = the sentence(s) to be put on the board or overhead   **C = the corrected sentence(s)**

38. peers

No paragraph – same topic
Types of sentences – 1) simple; 2) complex
Capitalization – capitalize names of languages
Commas – always surround "too" with commas when it means "also;" introductory phrase
Verb tense – "taught" is past tense of verb "to teach"; "knew" is past tense of verb "to know"
Spelling rules – homophones (to/too/two and gnu/knew/new); difficult word "taught"
Other skills – strong verb practice; negatives (no double negatives in English)

B – marie taught her **peers** a few words in french too. of course she taught them by pointing since she didn't know no english

C – Marie taught her **peers** a few words in French, too. Of course, she taught them by pointing since she knew no English.

39. camaraderie

No paragraph – same topic
Types of sentences – simple (compound object)
Capitalization – always capitalize the names of languages
Commas – introductory phrase; noun series
Verb tense – "taught" is past tense of verb "to teach"
Other skills – strong verb practice; use of colon before long series (*never* use colon after a verb); use of parentheses around translation (extra information)

B – in **camaraderie** marie taught her new friends the following words in french: le garçon (the boy) la fille (the girl) le crayon (the pencil) and mon livre (my book)

C – In **camaraderie**, Marie taught her new friends the following words in French: le garçon (the boy) (*luh garsaunh — do not pronounce the "n," it is nasal*), la fille (*the girl*) (*laah fiiiyuh*), le crayon (*the pencil*) (*luh crayaunh — do not pronounce the "n"*), and mon livre (*my book*) (*maunh leevruh — do not pronounce the "n"*).

NOTE: *Point out accent in French for which French children are responsible on their spelling tests!*

40. brief, respite

Paragraph – new time and topic
Types of sentences – complex
Punctuation – use of quotation marks around what is said out loud
Commas – noun series; subordinate clause at beginning of sentence
Verb tense – add "ed" to end of regular verbs to put in past tense
Spelling rules – consonant/vowel/consonant = double 2nd consonant when adding suffix
Possessives – use of plural and singular possessive (go over rules)
Other skills – strong verb practice; review preposition use (before, for, from)

B – when _____ _____ _____ _____ and willem returned from the boys lavatory just before lunch the class stopped for a **brief respite** from the mornings work

C – When _____, _____, _____, _____, and Willem returned from the boys' lavatory just before lunch, the class stopped for a **brief respite** from the morning's work.

B = the sentence(s) to be put on the board or overhead   **C** = the corrected sentence(s)

41. devoured, equipment

No paragraph – same topic (details)

Types of sentences – simple (compound verb)

Punctuation – use of quotation marks around words used out of context

Commas – verb series

Verb tense – add "ed" to end of regular verbs to put in past tense; "went" is past tense of irregular verb "to go"; "taught" is past tense of verb "to teach"

Spelling rules – compound words (playground, outdoor)

Other skills – strong verb practice

B – they **devoured** lunch went out to the playground played on the **equipment** visited with each other and taught willem and marie outdoor words like "tree" and "sky"

C – They **devoured** lunch, went out to the playground, played on the **equipment**, visited with each other, and taught Willem and Marie outdoor words like "tree" and "sky."

42. putrescent

Paragraph – new person speaking

Types of sentences – compound

Commas – two adjectives not separated by "and" where second is not age, size, or linked to noun

Verb tense – "was" is past tense of irregular verb "to be"; "felt" is past tense of verb "to feel"

Spelling rules – difficult word "beautiful;" compound word; consonant/vowel/consonant + suffix = double 2nd consonant (sunny)

Other skills – comparatives (good/better/best); review FANBOYS

B – it was a beautiful sunny day and willem felt better to be out of the **putrescent** bathroom

C –   It was a beautiful, sunny day, and Willem felt better to be out of the **putrescent** bathroom.

43. azure, shrilly

No paragraph – same topic (details)

Types of sentences – 1) simple; 2) complex

Verb tense – add "ed" to end of regular verbs to put in past tense; "flew" is past tense of irregular verb "to fly"

Spelling rules – most plurals are formed by adding "s;" homophone (flew/flue): compound word

Other skills – strong verb practice

Literary device – strong verb description; alliteration (few fluffy)

B – a few fluffy clouds floated across the **azure** sky. birds chirped **shrilly** as they flew overhead

C – A few fluffy clouds floated across the **azure** sky. Birds chirped **shrilly** as they flew overhead.

B = the sentence(s) to be put on the board or overhead   **C = the corrected sentence(s)**

44. cavorted

No paragraph – same topic (details)
Types of sentences – 1) simple (compound verb)
Verb tense – add "ed" to end of regular verbs to put in past tense
Spelling rules – difficult word "squirrel"
Other skills – strong verb practice
Literary device – strong verb description; personification (making a thing — the tree – do a human act); metaphor (arms for branches)

B – squirrels played and **cavorted** on the trunks and branches of oak trees that spread their wide arms towards the sky

C – Squirrels played and **cavorted** on the trunks and branches of oak trees that spread their wide arms towards the sky.

45. chattered, faintly

No paragraph – same topic (the description)
Types of sentences – both simple
Capitalization – always capitalize the first letter of a quote
Punctuation – use of quotation marks around what is said out loud
Commas – long introductory adverb (really two adverbs); before quote
Verb tense – add "ed" to end of regular verbs to put in past tense
Possessive – use of plural possessive in word that does not end in "s"
Other skills – strong verb practice
Literary device – strong verb description
Onomatopoeia – word that represents a sound ("beep")

B – happy childrens voices **chattered** all around willem. somewhere in the distance a car horn tooted **faintly** beep. beep

C – Happy children's voices **chattered** all around Willem. Somewhere in the distance, a car horn tooted **faintly**, "Beep. Beep."

46. embarrassment, mortification

No paragraph – same topic
Types of sentences – 1) simple; 2) simple (compound verb)
Commas – repeating word
Verb tense – add "ed" to end of regular verbs to put in past tense; "was" is past tense of irregular verb "to be"; "forgot" is past tense of verb "to forget"
Spelling rules – difficult word "beautiful"
Other skills – comparatives (good/better/best); never begin a sentence with a conjunction **(see NOTE with *Caught'ya* #30)**; possessive pronoun "his"

B – it was a beautiful day a day that would make anyone feel better. and willem breathed deeply and forgot his **embarrassment** and **mortification**

C – It was a beautiful day, a day that would make anyone feel better. Willem breathed deeply and forgot his **embarrassment** and **mortification**.

NOTE: *This might be a good place to teach simple possessive pronouns (my, your, his, her, its, our, their).*

B = the sentence(s) to be put on the board or overhead   **C = the corrected sentence(s)**

47. firm

Paragraph – new time

Types of sentences – compound

Commas – introductory adverb; compound sentence; two adjectives not separated by "and" where 2nd adjective is not age, color, or linked to noun

Verb tense – "was" is past tense of irregular verb "to be"; "had" is past tense of verb "to have"; "made" is past tense of verb "to make"; use of pluperfect tense (had made) to denote action that took place previous to this sentence

Spelling rules – homophones (gnu, new, knew)

Other skills – note hyphen between two words used as one; review FANBOYS

Literary device – alliteration ("firm friends")

B – too soon it was time to go inside but willem and marie had made **firm** friends in their new third-grade class

C –   Too soon, it was time to go inside, but Willem and Marie had made **firm** friends in their new, third-grade class.

---

48. shrill

2 Paragraphs – new subjects referred to (whistle and teacher)

Types of sentences – both simple quotes

Capitalization – always capitalize the first letter of a quote unless it is a continuation

Punctuation – use of quotation marks around what is said out loud

Commas – appositive (extra information about a noun); before quote; after quote

Verb tense – "blew" is past tense of verb "to blow"; switch to present tense for quote

Spelling rules – homophone (its/it's)

Other skills – never begin a sentence with a conjunction (FANBOYS); review FANBOYS; go over preposition use; abbreviations of titles (Mr., Ms., Miss, or Mrs. before the teacher's name)

Literary device – Onomatopoeia (word mimicking sound)

B – and the teacher _____ blew a **shrill** whistle tweeeet. its time to go in she said

C –   The teacher, _____, blew a **shrill** whistle, "Tweeeet."
      "It's time to go in," she said.

---

49. docile, dormice

Paragraph – new person speaking (narrator)

Types of sentences – simple

Commas – extra information (FYI – participial phrase)

Verb tense – add "ed" to end of regular verbs to put in past tense

Spelling rules – homophone (hole/whole); unusual plural of "mouse"

Other skills – strong verb practice

Literary device – simile

B – the hole class including willem and marie lined up at the door as quiet and **docile** as **dormice**

C –   The whole class, including Willem and Marie, lined up at the door as quiet and **docile** as **dormice**.

B = the sentence(s) to be put on the board or overhead   **C = the corrected sentence(s)**

190   CHAPTER 3

50. uneventfully, peers

Paragraph – new time

Types of sentences – 1) simple; 2) compound

Capitalization – always capitalize the names of languages

Commas – compound sentence

Verb tense – add "ed" to end of regular verbs to put in past tense; "taught" is past tense of irregular verb "to teach"

Other skills – strong verb practice; review FANBOYS

B – the rest of the day passed **uneventfully**. willem and marie learned even more english and they taught some french and dutch to their **peers** in return

C –   The rest of the day passed **uneventfully**. Willem and Marie learned even more English, and they taught some French and Dutch to their **peers** in return.

51. inventively, illustrations, instruct

No paragraph – same topic, same time

Types of sentences – 1) simple (compound subject); 2) simple

Punctuation – use of quotation marks around words used out of context; note periods and commas *always* go inside quotes

Commas – noun series; noun series

Verb tense – add "ed" to end of regular verbs to put in past tense

Spelling rules – homophones (their/there/they're)

Other skills – strong verb practice

Literary devices – simile with "like" (used for direct noun comparison only); alliteration (i, i, i)

B – _____ _____ _____ and _____ pointed out more nouns like "pig" "dog" and "cat." they **inventively** used **illustrations** in there reading books to **instruct** the foreigners

C – _____, _____, _____, and _____ pointed out more nouns like "pig," "dog," and "cat." They **inventively** used **illustrations** in their reading books to **instruct** the foreigners.

NOTE: *If you feel that your students can handle it, take out the quotation marks on "pig," "dog," and "cat" in the board version. They have seen this rule several times now.*

B = the sentence(s) to be put on the board or overhead   **C = the corrected sentence(s)**

52. expanding, adjectives

No paragraph – same time, same topic, same place

Types of sentences – 1) simple; 2) simple (compound object)

Punctuation – use of quotation marks around words out of context

Commas – always surround "too" with commas if it means "also"

Verb tense – add "ed" to end of regular verbs to put in past tense; "taught" is past tense of irregular verb "to teach"

Spelling rules – homophone (their/there/ they're)

Other skills – inform students of use of dash; strong verb practice; go over adverbs and adjectives

B – the teacher introduced a verb into their already **expanding** vocabulary — "to be." she taught willem and marie a few **adjectives** too

C – The teacher introduced a verb into their already **expanding** vocabulary — "to be." She taught Willem and Marie a few **adjectives**, too.

> **NOTE:** *This would be a good place to introduce the eight parts of speech. Nouns, interjections, prepositions, pronouns, adverbs, verbs, adjectives, conjunctions (NIPPAVAC). See the note in the* **Appendix** *on the parts of speech. A mini-lesson on adverbs and adjectives might be appropriate here.*

53. adjective

Paragraph – narrator aside to reader

Types of sentences – all simple questions

Punctuation – question marks needed after questions

Verb tense – switch to present tense for narrator aside

Spelling rules – most words become plural by adding "s"

Other skills – use article (adjective) "an" before a word that begins with a vowel; abbreviation of your title (Mr., Ms., Miss, or Mrs.)

Literary device – narrator aside

B – what is an **adjective**? can you name a few of them? what adjectives do you think _____ taught willem and marie

C –   What is an **adjective**? Can you name a few of them? What adjectives do you think _____ taught Willem and Marie?

> **NOTE:** *Use your name here so that you can discuss abbreviations.*

B = the sentence(s) to be put on the board or overhead   **C = the corrected sentence(s)**

54. utter

Paragraph – new time
Types of sentences – compound/complex
Capitalization – always capitalize the name of a language
Commas – compound/complex sentence
Verb tense – "could" is past tense of irregular verb "can"; "knew" is past tense of verb "to know"
Spelling rules – homophones (gnu/new/knew)
Other skills – "fewer" can be counted, "less" refers to vague things that cannot be counted ("fewer people" can be counted, but "less active" is a concept and can't be counted); difference between "then" (adverb) and "than" (comparative); write out numbers to 121

B – by the end of the day willem and marie could **utter** a few more things in english although they still knew fewer than fifty words in all and they new only 1 verb

C –   By the end of the day Willem and Marie could **utter** a few more things in English although they still knew fewer than fifty words in all, and they knew only one verb.

55. foreign, lavatory, portals

Paragraph – time change, subject change
Types of sentences – both simple
Punctuation – use of exclamation mark in exclamation
Commas – long introductory adverb
Verb tense – "could" is past tense of irregular verb "can"
Spelling rules – "i" before "e" except after "c," and n**ei**ghbor, w**ei**gh, and th**ei**r are w**ei**rd (along with quite a few other words)
Other skills – write out numbers to 121

B – by the end of the week the 2 **foreign** third graders could say a few sentences. now willem could read the words on the **lavatory portals**

C –   By the end of the week, the two **foreign** third graders could say a few sentences. Now Willem could read the words on the **lavatory portals**!

56. vocalize

Paragraph – new person introduced
Types of sentences – both simple (compound objects)
Capitalization – always capitalize the first letter of a quote unless it is a continuation (even in French and Dutch)
Punctuation – use of quotation marks around what is said out loud
Commas – before quotes and after quote
Verb tense – "knew" is past tense of irregular verb "to know"; "could" is past tense of verb "can"
Spelling rules – homophone (gnu/new/knew)

B – the rest of the class also gnu a few sentences in french and dutch. they could **vocalize** tu es un cochon moche in french and jij bent een lelijk varken in dutch

C –   The rest of the class also knew a few sentences in French and Dutch. They could **vocalize**, "Tu es un cochon moche," in French (*"too eh unh coshaunh mohsch"*) and "Jij bent een lelijk varken," in Dutch (*"yay bent ayn lay-līyke farken"*).

NOTE: *Translation in next Caught'ya....*

B = the sentence(s) to be put on the board or overhead   C = the corrected sentence(s)

57. affront

No paragraph – continuation
Types of sentences – 1) simple; 2) simple (compound verb)
Capitalization – always capitalize the first letter of a quote unless it is a continuation
Punctuation – use of quotation marks around what is said out loud
Commas – before quote; note no comma before "and" as it is not a compound sentence (no subject) only a compound verb
Verb tense – "meant" is past tense of verb "to mean"; "could" is past tense of verb "can"; switch to present tense for quote
Spelling rules – homophones (their/there/they're); form plural of nouns that end in consonant "ly" by getting rid of the "y" and adding "ies" (enemy/enemies)
Other skills – article (adjective) "an" must be used before word that begins with a vowel or a silent "h"

B – both meant you are an ugly pig. now the third graders could tease their friends and insult and **affront** there enemies

C – Both meant, "You are an ugly pig." Now the third graders could tease their friends and insult and **affront** their enemies.

58. peers

Paragraph – new time
Types of sentences – 1) simple; 2) simple (compound object)
Capitalization – always capitalize the name of a language
Verb tense – add "ed" to end of regular verbs to put in past tense; "went" is past tense of irregular verb "to go"
Spelling rules – homophones (there/their/they're)
Other skills – strong verb practice; review simple possessive pronouns (my, your, his, her, our, their)

B – weeks went by. marie and willem learned more and more english from there teacher and from their **peers**

C – Weeks went by. Marie and Willem learned more and more English from their teacher and from their **peers**.

59. a plethora of

No paragraph – same topic
Types of sentences – 1) simple; 2) complex
Capitalization – always capitalize the name of a language
Commas – interrupter
Verb tense – "could" is past tense of irregular verb "can"; "made" is past tense of verb "to make"; "spoke" is past tense of verb "to speak"
Spelling rules – "a lot" is two words (meaning of vocabulary word)
Other skills – strong verb practice

B – they could now speak in sentences. they still made **a plethora of** mistakes though when they spoke english

C – They could now speak in sentences. They still made **a plethora of** mistakes, though, when they spoke English.

B = the sentence(s) to be put on the board or overhead   **C = the corrected sentence(s)**

60. prepositions

Paragraph – now about Marie

Types of sentences – simple

Verb tense – "could" is past tense of irregular verb "can"

Spelling rules – homophones (straight/strait)

Other skills – *never* split verb parts or infinitives (*Star Trek's* "to boldly go" was wrong.); negatives

B – marie could never get the **prepositions** straight

C –   Marie never could get the **prepositions** straight.

> **NOTE:** *Now that it is halfway through the year, you might want to find a list of prepositions (in the* **Appendix** *of this book) and begin to have your students memorize them. This is a useful tool. Once young students have memorized the prepositions, it is easy to tell them not to capitalize them in a title. Prepositional phrases (simple phrases acting as adjectives and adverbs) can be understood and correctly used when a future teacher asks students to use more adjectives or adverbs to flesh out a story or essay. When the prepositions have been memorized, whenever one occurs in a subsequent Caught'ya, have your students recite them. Again, you will be very popular with the teachers who come after you. Note that, unlike the first grade story, I have not identified prepositions for the teachers.*

61. identical

No paragraph – same topic (details)

Types of sentences – compound with semicolon

Capitalization - capitalize names of languages

Punctuation – use of quotation marks around words out of context (I suggest taking out every other one as I did.); note that all commas and periods go inside quotes – always

Verb tense – "said" is past tense of verb "to say"; "were" is past tense of irregular verb "to be"

Other skills – use of semicolon instead of FANBOYS in a compound sentence; avoidance of direct quote by using "that"

B – she said that she "walked *of* home *at* school" instead of walked *from* home *to* school because "from" and of in french were the **identical** word; so were "at" and to

C – She said that she "walked *of* home *at* school" instead of "walked *from* home *to* school" because "from" and "of" in French are the **identical** word; so are "at" and "to."

62. persisted

No paragraph – same topic

Types of sentences – 1) complex ; 2) simple (compound object)

Capitalization – always capitalize names of languages

Punctuation – use of quotation marks around words that are out of context; note that all periods and commas go inside quotes

Commas – subordinate clause at beginning

Verb tense – add "ed" to end of regular verbs to put in past tense; "had" is past tense of irregular verb "to have"; use of present tense for truism

Other skills – article (adjective) "an" must be used before a vowel or a silent "h"

B – because the french place most adjectives after the noun marie had a hard time with adjectives. she **persisted** in saying "a pig ugly" instead of an ugly pig

C – Because the French place most adjectives after the noun, Marie had a hard time with adjectives. She **persisted** in saying "a pig ugly" instead of "an ugly pig."

B = the sentence(s) to be put on the board or overhead   **C = the corrected sentence(s)**

63. predicament

Paragraph – new topic (Willem)
Types of sentences – both simple
Capitalization – always capitalize the name of a
    language
Commas – interrupter
Verb tense – "had" is past tense of irregular verb
    "to have"; switch to present tense for truism

B – willem on the other hand had a
predicament with verbs. in dutch many
verbs go at the end of a sentence

C –   Willem, on the other hand, had a
predicament with verbs. In Dutch many
verbs go at the end of a sentence.

NOTE: *Now that we are halfway through the Caught'yas, I shall no longer list the need to capitalize the
names of countries and languages.*

---

64. pronunciation

No paragraph – same topic, same person
Types of sentences – both simple
Capitalization – always capitalize the first letter
    of a quote unless it is a continuation; always
    capitalize "I"
Punctuation – use of quotation marks around
    what is said out loud
Commas – before quote
Verb tense – "said" is past tense of verb "to say";
    "had" is past tense of irregular verb "to have"
Other skills – review prepositions

B – sometimes he said i to the lavatory need to
go. he also had trouble with **pronunciation**

C – Sometimes he said, "I to the lavatory need
to go." He also had trouble with
pronunciation.

---

65. amusing, foreign

Paragraph – new topic
Types of sentences – complex
Commas – subordinate clause at beginning;
    extra information about "class;" appositive
Verb tense – add "ed" to end of regular verbs to
    put in past tense; "was" is past tense of
    irregular verb "to be"
Plurals vs. possessives – possessive of singular
    noun
Other skills – abbreviations (in the title of your
    name); hyphen in two words acting as one
    adjective; learn ordinal numbers (first,
    second, third, fourth, etc.); write out numbers
    to 121; begin to teach collective nouns and
    pronouns like "everyone" and "everybody"
    (pronoun) and "class" (noun) that take
    singular form of verb and singular modifiers

B – since everyone was included in the language
lessons everybody in _____s
third-grade class including the teacher
learned a few **amusing** words and sentences
in two **foreign** languages french and dutch

C –   Since everyone was included in the
language lessons, everybody in
_____'s third-grade class, including
the teacher, learned a few **amusing** words
and sentences in two **foreign** languages,
French and Dutch.

---

66. keen, intelligent, attempted

Paragraph – same topic because quotes are indirect

Types of sentences – both simple

Capitalization – always capitalize the first letter of a quote unless it is a continuation

Punctuation – use of quotation marks around what is said out loud

Commas – two adjectives where the 2nd adjective is not age, color, or linked to noun; before and after quotes

Verb tense – add "ed" to end of regular verbs to put in past tense

Other skills – note use of infinitives; strong verb practice

B – the **keen intelligent** class learned to say ik ben prima in dutch. they **attempted** to say je suis formidable in french

C – The **keen, intelligent** class learned to say "Ik ben prima" (*pronounced as it looks*) in Dutch. They **attempted** to say, "Je suis formidable," (*juh swee formidaaabluh*) in French.

NOTE: *Translation in the next Caught'ya.....*

---

67. expressions, respective

No paragraph – continuation

Types of sentences – simple

Capitalization – always capitalize the first letter of a quote unless it is a continuation; always capitalize "I"

Punctuation – use of quotation marks around what is said out loud

Commas – before and after quote

Verb tense – "meant" is past tense of irregular verb "to mean"; switch to present tense for quote

Spelling rules – homophones (to/two/too and their/they're/there)

Other skills – write out numbers to 121; go over adjectives "this," "that," "these," and "those"

B – those 2 **expressions** meant i am super in their **respective** languages

C – Those two **expressions** meant, "I am super," in their **respective** languages.

B = the sentence(s) to be put on the board or overhead   C = the corrected sentence(s)

68. severe

No paragraph – continuation
Types of sentences – both simple quotes
Capitalization – always capitalize the first letter of a quote even in French
Punctuation – use of quotation marks around what is said out loud; quotes needed around idiomatic expression; *note quote within a quote and point it out to your students*
Commas – before and after quote; before quote
Verb tense – add "ed" to end of regular verbs to put in past tense; "meant" is past tense of irregular verb "to mean"; switch to present tense for quote
Possessive vs. plurals – possessive of singular noun
Literary device – use of idiomatic expression

B – the class also learned to say tu es casse-pieds in maries language. this meant you are a **severe** 'pain in the neck'

C – The class also learned to say, "Tu es casse-pieds." (*too eh cahss pee-ay — as in "lay"*) in Marie's language. This meant, "You are a **severe** 'pain in the neck.'"

69. declare

Paragraph – same topic but new expression being taught by someone else
Types of sentences – simple quote
Capitalization – always capitalize the first letter of a quote even in Dutch
Punctuation – use of quotation marks around what is said out loud
Commas – before quote
Verb tense – "taught" is past tense of irregular verb "to teach"
Spelling rules – difficult word "taught"

B – willem taught the class to **declare** jij bent een pijn in de achterste

C –   Willem taught the class to **declare**, "Jij bent een pijn in de achterste." (*yay bent aynn piyn in dee achterstuh — put the "ch" in the back of your throat*)

70. expression

Paragraph – new subject
Types of sentences – complex
Capitalization – always capitalize the first letter of a quote unless it is a continuation
Punctuation – use of quotation marks around what is said out loud
Commas – interrupter; before quote
Verb tense – add "ed" to end of regular verbs to put in past tense; "did" is past tense of irregular verb "to do"; switch to present tense for quote
Other skills – negative; use of parentheses for aside (*Note that I have put in the first one for the students. They can probably figure out that there must be a second at the end of the phrase.*)

B – the teacher however did not like this **expression** (even though it was in dutch because it meant you are a pain in the rear

C –   The teacher, however, did not like this **expression** (even though it was in Dutch) because it meant, "You are a pain in the rear."

B = the sentence(s) to be put on the board or overhead   **C = the corrected sentence(s)**

71. whispered, murmured

No paragraph – continuation
Types of sentences – complex
Verb tense – add "ed" to end of regular verbs to put in past tense; "thought" is past tense of irregular verb "to think
Spelling rules – note correct spelling of "themselves" if your students spell this word incorrectly (theirselves)
Other skills – strong verb practice; "between" refers to only two things or people while "among" refers to more than two; negative; teach object pronouns (me, you, him, her, us, them)

B – the class **whispered** and **murmured** it among themselves when they thought the teacher could not hear them

C – The class **whispered** and **murmured** it among themselves when they thought the teacher could not hear them.

72. exemplary

No paragraph – continuation
Types of sentences – complex
Commas – interrupter
Verb tense – "could" is past tense of irregular verb "can"; switch to present tense for truism
Spelling rules – homophones (here/hear)

B – she could hear them of course because teachers always have **exemplary** hearing

C – She could hear them, of course, because teachers always have **exemplary** hearing.

73. exhilarating, challenging, prove

Paragraph – new topic
Types of sentences – 1) simple; 2) compound
Punctuation – exclamation mark needed in exclamation
Commas – compound sentence
Verb tense – "was" is past tense of irregular verb "to be"; correct use of conditional tense (to denote something that might happen)
Spelling rules – "i" before "e" except after "c" and so on...
Literary device – foreshadowing, building suspense in story

B – it was fun learning words in a foreign language. it was **exhilarating** and **challenging** to teach willem and marie english but it also would **prove** to be dangerous

C – It was fun learning words in a foreign language. It was **exhilarating** and **challenging** to teach Willem and Marie English, but it also would **prove** to be dangerous!

74. concluded

No paragraph – same topic
Type of sentences – simple (compound subject)
Commas – noun series; introductory adverb (to independent clause); interrupter
Verb tense – add "ed" to end of regular verbs to put in past tense; "was" is past tense of irregular verb "to be"
Other skills – use of italics for emphasis

B – _____ _____ _____ and _____ **concluded** that so far this *was* indeed the best year yet

C – _____, _____, _____, and _____ **concluded** that so far, this *was*, indeed, the best year yet.

B = the sentence(s) to be put on the board or overhead   **C** = the corrected sentence(s)

75. appalling, ensue

Paragraph – new topic
Types of sentences – simple (compound object)
Comma – use of comma for clarity and effect
Verb tense – "did" is past tense of verb "to do";
    "were" is past tense of irregular verb "to be"
Spelling rules – consonant/vowel/consonant +
    suffix = double 2nd consonant; homophones
    (no/know)
Other skills – "between" refers to only two
    people or things, "among" refers to more
    than two
Literary device – foreshadowing, building
    suspense

B – they did not know the **appalling** problems
that were about to **ensue** among them and
the fifth grade all because of language
problems

C –   They did not know the **appalling**
problems that were about to **ensue** between
them and the fifth grade, all because of
language problems.

76. brisk

Paragraph – new time and subject
Types of sentences – both simple
Verb tense – "was" is past tense of irregular verb
    "to be"; "began" is past tense of verb "to
    begin"
Spelling rules – compound word; homophone
    (won/one)
Other skills – teach the use of "very" as an
    adverb that can tell you more about a verb,
    an adjective, or another adverb
Literary device – foreshadowing

B – it all began on the playground one **brisk**
winter day. willem was very excited

C –   It all began on the playground one
brisk winter day. Willem was very excited.

77. cronies

No paragraph – same topic
Types of sentences – both simple
Capitalization – always capitalize the first letter
    of the months and days and holidays
Commas – date, appositive (extra information
    about a noun); two adjectives where the 2nd
    is not age, color, or linked to noun
Verb tense – "was" is past tense of irregular verb
    "to be"
Spelling rules – homophone (gnu/new/knew)
Other skills – teach simple subject pronouns
    (I, you, he, she, it we, they)

B – it was december 5 2000. he was going to
share the dutch holiday saint nicholas day
with his new american **cronies**

C – It was December 5, 2000. He was going to
share the Dutch holiday, Saint Nicholas Day,
with his new, American **cronies**.

B = the sentence(s) to be put on the board or overhead   **C = the corrected sentence(s)**

78. anticipated

No paragraph – same topic
Types of sentences – compound
Punctuation – use of quotation marks around
  foreign word not in a quote
Commas – compound sentence; appositive
Verb tense – add "ed" to end of regular verbs to
  put in past tense; "had" is past tense of
  irregular verb "to have"
Spelling rules – if a noun ends in consonant "y"
  to make it plural, you get rid of the "y" and
  add "ies; homophone (whole/hole)
Other skills – review FANBOYS

B – willem had dutch "lekkers" or goodies for
the whole class and he **anticipated** a day of
fun

C – Willem had Dutch "lekkers," (*pronounced the
same as it looks*) or goodies, for the whole
class, and he **anticipated** a day of fun.

---

79. a plethora of, delicious, tradition

NOTE: *This would be a good place to discuss and explore some of our traditions.*

No paragraph – same topic (details)
Types of sentences – both simple
Capitalization – always capitalize the names of
  countries and holidays
Commas – none between two adjectives (big
  chocolate) as second adjective is linked to
  noun like "strawberry short-cake"); elaboration (extra information)
Verb tense – "had sent" is the pluperfect of the
  verb "to send" and is used here to indicate
  action that took place before this paragraph;
  "was" is past tense of irregular verb "to be"
Spelling rules – "a lot" is two words
Plurals vs. possessives – singular possessive
  noun
Other skills – use of "as" instead of "like" for
  comparison ("like" only compares two nouns
  — or pronouns — directly as in "a boy *like*
  Willem")

B – willems uncle in the netherlands had sent **a
plethora of** big chocolate letters one for the
first name of every student in willems class.
this was a **delicious** dutch **tradition** like
candy is at our halloween

C – Willem's uncle in the Netherlands had sent
a plethora of big chocolate letters, one for
the first name of every student in Willem's
class. This was a **delicious** Dutch **tradition**
as candy is at our Halloween.

---

80. whistled, warbled

Paragraph – new time
Types of sentences – complex
Commas – no comma as subordinate clause is
  at end of sentence
Verb tense – add "ed" to end of regular verbs to
  put in past tense
Spelling rules – compound word
Other skills – strong verb practice
Literary device – description; alliteration
  (whistled, warbled, walked)

B – that winter morning, Willem **whistled** and
warbled as he walked across the playground
to the school building

C –   That winter morning, Willem **whistled**
and **warbled** as he walked across the
playground to the school building.

B = the sentence(s) to be put on the board or overhead   **C = the corrected sentence(s)**

81. burlap

No paragraph – same description

Types of sentences – simple

Capitalization – always capitalize the name of a specific thing (not just any "sack" but a "Santa Sack")

Punctuation – use of quotation marks around what is said out loud

Verb tense – "was" is past tense of irregular verb "to be;" "hung" is past tense of irregular verb "to hang" (exception: "hanged is used to indicate a death by rope around the neck)

Spelling rules – if a noun ends in consonant "y," to make it plural you get rid of the "y" and add "ies"

Other skills – strong verb practice; use of parentheses for translation and further explanation (I suggest leaving out the end one for students to insert); "that" refers only to things

B – a **burlap** "sinterklaas zak (a santa sack that was filled with the chocolate goodies hung over his left shoulder

C – A **burlap** "Sinterklaas Zak" (*pronounced as it looks*) — a Santa sack — that was filled with the chocolate goodies hung over his left shoulder.

> **NOTE :** *A review of left and right would not be amiss. I am sure you still have students who do not know their right hand from their left. It doesn't hurt to review. I like to play "Simon Says" which lets me review without my students even knowing it... (FYI – In French it is pronounced Jacques ah dee and means "Jack has said.")*

82. anticipated

No paragraph – concluding sentence

Types of sentences – complex (subordinate clause at end = no comma)

Verb tense – add "ed" to end of regular verbs to put in past tense

Spelling rules – consonant/vowel/consonant + suffix = double 2nd consonant (getting)

Other skills – strong verb practice; discuss use of adverbs and adverbial phrases — adverbs of more than one word (happily, at school, at home, that evening, usually, on that date, in the Netherlands); noun needed for clarity (students use too many pronouns)

B – he happily **anticipated** the day at school and then getting presents at home that evening as he usually did on that date in the netherlands

C – Willem happily **anticipated** the day at school and then getting presents at home that evening as he usually did on that date in the Netherlands.

B = the sentence(s) to be put on the board or overhead   **C = the corrected sentence(s)**

83. surrounded, slung

Paragraph – new action

Types of sentences – both simple

Commas – introductory adverb

Verb tense – add "ed" to end of regular verbs to put in past tense; "slung" is past tense of irregular verb "to sling"

Other skills – strong verb practice; "that" refers only to things; go over ordinal numbers (first, second, third, fourth, fifth, etc.)

Literary device – suspense

B – suddenly big fifth graders **surrounded** Willem. they wanted to know what was in the sack that was **slung** over his shoulder

C –   Suddenly, big fifth graders **surrounded** Willem. They wanted to know what was in the sack that was **slung** over his shoulder.

---

84. panicked, croaked, precious

Paragraph – shift to new subject

Types of sentences – all three simple

Verb tense – add "ed" to end of regular verbs to put in past tense; "had learned" is pluperfect tense to indicate action that took place before this paragraph; "had" is past tense of irregular verb "to have"

Other skills – strong verb practice

Literary device – suspense

B – willem **panicked**. he forgot all the english he had learned. his voice **croaked** in fear of losing all the **precious** dutch chocolate he had in his sack

C –   Willem **panicked**. He forgot all the English he had learned. His voice **croaked** in fear of losing all the **precious** Dutch chocolate he had in his sack.

NOTE: *If you think your students can handle correcting a run-on sentence, remove all the periods and insert "and" instead. Warn them about the run-on sentence. You can do this whenever there are several simple sentences in a Caught'ya. Run-on sentences are the bane of student writing at any level!*

---

85. squeaked, attempted, evade

Paragraph – new person speaking (quotation)

Types of sentences – complex (with simple sentence quotes); subordinate clause at the end = no comma

Capitalization – always capitalize the first letter of a quote unless it is a continuation

Punctuation – use of quotation marks around what is said out loud; question marks needed for questions in quote

Verb tense – add "ed" to end of regular verbs to put in past tense; switch to present tense for quote (in Dutch)

Spelling rules – consonant/vowel/consonant + suffix = double 2nd consonant (bigger)

Other skills – strong verb practice; comparisons (big/bigger/biggest); use of too many adjectives for clarity — noun is necessary

Literary device – suspense

B – wat doet jij, daan? wat hebt jij nodig? he **squeaked** out as he **attempted** to **evade** the bigger boys by running into the school

C –   "Wat doet jij, daan? Wat hebt jij nodig?" (*Vaht do juh dahn? Vaht hebbt yay nodich — put the "ch" in the back of your throat*) Willem **squeaked** out as he **attempted** to **evade** the bigger boys by running into the school.

NOTE: *The Dutch is not translated in subsequent student Caught'yas, so you will have to translate it for your students. It means "What are you doing, then? What do you need (want)?"*

B = the sentence(s) to be put on the board or overhead   **C = the corrected sentence(s)**

86. safeguard, lekkers

Paragraph – narrator comment
Types of sentences – 1) simple; 2) compound
Punctuation – use of quotation marks around foreign word not known in English
Commas – compound sentence
Verb tense – "should have" needs to be used as a hypothetical case since "should of" (which students like to use) is incorrect and does not make sense
Spelling rules – homophone (to, too, two)
Contraction – didn't = did not
Other skills – review FANBOYS **(See *Caught'ya* #30)**; review prepositions

B – willem should have asked his father to walk him too school to **safeguard** the "**lekkers**. he should of spoken in english but he didnt

C –   Willem should have asked his father to walk him to school to **safeguard** the "**lekkers**." He should have spoken in English, but he didn't.

---

87. discern

Paragraph – back to fifth graders
Types of sentences – simple
Verb tense – "did" is past tense of irregular verb "to do"; use of pluperfect (had spoken) to denote action that took place before this paragraph
Spelling rules – homophones (know/no and new/gnu/knew); consonant/vowel/consonant + suffix = double 2nd consonant (bigger)
Other skills – comparatives (big/bigger/biggest); negatives

B – the bigger fifth graders did not no that willem was knew in this country. they did not **discern** that he had spoken in dutch

C –   The bigger fifth graders did not know that Willem was new in this country. They did not **discern** that he had spoken in Dutch.

---

88. rowdy, bullies, insulted

No paragraph – continuation
Types of sentences – both simple
Punctuation – use of quotation marks around untruths and words that were supposedly said out loud
Verb tense – add "ed" to end of regular verbs to put in past tense; "thought" is past tense of irregular verb "to think"; need for pluperfect (had insulted) to denote action that took place before this paragraph
Other skills – strong verb practice; avoiding direct quotes by inserting "that;" use of hyphen for two words acting as one adjective

B – the fifth-grade **rowdy bullies** thought that willem had **insulted** them. they thought that he had called them "dookies and "nothings

C – The fifth-grade **rowdy bullies** thought that Willem had **insulted** them. They thought that he had called them "dookies" and "nothings."

NOTE: *This and the following Caught'ya are other good places to practice run-on sentences if you wish.*

---

89. irate

No paragraph – same topic
Types of sentences – both simple
Verb tense – add "ed" to end of regular verbs to put in past tense; "made" is past tense of irregular verb "to make"
Spelling rules – compound word
Other skills – strong verb practice; note no hyphen in "fifth graders" since it is a noun; review ordinal numbers (first, second, etc.)
Literary device – building suspense

B – this made the angry fifth graders even more **irate**. they chased Willem all the way to his classroom

C – This made the angry fifth graders even more **irate**. They chased Willem all the way to his classroom.

---

90. fracas, sped

Paragraph – new person speaking
Types of sentences – complex (subordinate clause with compound verb at the end)
Capitalization – always capitalize the first letter of a quote unless it is a continuation
Punctuation – use of quotation marks around what is said out loud; question mark needed after quote that is a question
Commas – introductory word
Verb tense – switch to present tense for quote; add "ed" to end of regular verbs to put in past tense; "stood" is past tense of irregular verb "to stand"; "sped" is past tense of irregular verb "to speed"
Spelling rules – compound word; consonant/vowel/consonant + suffix = double second consonant (grabbed)
Plural vs. possessive – possessive of singular noun

B – well what is this **fracas** asked willems teacher as she stood in the doorway to the room and grabbed willem as he **sped** past her

C – "Well, what is this **fracas**?" asked Willem's teacher as she stood in the doorway to the room and grabbed Willem as he **sped** past her.

---

91. ruffians

No paragraph – same person speaking; Paragraph – new person speaking
Types of sentences – both simple quotes
Capitalization – always capitalize the first letter of a quote unless it is a continuation
Punctuation – use of quotation marks around what is said out loud
Commas – introductory word; after quote that is not a question
Verb tense – switch to present tense for quote; add "ed" to end of regular verbs to put in past tense; "said" is past tense of verb "to say"
Spelling rules – homophone (won/one)
Contraction – Ma'am = Madam
Other skills – strong verb practice; review simple possessive pronouns
Literary device – conversation

B – are you **ruffians** picking on one of my third graders she continued. no ma'am said won of the fifth graders

C – "Are you **ruffians** picking on one of my third graders?" she continued.
"No, Ma'am," said one of the fifth graders.

B = the sentence(s) to be put on the board or overhead   C = the corrected sentence(s)

92. insulted, blurted

Paragraph – new person speaking

Types of sentences – simple quote

Capitalization – always capitalize the first letter of a quote unless it is a continuation

Punctuation – use of quotation marks around what is said out loud

Commas – end of quote that is not a question or exclamation

Verb tense – add "ed" to end of regular verbs to put in past tense; note use of past tense in quote to indicate something that happened prior to this paragraph

Spelling rules – if a noun ends in consonant "y" to make it plural, you get rid of the "y" and add "ies"

Other skills – strong verb practice

B – he **insulted** us **blurted** out another of the bullies

C –   "He **insulted** us," **blurted** out another of the bullies.

---

93. intentionally

Paragraph – new person speaking

Types of sentences – both simple, second with compound verb

Capitalization – always capitalize the first letter of a quote unless it is a continuation; always capitalize "I"

Punctuation – use of quotation marks around what is said out loud

Commas – end of quote that is not a question or exclamation; direct address

Verb tense – switch to present tense for quote; "said" is past tense of irregular verb "to say"

Plural vs. possessive – possessive of singular noun

Contraction – don't = do not

Other skills – strong verb practice

B – i don't think willem would do that **intentionally** said willems teacher. go to class boys and leave my students alone

C –   "I don't think Willem would do that **intentionally**," said Willem's teacher. "Go to class, boys, and leave my students alone."

B = the sentence(s) to be put on the board or overhead   **C = the corrected sentence(s)**

94. dreadful, stare

Paragraph – new person speaking
Types of sentences – simple quote
Capitalization – always capitalize the first letter of a quote unless it is a continuation
Punctuation – use of quotation marks around what is said out loud
Commas – before quote; direct address with repeated word
Verb tense – add "ed" to end of regular verbs to put in past tense; "was" is past tense of irregular verb "to be"; switch to present tense for quote
Spelling rules – consonant/vowel/consonant + suffix = double 2nd consonant (biggest); homophone (know/no)
Contraction – we're = we are
Other skills – comparatives (big/bigger/biggest)
Literary device – building suspense again; Anadiplosis (repeating a word or phrase for emphasis); use of slang ("twerp")

B – the biggest fifth grader gave willem a **dreadful stare** that said were not finished with you you little twerp

C –   The biggest fifth grader gave Willem a **dreadful stare** that said, "We're not finished with you, you little twerp."

95. apprehensive

Paragraph – new subject
Types of sentences – simple
Commas – always put commas around "too" if it means "also"
Verb tense – "was" and "were" are past tense of irregular verb "to be"
Spelling rules – compound word; homophone (to/too/two)
Other skills – review simple possessive pronouns
Literary device – building suspense

B – willem was scared. his classmates were **apprehensive** to

C –   Willem was scared. His classmates were **apprehensive**, too.

96. bullied

No paragraph – same subject; continuation
Types of sentences – complex
Verb tense – note use of pluperfect (had bullied) to refer to action that took place prior to this paragraph; "was" is past tense of irregular verb "to be"
Spelling rules – compound word
Other skills – negative; comparative (big/bigger/biggest)

B – the big fifth graders had **bullied** them before whenever a teacher was not around

C – The big fifth graders had **bullied** them before whenever a teacher was not around.

B = the sentence(s) to be put on the board or overhead   **C = the corrected sentence(s)**

97. consumed, victims

No paragraph – same topic
Types of sentences – compound
Commas – introductory adverb; compound
   sentence
Verb tense – add "ed" to end of regular verbs to
   put in past tense; "took" is past tense of
   irregular verb "to take"
Spelling rules – consonant/vowel/consonant +
   suffix = double 2nd consonant (bigger); if a
   noun ends in consonant "y," to make it
   plural you get rid of the "y" and add "ies"
   (goodies/ cookies); homophone (right/write/
   rite); plural of noun that does not end in "s"
   (children); plurals of words ending in "ch"
Plural vs. possessive – possessive of plural noun
Other skills – strong verb practice; comparatives
   (big/bigger/biggest); note hyphen in "third-
   graders" because of two words acting as one
   adjective; review FANBOYS

B – sometimes some of the bigger children took
the best goodies and all the cookies from
third-graders lunches and they **consumed**
them write in front of the **victims**

C – Sometimes, some of the bigger children
took the best goodies and all the cookies
from third-graders' lunches, and they
consumed them right in front of the
victims.

98. whimpered

Paragraph – new person speaking (quotation)
Types of sentences – complex
Capitalization – always capitalize the first letter
   of a quote unless it is a continuation
Punctuation – use of quotation marks around
   what is said out loud; need for question mark
   at end of quote that is a question
Commas – no commas needed after "friend"
   since she probably has many friends and thus
   the name is necessary; unnecessary, extra
   information (restrictive vs. non-restrictive
   modifiers for you English buffs)
Verb tense – add "ed" to end of regular verbs to
   put in past tense; switch to present tense for
   quote
Spelling rules – "i" before "e" except after "c,"
   etc. (friend)
Other skills – strong verb practice; review
   prepositions

B – what can we do **whimpered** _____ to
her freind _____ as the teacher closed
the door of the classroom behind willem

C –   "What can we do?" **whimpered**
_____ to her friend _____ as
the teacher closed the door of the classroom
behind Willem.

---

99. proffered

Paragraph – new person speaking
Types of sentences – complex
Capitalization – always capitalize the first letter of a quote unless it is a continuation
Punctuation – use of quotation marks around what is said out loud
Commas – end of quote that is not a question or exclamation
Verb tense – future tense (will come); "could" is past tense of verb "can"
Spelling rules – homophone (here/hear)
Other skills – strong verb practice; negative; review adverb use

B – those big kids really will come after us now **proffered** _____ quietly so that the teacher could not hear

C – "Those big kids really will come after us now," **proffered** _____ quietly so that the teacher could not hear.

100. agitated

Paragraph – new topic; narrator now speaking
Types of sentences – compound
Commas – compound sentence
Verb tense – add "ed" to end of regular verbs to put in past tense; "became" is past tense of irregular verb "to become"; "were" is past tense of verb "to be"
Spelling rules – often confused words (quit/quiet/quite); plural of noun that does not end in "s;" if a noun ends in consonant "y," to make it plural you get rid of the "y" and add "ies (bullies); homophone (their/there/they're)
Other skills – review simple object pronouns (me, you, him, her, us, them); review FANBOYS

B – The children became quiet as the teacher began class but most of them were **agitated** by there fear of the bullies

C – The children became quiet as the teacher began class, but most of them were **agitated** by their fear of the bullies.

101. apprehensively

Paragraph – new subject
Types of sentences – simple with long introductory participial phrase
Commas – participial phrase
Verb tense – "went" is past tense of irregular verb "to go"
Spelling rules – compound word
Plurals vs. possessives – possessive of singular noun
Other skills – "good" is adjective and "well" is adverb; review adverbs; note hyphen in third-grade as it is two words acting as one adjective

B – except for a student occasionally looking **apprehensively** out the doorway the rest of the day went very good in _____s third-grade class

C – Except for a student occasionally looking **apprehensively** out the doorway, the rest of the day went very well in _____'s third-grade class.

B = the sentence(s) to be put on the board or overhead   C = the corrected sentence(s)

102. celebrated, traditions

Paragraph – new subject
Types of sentences – compound
Commas – compound sentence
Verb tense – add "ed" to end of regular verbs to put in past tense
Spelling rules – most nouns form plurals by adding "s"
Possessive vs. plural – possessive of singular noun
Other skills – strong verb practice; collective nouns and pronouns (everyone-pronoun) need singular verbs and referents (i.e. never use "their" with everyone); go over simple possessive pronouns; review FANBOYS

B – everyone enjoyed his or her chocolate letter from willems uncle in the netherlands and the class **celebrated** the dutch holiday of saint nicholas in the **traditional** way with poems and small gifts

C –   Everyone enjoyed his or her chocolate letter from Willem's uncle in the Netherlands, and the class **celebrated** the Dutch holiday of Saint Nicholas in the **traditional** way with poems and small gifts.

103. threatened, wary

No paragraph – same focus (day of students)
Types of sentences – 1) complex; 2) compound
Commas – compound sentence
Verb tense – add "ed" to end of regular verbs to put in past tense; "was" is past tense of irregular verb "to be"
Spelling rules – homophone (no/know)
Other skills – review FANBOYS

B – even after school nothing happened because the teacher walked everyone out. no third grader was **threatened** that day but they were still **wary**

C – Even after school nothing happened because the teacher walked everyone out. No third grader was **threatened** that day, but they were still **wary**.

104. predicament

Paragraph – new topic
Types of sentences – 1) complex; 2) simple
Commas – subordinate clause at beginning of complex sentence
Verb tense – add "ed" to end of regular verbs to put in past tense; "had" is past tense of irregular verb "to have"
Spelling rules – homophone (whole/hole); often misspelled word (since)

B – will decided that since this hole mess had been his fault he wanted to fix the **predicament**. he had a plan

C –   Will decided that since this whole mess had been his fault, he wanted to fix the **predicament**. He had a plan.

NOTE: *This is another good Caught'ya to practice run-on sentences if you wish.*

B = the sentence(s) to be put on the board or overhead   C = the corrected sentence(s)

105. peers

No paragraph – same topic
Types of sentences – complex
Commas – subordinate clause at beginning of
complex sentence
Verb tense – add "ed" to end of regular verbs to
put in past tense; "told" is past tense of
irregular verb "to tell"
Plurals vs. possessives – possessive of singular
noun
Other skills – strong verb practice; better to
change word so you don't use the same word
twice in a sentence (plan)

B – When Willem told his plan to his **peers**
Marie and the others offered to help put
Willems plan into action

C – When Willem told his plan to his **peers**,
Marie and the others offered to help put
Willem's idea into action.

NOTE: *Warn students that a word needs to be changed so that it is not repeated.*

---

106. relatives

Paragraph – new person speaking and new time
Types of sentences – 1) simple (compound
verb); 2) simple quote
Capitalization – always capitalize the first letter
of a quote unless it is a continuation
Punctuation – use of quotation marks around
what is said out loud; use of quotes around
word referred to in context (yes)
Commas – introductory adverb; before quote;
after quote; extra information (explanation);
no comma after "meant" as it is an indirect
quote
Verb tense – add "ed" to end of regular verbs to
put in past tense; "said" is past tense of
irregular verb "to say"; "meant" is past tense
of the verb "to mean"
Spelling rules – homophone (their/there/
they're)
Other skills – strong verb practice; comparatives;
go over adjectives (this, that, these, and
those)

B – that night willem and marie called they're
relatives in the netherlands and in france
and asked a big favor. their **relatives** said ya
and oui both of which meant yes

C –
That night, Willem and Marie called
their **relatives** in the Netherlands and in
France and asked a big favor. Their **relatives**
said, "Ya," and "Oui," (*wee*) both of which
meant "Yes."

B = the sentence(s) to be put on the board or overhead   **C = the corrected sentence(s)**

107. ongoing, dilemma

2 Paragraphs – new person enters and then new person speaking

Types of sentences – 1) simple; 2) simple quote

Capitalization – always capitalize the first letter of a quote unless it is a continuation

Punctuation – use of quotation marks around what is said out loud

Commas – appositive (extra information about a noun); put commas around "too" if it means "also;" before quote

Verb tense – add "ed" to end of regular verbs to put in past tense; "said" is past tense of irregular verb "to say"

Spelling rules – homophones (to/too/two and their/there/they're)

Other skills – strong verb practice; note use of hyphen in two words acting as one adjective; collective noun "class" needs singular verb and referents

Literary device – building of mystery

B – the class explained the **ongoing dilemma** with the fifth graders and asked the help of their teacher _____.
she too said yes

C – 　　　The class explained the **ongoing dilemma** with the fifth graders and asked the help of their teacher, _____.
　　She, too, said, "Yes."

108. toiled

Paragraph – new time

Types of sentences – simple (compound verb)

Commas – long introductory adverb; verb series

Verb tense – add "ed" to end of regular verbs to put in past tense

Spelling rules – consonant/vowel/consonant + suffix = double 2nd consonant (planned)

Plural vs. possessive – possessive of singular noun

Other skills – strong verb practice; write out numbers to 121; hyphen needed in two words acting as one adjective

B – for the next 3 weeks _____s third-grade class planned prepared **toiled** and worked

C – 　　　For the next three weeks, _____'s third-grade class planned, prepared, **toiled**, and worked.

---

109. occasionally, glared

No paragraph – same time
Types of sentences – compound
Commas – long introductory adverb; compound
  sentence
Verb tense – add "ed" to end of regular verbs to
  put in past tense
Spelling rules – if a noun ends in consonant "y,"
  to make it plural you get rid of the "y" and
  add "ies" (bullies)
Plural vs. possessive – possessive of singular
  noun
Other skills – strong verb practice; write out
  numbers to 121; use "like" only to compare
  two nouns (or pronouns) directly (Dogs are
  like cats in many ways.); review adverbs;
  review FANBOYS
Literary device – building of suspense

B – for those three weeks the bullies
occasionally snatched a yummy cookie
from a third-graders lunch box or teased
other students but they always **glared** at
Willem as if they wanted to beat him up

C – For those three weeks, the bullies
occasionally snatched a yummy cookie
from a third-grader's lunch box or teased
other students, but they always **glared** at
Willem as if they wanted to beat him up.

110. implied, threat

No paragraph – same topic
Types of sentences – complex
Commas – interrupter
Verb tense – "could" is past tense of irregular
  verb "can"; "hung" is past tense of verb "to
  hang"
Spelling rules – if a noun ends in consonant "y,"
  to make it plural you get rid of the "y" and
  add "ies" (bullies); homophone (their/there/
  they're)
Other skills – negative; never split verb parts nor
  infinitives; comparatives (large/larger/largest)

B – the larger bullies could never carry out there
implied threat however because all the
other third graders hung around Willem all
the time

C – The larger bullies never could carry out their
implied threat, however, because all the
other third graders hung around Willem all
the time.

111. unaccompanied, whenever

No paragraph – same topic
Types of sentences – 1) simple; 2) complex
Verb tense – "was" and "were" are past tense of
  irregular verb "to be"
Spelling rules – homophone (their/there/
  they're); compound words
Other skills – write out numbers to 121; hyphen
  in between two words acting as one adjective

B – willem was never **unaccompanied** at
school. they're were always at least 10 other
third-grade students around him **whenever**
he was out of the classroom

C – Willem was never **unaccompanied** at
school. There were always at least ten other
third-grade students around him **whenever**
he was out of the classroom.

B = the sentence(s) to be put on the board or overhead   C = the corrected sentence(s)

112. drafted, via, epistle

Paragraph – new time

Types of sentences – 1) simple; 2) simple (compound verb)

Commas – introductory adverb (optional here)

Verb tense – add "ed" to end of regular verbs to put in past tense; "was" is past tense of irregular verb "to be"; "sent" is past tense of verb "to send"

Spelling rules – homophones (their/they're/ there and write/rite/right)

Other skills – no hyphen needed in "third grade" since it is a noun; hyphen needed in "fifth-grade" since together the two words are one adjective

B – finally everything was ready. the third grade **drafted** a letter to the fifth-grade students and sent it **via** their teacher who helped them write the **epistle**

C –   Finally, everything was ready. The third grade **drafted** a letter to the fifth-grade students and sent it **via** their teacher who helped them write the **epistle**.

B = the sentence(s) to be put on the board or overhead　　　　**C = the corrected sentence(s)**

113. misunderstanding, foreign

> **NOTE:** *This is a longer Caught'ya due to its nature as a letter. You may want to spend an hour on it followed by a brief, end-of-the-year letter-writing unit and have students exchange letters or write a letter to himself/herself. You could collect these letters, save them, and return them to the students when they leave your school two years from now. Emphasize elaboration and correct letter-writing format. The middle-school teachers beg you to make sure that students learn not to indent the greeting. For some reason, children arrive in middle school with this incorrect habit ingrained in their minds. It really is hard to break them of it.*

2 Paragraphs – letter beginning (do not indent greeting); new topic

Types of sentences – 1) simple; 2) compound; 3) simple (compound verb); 4) simple; 5) simple; 6) simple

Capitalization – in greeting capitalize every word; in closing capitalize only the first word; rules for normal capitalization of proper noun apply to headings and signatures

Commas – between city and state; in date; after greeting in friendly letter; appositive (more information about a noun – Willem); compound sentence; after closing of letter

Verb tense – switch to present tense for invitation which is technically a quote

Spelling rules – homophone (its/it's); compound words; if a noun ends in consonant "y," to make it plural you get rid of the "y" and add "ies" (cookies); difficult word (o'clock)

Plurals vs. possessive – possessive of singular noun

Other skills – letter-writing format; do not begin a sentence with a FANBOYS (conjunction); write out numbers to 121; abbreviation "p.m."; hyphen needed when two words acting as one

Literary device – letter within story

B –

_____ elementary school
put your school's address here
your city, your state your zip code
may _____ _____ (put the correct date)

the fifth-grade class
_____ elementary school
put your school's address here
your city your state your zip code

dear fifth graders
we apologize for the **misunderstanding** you had with willem one of our two new **foreign** students. we know that some of you have been mean to us in the past but maybe its because you like our cookies. so we invite you to a party to let you meet willem and marie and to share some really yummy dutch and french cookies with us please come to our classroom friday at 2 o'clock p m. we want to get to know you too. we also want to know what it is like to be a big fifth grader
      sincerely yours

_____s third-grade class

C –

_____ Elementary School
Put your school's address here
Your city, your state your zip code
May _____, _____ (put the correct date)

The Fifth-grade Class
_____ Elementary School
Put your school's address here
Your city, your state your zip code

Dear Fifth Graders,
    We apologize for the **misunderstanding** you had with Willem, one of our two new **foreign** students. We know that some of you have been mean to us in the past, but maybe it's because you like our cookies. We invite you to a party to let you meet Willem and Marie and to share some really yummy Dutch and French cookies with us.
    Please come to our classroom Friday at two o'clock p.m. We want to get to know you, too. We also want to know what it is like to be a big fifth grader.

      Sincerely yours,
      _____'s Third-grade Class

B = the sentence(s) to be put on the board or overhead　　　**C = the corrected sentence(s)**

114. epistle

Paragraph – new time
Types of sentences – simple
Commas – introductory adverb (optional)
Verb tense – add "ed" to end of regular verbs to
    put in past tense
Spelling rules – "i" before "e" except after "c,"
    etc.; homophone (their/they're/there)
Plurals vs. possessives – possessive of singular
    noun
Other skills – strong verb practice; hyphen
    needed between two words acting as one
    adjective

B – the next day _____s third-grade class
received a reply to their **epistle**

C –   The next day, _____'s third-grade
class received a reply to their **epistle**.

115. accept, invitation, affable

Paragraph – letter beginning (do not indent
    greeting)
Types of sentences – all simple
Capitalization – in greeting capitalize every word;
    in closing capitalize only the first word; rules
    for normal capitalization of proper noun apply
    to headings and signatures
Punctuation – question mark needed in
    question
Commas – between city and state; in date; after
    greeting in friendly letter; two adjectives not
    separated by "and" where 2nd is not age, color,
    or linked to noun; after closing of letter
Verb tense – switch to future tense for acceptance
    of invitation which is technically a quote
Spelling rules – homophone (its/it's); if a noun
    ends in consonant "y," to make it plural you get
    rid of the "y" and add "ies" (cookies); difficult
    word (o'clock)
Commonly confused – accept/except
Plurals vs. possessive – possessive of singular noun
Conjunction – we'll = we will
Other skills – letter-writing format; often-confused
    words (accept vs. except); write out numbers to
    121; abbreviation "p.m.;" use of parentheses for
    nickname hyphen needed when two words are
    acting as one adjective
Literary device – letter within story

B –   _____ elementary school
      put your school's address here
      your city your state your zip code
      may ____ _____ (put the correct date)

the third-grade class
_____ elementary school
put your school's address here
your city your state your zip code

dear third graders
we will **accept** your **invitation**. its a nice **affable**
surprise for us. well come to your classroom friday
at 2 o'clock p.m. did you say cookies

            _____s fifth-grade class
            (the cookie monsters)

C –   _____ Elementary School
      Put your school's address here
      Your city, your state your zip code
      May ____, _____ (put the correct date)

The Third-grade Class
_____ Elementary School
Put your school's address here
Your city, your state your zip code

Dear Third Graders,

   We will **accept** your **invitation**. It's a nice, **affable**
surprise for us. We'll come to your classroom Friday
at two o'clock p.m. Did you say cookies?

            _____'s Fifth Grade Class.
            (the Cookie Monsters)

> **NOTE:** *This is a longer Caught'ya. Plan to spend at least an hour on it. You may want to have your students write a letter to the fourth graders at your school asking them what it will be like next year in the fourth grade. Again, emphasize elaboration as well as not indenting the greeting.*

B = the sentence(s) to be put on the board or overhead　　　　**C = the corrected sentence(s)**

116. parcel

Paragraph – new time
Types of sentences – all simple
Verb tense – add "ed" to end of regular verbs to put in past tense; "came" is past tense of irregular verb "to come"
Spelling rules – often misspelled word (finally)
Plural vs. possessive – possessive of singular noun
Other skills – strong verb practice; collective pronoun requires singular verb and referents (like possessive pronouns); need for hyphen as two words acting as one adjective; subject-verb agreement ("each student" is singular and thus you cannot use "their" which is plural)

B – friday finally arrived. everyone in _____s third-grade class came in early. each student carried their **parcel**

C – ⎯ Friday finally arrived. Everyone in _____'s third-grade class came in early. Each student carried a **parcel**.

117. prodigious

No paragraph – same topic (detail)
Types of sentences – simple (compound verb)
Capitalization – do not capitalize the names of subjects unless they are the name of a language (English, French, Dutch)
Commas – interrupter of extra information; noun series within interrupter
Verb tense – add "ed" to end of regular verbs to put in past tense
Other skills – strong verb practice; collective noun (class) takes singular verb, etc.

B – all day long instead of math science social studies and language arts the class practiced greetings in french and dutch and prepared for the **prodigious** party

C – All day long, instead of math, science, social studies, and language arts, the class practiced greetings in French and Dutch and prepared for the **prodigious** party.

118. precisely

Paragraph – new time
Types of sentences – 1) simple (compound subject); 2) simple
Commas – long introductory adverb
Verb tense – add "ed" to end of regular verbs to put in past tense; "was" is past tense of irregular verb "to be"
Spelling rules – homophone (their/there/they're); difficult word (o'clock)
Other skills – write out numbers to 121; review adverbs; review subject and object pronouns (the error in this one should be obvious to your students)
Literary device – suspense building

B – At two o'clock **precisely** the fifth graders and theyre teacher arrived at the door. Everything was ready for they

C – ⎯ At two o'clock **precisely**, the fifth graders and their teacher arrived at the door. Everything was ready for them.

B = the sentence(s) to be put on the board or overhead   **C** = the corrected sentence(s)

119. guests

Paragraph – new action with people speaking

Types of sentences – complex (subordinate clause at beginning)

Capitalization – always capitalize the first letter of a quote unless it is a continuation

Punctuation – use of quotation marks around what is said out loud

Commas – subordinate clause at beginning; noun series; no comma after "of" and "and" since these are indirect quotes

Verb tense – add "ed" to end of regular verbs to put in past tense

Spelling rules – compound word; homophone (their/there/they're); if a noun ends in consonant "y," to make it plural you get rid of the "y" and add "ies" (cries)

Other skills – strong verb practice

B – as they opened the door of the classroom willem marie and all the third graders greeted there **guests** with cries of bienvenue and welkom

C – As they opened the door of the classroom, Willem, Marie, and all the third graders greeted their **guests** with cries of "Bienvenue" (*pronounced biehnvenoo — don't pronounce the "n," stress the last syllable, and the "noo" rhymes with "moo"*) and "Welkom." (*pronounced velcome*)

120. decorated, confections, perched, decoratively

No paragraph – same topic

Types of sentences – 1) simple (compound subject); 2) simple (compound verb)

Commas – noun series

Verb tense – add "ed" to end of regular verbs to put in past tense; "had" is past tense of irregular verb "to have"; "were" is past tense of "to be"

Spelling rules – most nouns form plurals by adding "s"

Plural vs. Possessive – possessive of singular nouns

Other skills – strong-verb practice

Literary device – strong-verb description

B – pictures flags and posters of france and the netherlands **decorated** the room. hundreds and hundreds of dutch and french **confections perched decoratively** on the desks. they had come from france and holland or been made according to the recipes of maries and willems relatives

C – Pictures, flags, and posters of France and the Netherlands **decorated** the room. Hundreds and hundreds of Dutch and French **confections perched decoratively** on the desks. They had come from France and Holland or been made according to the recipes of Marie's and Willem's relatives.

B = the sentence(s) to be put on the board or overhead   **C = the corrected sentence(s)**

121. transported, directly

No paragraph – same topic

Types of sentences – simple

Capitalization – capitalize the names of
  continents

Punctuation – exclamation mark needed for
  emphasis

Verb tense – add "ed" to end of regular verbs to
  put in past tense; "had been" is pluperfect of
  the verb "to have" and is needed here to
  refer to action that took place before this
  paragraph

Other skills – use "as if" not "like" because
  "like" directly compares only two nouns or
  pronouns (use "as if" if a verb is involved);
  strong verb use

Literary device – description; simile with "as"

B – the room looked like it had been
transported directly from europe

C – The room looked as if it had been
transported directly from Europe!

---

122. astonished, delighted, confections

Paragraph – new subject (now talking about
  fifth graders)

Types of sentences – 1) simple (compound
  object); 2) simple

Verb tense – "were" is past tense of irregular verb
  "to be"; "ate" is past tense of verb "to eat"

Spelling rules – often confused words (were/
  we're)

Other skills – review ordinal numbers (first,
  second, etc.); review simple subject pronouns
  (I, you, he, she, we, they)

B – the fifth graders were **astonished** and
delighted. they ate the **confections**

C – The fifth graders were **astonished** and
delighted. They ate the **confections**.

---

123. established, friendships

No paragraph – same topic

Types of sentences – compound

Commas – compound sentence; two adjectives
  not separated by "and" where second adjective is not age, color, or linked to noun

Verb tense – add "ed" to end of regular verbs to
  put in past tense

Spelling rules – homophone (gnu/new/knew)

Other skills – strong verb practice; too many
  pronouns for clarity (substitute noun);
  review ordinal numbers; comparatives
  (young/younger/youngest and small/smaller/
  smallest); review FANBOYS

B – they learned to sing songs in french
and dutch and they **established** gnu
friendships with the younger smaller
students

C – The fifth graders learned to sing songs in
French and Dutch, and they **established**
new **friendships** with the younger, smaller
students.

B = the sentence(s) to be put on the board or overhead   C = the corrected sentence(s)

124. misdeeds, mistreat

No paragraph – same topic (detail)

Types of sentences – simple (compound verb)

Commas – no comma needed since sentence is
not compound (no subject)

Verb tense – add "ed" to end of regular verbs to
put in past tense

Spelling rules – homophones(their/there/they're
and to/too/two)

Other skills – strong verb practice; do not begin
a sentence with a conjunction (FANBOYS);
too many pronouns for clarity (substitute
noun); review ordinal numbers

B – and they apologized for there past
misdeeds and promised never too **mistreat**
third graders again

C – The fifth graders apologized for their past
misdeeds and promised never to **mistreat**
third graders again.

125. pompous; entirely

Paragraph – new topic

Punctuation – use of dots to indicate possible
future action

Commas – introductory adverb (optional);
relative pronoun clause (not necessary)

Verb tense – "were" is past tense of irregular verb
"to be"

Other skills – review ordinal numbers; review
adjectives and adverbs; relative pronouns
"who" and "whom" ("who" is subject, and
"whom" is the object)

Literary device – leave your reader hanging

B – now the second graders who were a
pompous group were another matter
entirely

C – Now, the second graders, who were a
pompous group, were another matter
entirely...

NOTE: *Now invite your students to write a sequel to the story. What is going to happen to Willem and
Marie? Will the friendship among the third and fifth graders continue?*

B = the sentence(s) to be put on the board or overhead   C = the corrected sentence(s)

NINE
SUGGESTIONS

**Pre-writing and Writing Activities to Prepare
Primary Students for Writing Assessment
and Standardized Tests That Require Writing**

Introduction

With all the emphasis on state writing assessment tests (currently instituted in thirty-nine states) and on standardized tests that require the writing of paragraphs even in the math part, the ability to express oneself clearly and effectively in writing finally is being treated with the importance and seriousness it always deserved. Students learn to read by reading, and they learn to write by writing.

First graders, if given a lot of practice, can produce some short but excellent pieces of expository/clarification, descriptive, and narrative writing. If students write from day one in school, by the time they are in the fifth grade, they can write better than many adults. (I know. I taught fifth grade for many years in a school that encouraged writing at every grade level.) All young students need is practice and direction. The response journal in which primary students write after they complete the daily *Caught'ya* is a start on this road to fluent and excellent writing.

Kindergartners, first, second, and third graders should write *every* day not only in their response journal but in at least one other writing activity. This is the key. Yes, you will have to read those writing efforts, but at the primary level, where you are looking only at content or a targeted skill (to be explained later in **Suggestion #5, Afterwards**), this does not take long.

Regardless of the demographics of the student population, schools which require daily writing at *all* grade levels, achieve much higher scores on the fourth-grade state writing test than schools which require a minimum of writing. In fact, you may be amazed at what first graders can produce when given plenty of practice and encouragement.

Those of us who teach in the grades that are tested — 4, 7-8 and 10 in most states — depend on those teachers who precede us. If our students do not arrive in our classrooms in August convinced that writing is a daily part of their lives and aware that expository/clarification, descriptive, narrative, and persuasive writing differ from each other, we cannot instill in them the writing skills they need in the short time before the state writing test. In fact, some states, like Wisconsin for example, already have figured out that the test should be scheduled early in the year (in October). In that way the onus does not fall entirely on the current teacher, but rather on those of preceding grades.

With all this in mind, here are a few suggestions for writing activities that go beyond the daily response-journal entry. I repeat: students learn to read by reading and learn to write by writing. Like learning a foreign language or a sport, the more writing practice children have at an early age, the more proficient and fluent they will be when they are older and the less chance they will have to lose those skills in adulthood.

Nine Ideas and Activities for Writing

(Activities specifically designed to help raise your school's scores on the state writing assessment test.)

Suggestion #1

Some fruitful sources of ideas for writing and for setting up a viable "writing community" in the primary classroom.

It is important that you establish, even as early as kindergarten, a writing community in your classroom, a workshop atmosphere that fosters and encourages constant writing practice. There are some really good books on the market that address this concern for elementary school teachers. The most effective ones (obviously) were written by teachers who already have used the ideas with their own students. See the **Bibliography** for a list of helpful resources. I have put hearts (❤) after the books with great writing suggestions.

Suggestion #2

Distinguishing and identifying the three (or four in some states) types of writing that students must produce by fourth grade — expository/clarification, descriptive, narrative, (and in one or two states, persuasive as well).

> **NOTE:** *Since so few states require their elementary students to write in the persuasive mode, and since, in my opinion, persuasive writing is too sophisticated an idea for primary children to comprehend, I do not suggest including the teaching of that genre unless absolutely necessary.*

Another important thing to keep in mind is that children arrive in kindergarten speaking (and potentially writing) expository/clarification and descriptive essays. They explain how their mothers make dinner. They describe their dogs and cats. They explain why they are mad at their little brothers and sisters. They describe their house. Yet, when fourth-grade students take the writing assessment test, they score lower on the expository/clarification and descriptive essays than on the narrative stories.

Somehow between kindergarten and fourth grade expository/clarification and descriptive writing diminishes in favor of narrative stories. Young children read mostly narrative books, and their writing eventually follows that genre. We need to offer an equal number of selections of non-fiction expository/clarification and descriptive writing from books which abound in your school library.

Equal exposure to the three types of writing — expository/clarification, descriptive, and narrative — should be emphasized at the primary level. For high scores on the state writing tests and for future writing habits, it is most important that, at a very early age, students be able to distinguish and identify each of the three types of writing, adding the fourth type (persuasive) in the second semester of fourth grade.

Here are some useful activities to help teach students the differences among the types of writing asked for on most writing tests:

1) Compile a list of expository/clarification, descriptive, and narrative topics. These can be found either by writing your own, or by brainstorming with other teachers, or by purchasing a copy of *Blowing Away the State Writing Assessment Test* (Kiester, 1996).

Prompts are easy to compose. For expository/clarification topics, just include the word "explain" or "clarify." For narrative prompts, include the words "tell a story about." For descriptive, include the words "describe so that your reader can picture it." Then think of things that are near and dear to your students — their families, their classroom, their toys, their pets, etc. Use them as the focus of the prompts (topics).

Once you have a variety of prompts of the three types of writing, type them up, cut out each prompt separately, fold them, and place them in a hat. Each day, ask a student to draw a prompt from the hat for the class to decide whether the prompt is expository/clarification, narrative, or descriptive. Ask the class to identify the key words that clued them to the type of topic and also what the prompt wants the writer to do. You can do this exercise as early as kindergarten.

2) Use the same list of prompts in a separate activity. This time, again ask a student to pick a topic from the hat for the class and to list the many nitty-gritty details that could be included in an essay or story written from that prompt. Write these details on the board or overhead for a group effort. Since most primary students cannot grasp the idea of clustering or mapping out a composition before the end of second grade, this is an alternative approach that both avoids written clusters and introduces the pre-writing they must learn to do by the fourth grade.

Those of you who teach third grade can cluster with your students the prompt that was drawn from the hat. Be sure to use the circle cluster for narrative topics and the rocket cluster for expository/clarification and descriptive ones. If you are not familiar with these types of clusters, they are fully explained in *Blowing Away the State Writing Assessment Test* (Kiester, 1996). I have reproduced just the examples of the two types of clusters on the following page.

3) Challenge your students to a game of "You are the Writer." Divide the class in half or in quarters. Each group takes turns coming up with an appropriate topic as you call out, "Expository/Clarification," "Narrative," or "Descriptive." The group that is on the spot tries to come up with a topic like: Expository/Clarification — "Explain why I like my dog." You are the moderator. At the second- and third-grade level, this could be a writing activity after playing the game orally several times.

4) Every day put a topic (prompt) on the board, and immediately after teaching the *Caught'ya*, ask students to identify the prompt as expository/clarification, narrative, or descriptive. Students quickly pick up on the key words (see #2 of this **Suggestion**) and learn to identify the type of topic. Students then can suggest the next day's topic and wait for the next day to identify the type of writing that prompt demands.

Suggestion #3

Clustering, mapping, and pre-planning before writing.

While some sort of pre-planning is an absolutely necessary skill for a good writer, younger children can do this only on a very basic level, if at all. To get the basic idea across to kindergarteners, first graders, and the first-term second-grade students, pair up the children so that they can talk out their compositions before they begin to write. This activity establishes the need for pre-planning. Talking out a story or an essay with a peer, as they do in the imaginary games they play, helps them with organization, order, and elaboration (the banes of primary teachers).

Set a timer for the pre-planning conversations so that students know that they must keep on task. Instruct students to use the words "first," second," "third," "next," etc., to help organize their verbal plans.

By the age of about seven-and-a-half, most students can learn to plan a paper before they write and then to use that plan for help in their writing. I prefer two simple plans, one for narrative writing (a circle cluster) and the other for expository/clarification, descriptive, and persuasive writing (a rocket cluster). Again, if you are not familiar with these types of clusters, they are explained fully in *Blowing Away the State Writing Assessment Test* (Kiester, 1996). A small sample of both can be found on the following page.

Suggestion #4

Writing strong-verb sentences and paragraphs.

The ability to compose strong-verb sentences and paragraphs is an important tool to developing good, fluent writing. As primary teachers, you have the advantage of teaching children at a young age when they are just beginning to develop their writing habits. If you are successful in encouraging your students to use more "strong verbs" (action verbs) rather than "dead" ones (*am, are, be, is, was, were, had, has, have, "ing" verbs, act, feel, become, seems*), student writing in your school will improve dramatically, and high test scores will follow.

Circle Clusters for Narrative Stories

Topic cluster:

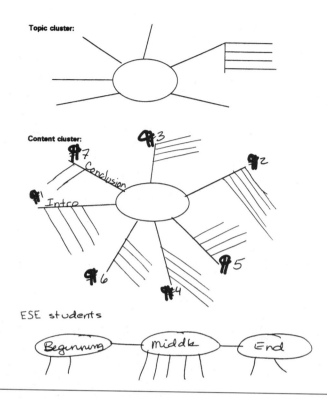

Content cluster:

#3

#7

Conclusion

#2

#1 Intro

#6

#4 #5

ESE students

Beginning — middle — End

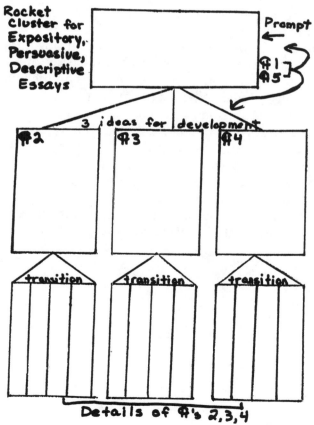

Rocket Cluster for Expository, Persuasive, Descriptive Essays

Prompt

#1
#5

3 ideas for development

#2   #3   #4

transition   transition   transition

Details of #'s 2, 3, 4

The secret is that all good literature uses active verbs. The "grammar checkers" on computers even check for active verbs. Writing flows more smoothly and paints better pictures when "strong," active verbs are used.

Unless otherwise trained, by the time students reach the fourth grade, even the most fluent writers among them confine themselves to only one or two verbs. "Is" and "was" are their favorites. Look at your students' writing. The verb "to be" is the first verb children learn to write. Thus, using this verb almost exclusively is natural. However, even before students have mastered the verb "to be," you can introduce the use of active verbs (as good vocabulary) and encourage their use in writing. How? Follow these steps.

1) Make a bulletin board with a graveyard showing the "dead" verbs on it. You can use the list, located on the page following this suggestion, to help you. Then, meet with your fellow primary teachers and decide which grade level gets the honor of *actually* burying the verbs in the ground. The decision should be based on which grade level would be able to understand *why* they are participating in this activity. You teachers know better than anyone else the relative maturity of the students in your school. The teachers of grade levels that do not bury the "dead" verbs simply can refer to the bulletin board to remind students which verbs to avoid.

Anyway, having picked the lucky grade level, borrow a shovel, have students write the "dead" verbs on a piece of paper and put each of them in a separate envelope or in tiny paper "coffins" (if you can show your students how to make them).

On the appointed day (with, perhaps, a parent or administrative volunteer — rope your principal into this if he/she has a good sense of humor) everyone dresses lugubriously in dark, somber colors. (The words in bold type are good vocabulary to teach to students and to use over and over on that day.) You and your students then take the envelopes or coffins outside and bury them while singing the "dead" verbs to the tune of the "Volga Boatman's Song," "Where Will We All Be 1000 Years from Now?" or some other funereal-sounding song in a minor key. By repeatedly singing the "dead" verbs, students learn them easily. With the bulletin board to remind them plus frequent singing of them in the ensuing weeks, students will never forget the verbs they need to be careful not to overuse.

Once the "dead" verbs are learned, students can begin learning the strong, active verbs that render writing so much more effective and help raise scores astronomically on the state writing test in the fourth grade. Put lists of good, strong, active verbs on the board; use the ones you hear the children say. It is a good idea to have a designated place in your classroom where you can write the strong, active verbs as soon as students utter them.

When your ears are attuned, you will be surprised at what verbs young children can use. Add really "cool" verbs to your list whenever you think of them, verbs that will appeal to your students like "reeks" instead of "smells" and "ambled" instead of "walked." Any student who has read *Babar* knows the word "perambulator" and what it is (a carriage for *walking* the baby elephants). The leap to "amble" should be simple.

The two next steps will give you some activities to acquaint students with writing strong, active verbs and with substituting "strong" verbs for "dead" ones.

"Dead" and "Dying" Verbs to Avoid

"Dead" Verbs

am
are
be
had
has
have
is
was
were
any verb ending in "ing"

...*and*, for third grade, the sense verbs — (looks, smells, tastes, sounds, feels)

"Dying" Verbs (act as helping verbs)

become/became
act/acted
seem/seemed
feel/feels

2) Use the Primary Strong-verb Practice Sentences on the following page and then make up your own "dead verb" sentences for further practice in rewriting them with strong, active verbs. The more practice students have, the sooner they will begin using the active verbs in their writing, cutting back on their use of "is," "was," or "were." Do the first practice sheet orally. You can complete one or two sentences a day and then ask students to come up with "dead verb" sentences from their own writing that you then put on the board. A set of possible answers follows the **Primary Strong-verb Practice Sentences**. Please keep in mind that there are many other possible verbs to use when rewriting the sentences.

Second and third graders can do the **Primary Strong-verb Practice Sentences** sheet orally and then write the answers. This gets them used to writing action verbs. It is a good idea to follow this activity with a short, daily practice in writing sentences with strong, active verbs.

3) When you feel your students are ready, copy one or two "dead verb" sentences a day on the board from the **Dead-verb Practice Sentences to Rewrite** sheet. When your second and third graders are comfortable rewriting these sentences as a large group, make a copy of the sheet and instruct your students to rewrite them, one or two a day, in their editing journals. Ask them to show by descriptive detail just how mad, sad, happy, or fun something or someone is. A set of possible answers follows the practice sentences, but please recall that there are *many* ways to change each sentence.

Primary Strong-verb Practice Sentences

1. The cat _____ in the chair.

2. A big brown dog _____ at the little cat.

3. The big dog then _____ the cat around

   the house.

4. My teacher _____ when the class talks

   too much.

5. Rabbits _____ when they smell danger.

6. The smelly, black and white skunk _____

   on the dog when the dog _____ it.

7. Our teacher _____ us how to write.

8. A yellow ball _____ down the stairs.

9. I _____ my best friend.

10. My friend _____ to school with me.

11. A big blue bird _____ in the window.

12. When the teacher _____, I

    _____.

Possible (but not the only) Answers To Primary Strong-verb Practice Sentences

1. The cat **curled up** in the chair.
    (sat, yawned, slept, etc.)

2. A big brown dog **barked** at the little cat.
    (growled, whined, etc.)

3. The big dog then **chased** the cat around the house.
    (pursued, followed, etc.)

4. My teacher **frowns** when the class **talks** too much.
    (yells, sighs, shouts, etc.)   (chatters, prattles, etc.)

5. Rabbits **run** when they **smell** danger.
    (scamper off, quiver in fear, etc.) (sense, notice, etc.)

6. The smelly, black and white skunk **sprayed** the dog when the dog **attacked** it.
    (peed on, bit, etc.)   (growled at, chased, etc.)

7. Our teacher **teaches** us how to write.
    (shows, demonstrates to, etc.)

8. A yellow ball **bounced** down the stairs.
    (rolled, fell, etc.)

9. I **hugged** my best friend.
    (love, played with, etc.)

10. My friend **walked** to school with me.
    (ambled, skipped, came, etc.)

11. A big blue bird **tapped on** the window.
    (pecked at, hit, etc.)

12. When the teacher **talks,** I **listen**.
    (yells, teaches, etc.) (learn, cringe, pay attention, etc.)

Dead-verb Practice Sentences to Rewrite

NOTE — *The key is to show just how lonely, sad, happy, etc., the person is by telling something he or she would do. What do you do when you are sad? mad? happy? lonely?*

1.   The boy was lonely.

2.   The little girl was sad.

3.   The girl in the red dress was happy.

4.   My teacher is slightly crazy and lots of fun.

5.   My mom is mad at me.

6.   My friend is mean to his sister.

7.   These sentences are stupid.

8.   The calico cat was a nice cat.

9.   The little dog with the floppy ears was cute.

10. When I go to my grandparents' house, I am happy.

11. School is sometimes boring.

12. My room is a mess.

13. She is my best friend, and we have fun together.

14. The sky is blue with lots of fluffy clouds.

15. There are nasty brown roaches in my backpack.

16. The classroom was noisy

17. The birthday party was awesome.

18. The skunk is smelly.

19. I am mad today.

20. It was fun.

Several Possible (but not the only) Answers to Each of the Dead-verb Practice Sentences to Rewrite

1. The lonely boy **sat** in the corner and **cried**.
    The lonely boy **played** all by himself.

2. The sad little girl **cried** piteously.
    The sad little girl **ran** to her mother and **sobbed** in her arms.

3. The girl in the red dress **danced** with joy.
    The girl in the red dress **twirled** around the room from happiness.

4. My crazy, fun teacher **plays** with us on the jungle gym.
    My crazy, fun teacher **likes** skunks.

5. My mom sometimes **yells** at me angrily.
    My angry mom **puts** me in my room when I **do** something bad.

6. My friend **hits** and **teases** his sister.
    My friend **takes** his sister's dolls and **breaks** them.

7. These stupid sentences **take** a long time to do.
    These stupid sentences **teach** me about strong verbs.

8. The nice calico cat **licked** my hand.
    The nice calico cat **curled up** in my lap and **purred**.

9. The cute little dog with the floppy ears **chased** its tail.
    The cute little dog with the floppy ears **rolled** on its back and **waved** its paws in the air.

10. When I go to my grandparents' house, I **get** anything I ask for.
    I **love** going to my grandparents' house because they **play** with me and **love** me a lot.

11. School **bores** me when I **must do** worksheets.
    Doing math problems **puts** me to sleep.

12. My clothes **litter** the floor of my messy room.
    In my messy room clothes **cover** the floor and math papers **spill out of** the trash can.

13. My best friend and I **play** games together all the time.
    My best friend and I **visit** each other's houses every day.

> **NOTE** — *Sometimes you need to reverse the parts of the sentence.*

14. Lots of fluffy clouds **dot** the blue sky.
    Lots of fluffy clouds **float** in the beautiful blue sky overhead.

15. Nasty brown roaches **live** in my backpack.
    Nasty brown roaches **eat** my lunch in my backpack.

16. The noisy classroom **hummed** with students at their learning centers.
    The students **talked**, **shouted** at each other, and **laughed** happily as they played in the noisy classroom.

17. We **stayed** up late at the awesome birthday party.
    A clown and lots of animals **came** to the awesome birthday party.

18. The smelly skunk **sprayed on** the mean kid.
    The smelly skunk still **reeked** from spraying a dog.

> **NOTE —** *Sometimes you may want to take a totally different tack that doesn't even mention the adjective, but just demonstrates it with action.*

19. In my anger, I **want** to hit and yell at everyone today.
    My face **frowns** and **scrunches** up in anger.

20. My hair **stood** on end, and I **laughed** and **screamed** on the roller coaster ride.
    At Disney World, we **rode** on lots of rides and **met** Mickey Mouse.

4) When your students can comfortably change a telling sentence (one with a "dead verb") to one with a strong, action verb (a "showing" sentence), they are ready to go on to the next step. This next step is to introduce the idea of strong-verb paragraphs. These paragraphs are very simple and can be expository/clarification or descriptive. You and your students can plan each paragraph by using a simple circle cluster like the one below. In this type of cluster, you and your students write only the subject and verb of each planned strong-verb sentence. You do this on the arms of the cluster. You and your students then can use numbers by each subject/ verb to plan the order of the sentences in the paragraph.

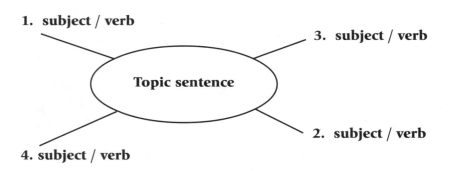

The first sentence of each paragraph is a sentence with a "dead" verb.

> **NOTE** — *After advanced second graders or "average" third graders have mastered the paragraphs in a large group and perhaps even in small groups, you can begin asking them to rewrite the boring, dead-verb topic sentence into an interesting "grabber." For example: Change "It was fun" to "Wow! This year's trip to Disney topped every other trip we've ever taken for excitement and strange adventures!"*

The middle sentences (the number to be determined by you — no fewer than two and no more than four) must contain only strong, active verbs. No "dead" verbs may be used even in subordinate (dependent) clauses. Primary students keep these sentences very simple. They usually stick to the subject and verb plus an adjective or two and maybe an adverb. This is fine. More complicated sentences (compound and complex) can be added later as the children become more sophisticated writers. Concentrate at first on teaching elaboration and nitty-gritty detail in these paragraphs. Fourth-grade teachers will be very grateful!

The last sentence in the strong-verb paragraph is a conclusion and restates the first sentence but in a little different way, even if it means adding only one word. Writing a conclusion trains students in the art of repeating the beginning premise in different words, a vital skill for good writing (and good scores on a state writing test).

The entire strong-verb paragraph is a microcosm of the essays and stories demanded on the writing test. Each paragraph must have a beginning, a detailed and elaborated middle that supports the beginning, and a conclusion. You also will want to encourage the use of similes (even require them). The earlier students get used to using figurative language, the more likely they are to use them on the state writing test in the fourth grade. Sample paragraphs follow.

Examples of Basic, Primary
Strong-verb Paragraphs

The Happy Girl

Mary *is* happy. She **smiles**. She **laughs** at everything. She **plays** with her toys. Mary *is* very happy today.

My Heart

A heart *is* in my body. It **pumps** my blood. It **runs** my blood around my body. It **makes** a noise thump thump when my doctor listens to it. I *have* a good heart.

The Sad Boy

John *is* sad. He **cries** all the time like a baby. He **frowns**, and he never **smiles**. He **sits** by himself in the corner. John *is* very sad today.

My Sister

My sister *is* a pain. She **takes** stuff out of my room. She **hurts** me by kicking me. She always **comes** in my room when I don't ask her. She **hogs** the t.v. too. That *is* why my big sister is a pain. (She really is not a pain.)

The Funny Dog

The dog *was* very funny. It **chased** its tail round and round, and it never **caught** it. When the funny dog **woofed**, its ears **flopped**. The dog **wagged** its tail so fast it was **like a flag in a big wind**. This dog *was* so funny I bought it.

5) I suggest sharing the previous examples with your students and then writing at least ten paragraphs as a whole class with the children dictating to you as you write on the board or overhead. If possible, ask the children to copy the finished products.

Then, when you feel that students are ready, break up your class into heterogeneous groups of three or four and give them a topic sentence for a paragraph. Each group must choose a "recorder" to write the group-effort paragraph, a "nagger" to keep the group on task, a "strong-verb person" to make suggestions, and a person who has the job to raise his or her hand if the group gets into trouble.

Once each student has a role in his/her group, then, as a group, students write a strong-verb paragraph, using the topic sentence you give them and writing the number of strong-verb sentences you require, a conclusion, and a title. Assign at least five more of these group compositions for practice.

When students in groups show proficiency in the art of strong-verb paragraph writing, they are ready to write the paragraphs on their own. This probably will not occur until the last semester of the second grade. While students write their paragraphs in class, I suggest that you circulate around the room with a big, brightly colored Crayola marker and put checks over correct strong-verb sentences. This has the double advantage of encouraging the children as well as grading the papers during class!

Suggestion #5

Fun writing activities that can be adapted for all three types of writing.

1) Cut out interesting pictures (of *things* and *places*, not people) from magazines, one for each student plus five extra — pictures of different foods; pictures of places such as beaches, forests, mountain scenes; etc.

or

2) Bring in lots of interesting *objects*, one for each student plus five extra — rubber duckies, chickens, and other equally cute rubber or cloth animals (unless your students like revolting rats, spiders, and the like); spatulas; rocks; egg beaters; baskets; interesting refrigerator magnets; dog toys; pieces of bushes; flowers; etc. You get the idea.

or

3) Write some strong, *active verbs in large print*, enough so that you have at least one for each student plus five extra — drive; swim; amble; bark; shout; cry; laugh, etc., any active verb that your students will recognize.

Each student picks one picture, object, or card from the medium you chose to use for the activity. Individually, students examine their choice of the objects, cards, or pictures and write about it. Since you have three categories to choose from and an infinite number of writing ideas (a few are listed below), you can repeat this activity many times during the year, varying the medium and the writing assignment. When you repeat a medium, instruct the children to choose a different picture/object/verb, one they have not written about previously.

Possible Topics to Use with Pictures/Objects/Verb Cards

1) Expository/Clarification —

- Explain why you chose this picture/object/verb.

- Explain what you like about this picture/object/verb.

- Explain some memory that comes to your mind when you see this picture/object/verb.

2) Narrative —

- Write a story about this picture/object/verb.

- Write a story that refers to what is in the picture, includes the object, or uses the verb several times.

- Imagine that this picture/object (you cannot use the verb cards for this one) came alive/ real in your hands right here in the classroom. Write a story about what might happen.

3) Descriptive —

- Describe the picture so that your reader can see it in his or her mind. Describe it from more than one aspect like size, shape, color, background, and so on.

- Describe the object so that your reader can picture it.

- Describe a place or an action about which the verb reminds you so that your reader can picture it very clearly as he/she reads. For example, "skip" might call to mind the play ground where the children skip rope or "munches" might make a student remember a trip to the zoo where the elephant munched on some hay.

Afterwards

When students have completed their compositions, they need to have what Marcia Freeman calls "knee-to-knee conferences" and I call "shoulder-to-shoulder conferences." Two students sit next to each other, practically touching shoulders. Their essays or stories sit on the desks in front of them both. Each pair pours over each other's paper, looking for an example of a skill that you have targeted — good vocabulary, strong verbs, a remembrance, elaboration, great "grabber" and conclusion, a simile, anything *you* want your students to look for and note.

I suggest that at the first-grade level, you have students look for only one thing. Older children can look for two or three things. (Remember those increments that first-to-eighth-grade teacher mentioned.)

Give each child a big, colorful marker or some "paste-em" dots or stars and instruct your students to put a mark with the marker, or paste one of the dots or stars by the targeted skill, every time they find that skill. The author reads the paper aloud to his/her partner while the partner looks on and marks or pastes wherever appropriate.

Marcia assured me that first graders *love* doing this activity. I know my eighth graders certainly do!! Only the increments are different for the different grade levels and ages. Please, if you ever meet any of my eighth graders, do not tell them that they do many activities designed for primary students!

Suggestion #6

Writing about what students know or can see.

1) Descriptive

- Ask them to make a tracing of their hand or foot then describe it from three different angles.

- Suggest that they describe *you* on paper. Instruct them to describe you from three different focal points — color, movement, the whole panorama.

- Instruct students to draw and color a monster on a piece of paper using geometric shapes (squares, circles, rectangles, triangles, ovals — whatever shapes they know). For spelling and copying purposes, put the shapes they can use on the board. Make sure that the children keep their monster a secret and that no one else sees it.

After students have drawn and colored in their monsters, they then *write* a description of the monster on a different sheet of paper. Ask them to describe it from at least two to three focal points — shapes, colors, appendages, etc.

When they are finished with both the drawn monster and its corresponding written description, students give the graphic monster to you, and they keep the written description. Be certain that students put their names on both the drawn monster that they give to you and the written description that they keep. Students then give the written description to a friend. Distribute drawing paper and crayons and instruct the partners to try to draw the monster from the written description. Compare the results with the original drawings. Try again! Students love this activity.

2) Expository/Clarification

- Explain, in gory detail, how to make a peanut-butter sandwich. Instruct them to start with opening the jar, getting the knife and bread, and proceeding from there. When students finish their directions for making the sandwich, you read their descriptions to the class while trying to make the sandwich from the instructions. Be absolutely precise and take all directions literally. For example, if the student does not instruct you to open the jar, try to jab the knife into the closed jar... The results are hilarious. Students then write the instructions again, putting in directions they forgot the first time. Of course, there are other how-to topics besides making peanut-butter sandwiches: how to put on a shirt, how to tie a shoe, and so on.

- Explain how to take out the trash (or any chore the child is assigned at home). Use life at home to generate many how-to expository/clarification essays. For example: Explain how to care for your pet; explain how to tidy up your room.

3) Narrative

- Ask students to write a story about themselves and their families when they do something unusual like ride a bike for the first time or go on a trip, etc.

- Use the classroom and objects in it to generate topics such as: Imagine if the blackboard could talk back. What would it say? What does it see all day?

When the children have completed their compositions, I again suggest "shoulder to shoulder conferences" (see **Suggestion #5**). The partners look for a targeted skill and mark it with a Crayola marker or paste a dot or star near it.

Suggestion #7

Using thematic units to generate topics of interest in the content areas of science and social studies.

Use your social studies and science units and the information in them to generate writing topics. These can be descriptive, expository/clarification, or even narrative. Here are a few examples. I do not know what science and social studies units you teach, but the following ideas may give you food for thought.

1) Expository/Clarification

Science —
- Explain the food chain.
- Explain what you know about sharks.

Social Studies —
- Explain what you know about France.
- Explain how the pilgrims made candles.
- Explain how the first Thanksgiving took place.

Simply use whatever you are currently studying and assign expository/clarification essays on an aspect of that topic, something that asks the children to explain a concept they have learned.

2) Descriptive

> **NOTE:** *Ask students to look at the place or object from three different focal points, like a panorama, color, shape, movement, background, front, back, etc.*

Science —
- Describe a shark so that your reader can picture it.
- Describe an estuary (or whatever is near your school).

Social Studies —
- Describe a pilgrim log cabin from front, back, and inside.
- Describe what the table must have looked like at the first Thanksgiving so that your reader can picture it. What was on the table? Who was sitting at the table? What was around the table?

3) Narrative

Science —
- Tell a story about a fish in an estuary (any animal in the woods, a cockroach in your house, etc.)

Social Studies —
- Imagine you were at the first Thanksgiving, write a story about your experience.
- Imagine you were one of the pioneers. Tell a story about your ride in a covered wagon.

When the children have completed their compositions, I again suggest "shoulder-to-shoulder conferences" (see **Suggestion #5**). The partners look for a targeted skill and mark it with a Crayola marker or paste a dot or star near it.

Suggestion #8

Writing in response journals.

Students (and adults, especially we teachers) should write in a daily journal. At the primary level, I have linked the journals (called response journals) to the daily *Caught'ya* in order to give you time to get around to each child and to accustom students to write in a daily journal at a very young age. Habits like this, begun very early, tend to last into adulthood.

As for the topic of the daily journals, let the subject or a word in the daily *Caught'ya* inspire you and your students. Ask your children to write about a positive thing that happened at home (or school) the previous day. Offer a topic on the board that students can use if they cannot think of one of their own.

The ultimate goal is to have students write for a minimum of ten minutes daily in their response journals on a topic that they choose. They may want to rage about an injustice, brag about a triumph, complain about a sibling, or joyfully tell about a happy experience. When students can think of their own topic without hesitation or long dithering, it really helps them in the third or fourth grade (depending on your state) when they face a topic/prompt which they hate or cannot relate to on the state writing test. Students will know that they easily can come up with details for the prompt since they have done so daily for their own ideas and thus have acquired the confidence to do so. This will keep the third or fourth graders (depending on your state) from "clutching" on the actual day of the test.

Of course, you do not have "shoulder-to-shoulder conferences" for the journal entries. Simply collect the journals at a convenient time for you (or quickly read them silently in class as you walk around for the *Caught'ya*) and write a short, positive comment next to several entries. Ask the student a question that might generate future entries. Enter into a written dialogue with each student. This does not have to be long; a sentence or two will suffice. Students love the personal interaction and can see the value of the written word — to communicate privately!

Suggestion #9

Debunking the great spelling myth.

For years we teachers have taught our students spelling out of a formal speller that comes with twenty or so words for each week plus many exercises that use those words. I have done a lot of research on the subject of spelling for my first book, *Caught'ya! Grammar with a Giggle* (Kiester, 1990). From articles, books, and personal observation after many years of teaching, I have found that people are born good spellers or bad spellers. It is in the genes. It also has little to do with academic ability or intelligence. In fact, unless there is some learning disability, usually the more creative a child is, the worse a speller he/she tends to be.

In other words, throw away those traditional spelling books. They do not work. Those same students who cannot spell "girl" for you in the first grade cannot spell it by eighth grade. Bright students can memorize twenty or so words the night before in order to ace a spelling test on Friday, but the next time they want to write those words in a composition, they continue to misspell them. They have put the spelling words only in their short-term memory. I know this from personal experience since I am a rotten speller who aced every spelling test my teachers gave me.

So, what do we do? I suggest two things. Target the specific words that each child misspells in his/her compositions and have students (or you) make up an individualized spelling list (and this is of utmost importance) of *no more than twenty to thirty words a year*. The students are responsible *only* for the words that *they* misspell consistently in their writing. This kind of spelling makes students sit up and take notice. This list is not a generic one. (Those who can't spell know they can't spell and pay no attention to generic lists.) This list is individual to each child, a wake-up call. "Hey, you, learn these few words this year, add thirty to fifty more next year, and by the time you reach middle school, you might have the basic words down." Students must spell them correctly in their compositions and in the *Caught'ya*s. Few gifted eighth graders can spell "Wednesday" correctly, and this is a "third-grade word".

Although on most state writing tests incorrect spelling does not count heavily against an essay or story unless it interferes with the understanding of the essay or story, for future school and employment, students must know how to spell the core group of words that they use. Some states give two scores on the state writing test, one for content and one for mechanics/spelling.

I also suggest a final method that I just found last year. This is a book that was written by teachers and published by teachers. There are several books for the different levels. The book for the primary level is called *QUICK-WORD Handbook for Beginning Writers* (Sitton and Forest, 1994), and for third grade *QUICK-WORD Handbook for Everyday Writers* (Sitton and Forest,

1994). The phone number for the company (Curriculum Associates, Inc.) is 1-800-225-0248. They will send a complimentary copy to you at your school if you are interested (at least they sent me one when I called). Use the words as you see fit.

Using these books, I suggest giving pre-tests to your students to find the words that each student cannot yet spell. Then, make students responsible *only* for the first twenty or thirty words they misspelled in the book. Teachers can pass on the booklets to the following year's teachers so that they may ask students to learn the next twenty or thirty words, and so on. This is the only method I have ever used that actually teaches students to spell correctly the words they use in their writing.

Conclusion

These nine suggestions will help prepare your students so that your school's average on the state writing test and on those subject-area tests that require writing will soar. Writing in general will improve, and students will think of writing as fun, not drudgery.

APPENDIX

Everything You Never Wanted to Know about *Grammar, Mechanics, and Usage* But I'm Going to Tell You Anyway

Introductory Notes

Those of us who are familiar with some topic or idea sometimes forget that not everyone else has the same knowledge. This is why I included this Appendix. Unless you have taught English for a year at eighth-grade level or higher, unless you have had a teacher somewhere along the way who has successfully taught you all the terms, or unless you have studied a grammar book from cover to cover and have kept up with all the changes, there is no way that you can know the rules of English grammar and usage and its many technical terms.

Complex as the language is, even we English teachers have trouble with some of the picky mechanical points of the language. We also disagree!

English is a fluid language. It changes with use. Thirty years ago we strewed commas with near abandon. Now we are eliminating many of them. People begin sentences with conjunctions. I have real trouble with this. Conjunctions are for joining ideas, not starting them. What teachers once called a dependent clause is now lumped under the heading of subordinate clause, and so on. Because of this, we all do not follow identical rules and terms, yet all of us still can be officially correct at the same time.

Do not be afraid to disagree with me. Many points of mechanics, especially the use of some commas, are highly debatable, extremely personal, and sometimes linked to a particular generation. When I participated in writing the English curriculum for the middle schools in my county, seven English teachers sat around a table and argued various points. Each of us always could find a book that would support a specific opinion. After a few hot debates, we finally had to agree to use one standard book for reference.

When Maupin House asked me to include a section that could serve as a reference for the grammar, mechanics, and usage terms, frankly, I was apprehensive. It seemed to be a dangerous task for one person to attempt. Grammar books are usually written by committees and still have errors in them. I solicited the help of my mother and several of my colleagues, all excellent grammarians, to ensure accuracy.

Do not feel inadequate or undereducated if you find yourself frequently referring to this Appendix. Many of you, like me, probably did not major in English in college and do not read grammar textbooks for pleasure. This **Appendix** will help you understand the whys and wherefores of a sentence so that you can explain it to your children in a way that makes sense to them. Once students understand the underlying concept of a rule, they can apply that rule to their own sentences when they write.

The terms are listed in alphabetical order for easier reference. If you do not fully understand a term used in one explanation, you can look it up under its own heading. All the terms that a non-English major might need for clarity are cross-referenced. Also included in the **Appendix** are some tips for teaching some of these concepts. I hope you find these suggestions useful. All of these teaching tips have proven successful with students.

Examples are included for each concept. If, after reading the explanation of a concept, you still do not feel comfortable with it, study the examples. Right here, I feel the need to apologize for the truly uninspired examples. The majority of them concern my dogs and cats. They are always present when I write, like furry muses.

While I am aware that the current trend is to abandon the teaching of certain concepts and terms such as the parts of speech, as a foreign language teacher I know that students need to be familiar with these terms to learn the new language. If a student is aware of the difference, for example, between a subject pronoun and an object pronoun, then French pronouns do not hold much horror.

In my French classes, I often find myself having to teach the parts of speech just so my students and I can have a common frame of reference. It is hard enough to learn a different vocabulary in another language. If, in addition, students have to learn basic grammar terms as well, it makes the task much more difficult. The grammar of languages based on Indo-European is basically similar. The verb may come at the end of a sentence in German or at the end of a subordinate clause in Dutch, or there may be an extra verb tense to learn in Spanish and French. The basic concepts and parts of speech, however, are the same in all these languages.

I believe, too, in the teaching of sentence diagramming to help students to think and to use logic. Diagramming reaches some left-brain students who otherwise might never understand sentence structure.

After teaching rudimentary sentence diagramming through the Caught'yas, I almost can see the light bulb go on in some students' eyes. I do not believe, however, in teaching all the picky points of English like infinitive phrases, gerund phrases, etc. unless there is a reason for learning them, like learning the appropriate placement of commas.

Even then, when teaching the picky points is unavoidable, I advise trying to avoid using the abstruse, esoteric grammar terms. Instead, explain these points in simpler terms, using the eight parts of speech for reference. I don't say to students, for example, "If a participial phrase begins or interrupts a sentence, you need to set it off by commas. You need to know that a participial phrase is . . . " Even after you explain what a participial phrase is, your students probably are gazing out the window, minds elsewhere.

Try something like this instead. "See this phrase. What part of speech is it? An adjective? Right! You know the parts of speech! Well, look at it. It contains a form of a verb. If you see a group of words like this at the beginning of a sentence or in the middle of a sentence, you need to put commas after it or around it." That gets their attention because it is something that makes sense to them. I do mention the words "participial phrase" so that students may recognize the term in the future in case other English teachers use it, but I stress the concept and not the specific term.

Other examples: instead of talking about "gerunds," you can teach your students to use a verb or a verb phrase as a noun. In teaching verbs like "lie" and "lay," "sit" and "set," and "rise" and "raise," a teacher can explain the use of each verb by talking about verbs that take direct objects and verbs that do not, instead of introducing new labels "transitive" and "intransitive."

Basically, the bottom line is to write correctly, not to memorize the names for everything or to identify certain phrases or clauses. When a student writes a sentence, the labels are useless. The task of English teachers is not to teach rules and technical terms, but to teach correct writing and editing skills.

Those of you who teach basic skills classes or younger children will want to avoid the more complicated concepts anyway. Use your own judgement as to how much your students can comprehend and transfer to their writing. Each class is different. Each group has different needs. You know them best.

If you are writing your own sentences, you will want to keep this book open to the **Appendix** as you write. Make certain that you include in your story the grammar, mechanics, and usage that you know your students can grasp comfortably. The list is comprehensive so that this book can be used at any level. I hope that all of you find this **Appendix** a useful tool in teaching this beautiful language of ours.

Abbreviations

Most abbreviations are followed by a period.

Examples: Mr., Mrs.

If, however, all the letters of the abbreviation are capitals, a period is not used.

Examples: NATO, USSR, USA

Usually abbreviations begin with a capital letter. Abbreviations of units of measure, however, do not begin with capital letters. They also do not require periods. The only exception is the abbreviation for inch.

Examples: mph, hp, l, km, and so on.

Exception: in.

Common abbreviations: Mr., Mrs., Ms., Dr., St., Rd., Ave., Co., Inc., days of the week, months of the year, A.M., P.M., O.K.,etc.

State abbreviations: The United States Postal Service now uses special abbreviations for each state. These are always two letters, both capitalized, without any periods. The postal code of twenty-nine states is the first two letters of the state. If the state has two words, the first letter of each word is used.

States that follow this rule: AL, AR, CA, CO, DE, FL, ID, IL, IN, MA, MI, NE, NH, NJ, NM, NY, NC, ND, OH, OK, OR, RI, SC, SD, UT, WA, WV, WI, and WY

Exceptions: Alaska (AK), Arizona (AZ), Connecticut (CT), Georgia (GA), Hawaii (HI), Iowa (IA), Kansas (KS), Kentucky (KY), Louisiana (LA), Maine (ME), Maryland (MD), Minnesota (MN), Mississippi (MS), Missouri (MO), Montana (MT), Nevada (NV), Pennsylvania (PA), Tennessee (TN), Texas (TX), Vermont (VT), and Virginia (VA).

Accept/Except

These two words often are confusing for students since they are so close in sound. Every time one of them appears in a Caught'ya, you can explain the difference.

1. Accept is a verb that means "to receive willingly."

Example: The fat Rottweiler surely **will accept** the bone.

2. Except is a preposition that means "excluding" or "other than." It also can be used as a verb that means "to leave out" or "exclude."

Examples: The fat Rottweiler eats everything **except** onions. (preposition)

The fire department will **except** men over seventy-two inches from that kind of duty. (verb)

Active vs Passive Verb Voices

1. **Active**: In the active voice, the subject does the action. Active voice is always better for more effective writing.

Example: The owner **pets** the happy dog on the head.

2. **Passive**: In the passive voice, the subject **receives** the action. Encourage students to try to avoid passive voice if at all possible. It weakens writing and often muddies the meaning in a sentence.

Example: The happy dog **was petted** on the head by the owner.

Adjective

An adjective describes a noun; it gives information about a noun.

Examples: ugly, pretty, big, little, this, four

An adjective answers one of the following three questions about a noun:

1) which one?

2) what kind?

3) how many?

Example: **The amazing English** teacher taught **two** grade levels. (which teacher? **the English** teacher; what kind of teacher? an **amazing** teacher; how many grade levels? **two** grade levels.)

Adjective Clauses

An adjective clause is any subordinate clause (a complete sentence made into an incomplete sentence by the addition of a subordinating conjunction) that acts as an adjective in a sentence.

Example: The house **where she lives** is filled with animals. ("She lives." would be a complete sentence without the addition of "where." "Where she lives" modifies the noun "house.")

Adjective clauses also can begin with a relative pronoun: who, whom, whose, which, that, where, or when.

Examples: The oven **which was small and dirty** could not be used.

This is the school **where my child is a student**.

The school **that my child attends** is a good one.

The teacher **who loves to laugh** has more fun.

Monday is the day **when we always write in our journals**.

The teacher **whom we admire** is retiring.

Jane Kiester, **whose dogs are obese**, teaches middle school.

Adverb

An adverb is any word, phrase or clause that tells more about a verb; many of the single word adverbs end in "ly."

An adverb also tells to what extent an adjective or another adverb is true (very, extremely, and so on). This is called an intensifier.

Examples: a **very** hungry dog, an **extremely** sleepy cat

An adverb answers one of the following six questions about a verb, an adjective, or another adverb: where, when, why, how, how often, or to what extent it happened.

Examples: Where? The students learned grammar **at home**. (phrase)

When? **Yesterday** the teacher was absent.

How? The students **quickly** intimidated the substitute.

How often? The student yawned **four times** during class. (phrase)

To what extent? The teacher was **very** angry. (modifies the adjective "angry")

Why? She yelled **because she was angry**. (clause)

Adverb Clauses

In the "olden days," an adverb clause was called an adverbial clause.

An adverb (or adverbial) clause is a subordinate clause that cannot stand on its own in a sentence. It acts as an adverb in a sentence.

Adverb clauses begin with a subordinating conjunction (see list under "Subordinating Conjunctions")

Examples: **Whenever the teacher taught grammar,** the students groaned. (When did the students groan? "Whenever the teacher . . .")

The students went home **when the last bell rang**. (When did the students go home? "when the bell rang.")

Affect/Effect

"Affect" and "effect" are two more words that many people confuse. If students have trouble with the correct use of these two words, use them in the Caught'yas and discuss their meanings.

1. Affect is a verb that means "to influence." It cannot be used as a noun.

Example: The eating habits of the fat Rottweiler will **affect** her girth.

2. Effect can be a noun or a verb. As a noun it means "the result of an action." As a verb it means "to cause to happen."

Examples: The **effect** of overeating is obvious in the width of the dog's belly. (noun)

The fat dog's owner **will effect** a new rule this week — no more scraps. (verb)

Agreement

1. **Antecedent and pronoun**: It is important that everything agrees in a sentence. If the subject is singular, then the pronoun used later in the sentence also must be singular. If the subject is plural, the pronoun should be plural.

Example of incorrect agreement: **Everyone** ate **their** pizza. (The indefinite pronoun "everyone" is singular and thus the possessive pronoun which refers to it also must be singular.

Examples of correct agreement: **Everyone** ate **his** or **her** pizza.

Each finished **his** or **her** lunch.

The **teachers** ate **their** lunch.

The **teacher** ate **his** lunch.

2. **Subject and verb**: If the subject is singular, then the verb must also be singular. If the subject is plural, then the verb must be plural.

Examples: The **dog bays** at the full moon. (singular)

The **dogs bay** at the full moon. (plural)

3. **Verbs in a story**: When writing a story an author must keep all the verbs in the same tense. If the story starts in the present tense, it must continue in the present tense (unless, of course, there is a flashback or a reference to something general). If a story begins in the past, it must remain in the past, and so on.

Among and Between

"Among" and "between" are two prepositions that students often confuse, but they cease to be a problem very quickly after you point out the difference.

1. **Between** refers to two people, things, or groups.

Example: The cat slept **between** the two huge dogs.

2. **Among** refers to more than two people, things, or groups.

Example: The foolish cat slept **among** the four dogs.

Antecedents (*See also* Collective Nouns)

These are the words that come before a given word in a sentence, as in "antecedent/pronoun agreement," and are referred to by the given word. Thus, they must agree with each other. If one is singular, the other also must be singular, etc.

Example: The **pack** (antecedent) of dogs forsook **its** (pronoun) mistress. ("Pack" is singular and thus must be followed by a singular pronoun.)

Apostrophes

1. Contractions always contain apostrophes. A contraction comprises two words that are combined into one by omitting one or more letters. (*See* Contractions for more information and examples.)

Common contractions: I'm, I've, can't, don't, haven't, isn't, it's, let's, they're, we're, we've, won't, you're

2. **Possessive nouns** always contain apostrophes. A possessive noun is a noun that shows ownership of something.

Singular: Always add 's to the noun.

Examples: The **dog's** growl is ferocious. (The growl belongs to the dog.)

The **glass's** rim is dirty. (The rim belongs to the glass.)

Plural: Add ' after the noun if the noun ends in "s."

Add 's to the noun if the plural does not end in "s."

Examples: The **dogs'** growls are ferocious. (Several dogs "own" their growls.)

The **children's** laughter fills the room. (Several children "own" the laughter.

3. **Plurals of letters**: Form the plural of single letters by adding apostrophe "s."

Examples: You will find more "**E's**" in words than any other letter.

She received all "**A's**" on her report card.

Appositive

An appositive is a noun or a noun phrase that means the same thing as the noun that comes before it.

Appositives are set off by commas if they occur in the middle or end of a sentence and are not necessary to the meaning of the sentence.

Examples: Dino, **the Doberman with the floppy ears**, loves to eat bananas.

The dog who craves bananas is Dino, **the Doberman with the floppy ears**.

Appositives are set off by commas if the appositive is extra information and is not needed to complete the meaning of the sentence.

Examples: Jane Kiester, **an English teacher at Westwood**, loves dogs.

Always by her side are her two dogs, **a wimpy Rottweiler and an oversized Doberman**.

Appositives are not set off by commas if the information given is needed to identify the noun.

Example: Mrs. Kiester's son **John** loves to tease his mother.

(There are no commas to set off this appositive because Mrs. Kiester has more than one son. The name is necessary to determine to which son the sentence refers. Technically, this is called a restrictive modifier. If Mrs. Kiester has only one son, the comma is needed because the information is *not* necessary. This is called a non-restrictive modifier.)

(*See* Modifiers and Misplaced Modifiers for more information and examples of restrictive and non-restrictive appositives.)

Articles

These are simply the three most commonly used adjectives. They are also called noun markers since they signal the arrival of a noun.

List of articles: a, an, the

1. Use "a" before a word that begins with a consonant.

Example: There is a lazy dog and a sleepy cat on the floor.

2. Use "an" before a word that begins with a vowel.

Example: **An** obnoxious black and white cat howled until someone let him out the door.

These three adjectives answer the question "which one?" (*See* Noun Markers.)

Bad and Badly

These words often cause confusion. "Bad" is the adjective and should modify a noun. "Badly" is the adverb and should tell about a verb.

Examples: The **bad** dog begged for forgiveness. (adjective tells what kind of dog)

The poor dog **badly** wanted a bone. (adverb tells to what extent it wanted the bone)

When a sense verb such as "feel" functions as a verb of being, it is often followed by a predicate adjective. Thus, one would use the adjective form after such a verb.

Example: I feel **bad**. (Not "I feel badly," since one would not say "I am badly.")

Because and Since

If you never put a comma before "because" and "since," you will be right 98 percent of the time. While there are some exceptions to this, they are rare. The words "because" and "since" begin adverb clauses. An adverb clause that begins a sentence needs a comma, but an adverb clause that follows the independent clause usually does not need a comma. Saying the sentence aloud is a good test.

About the only exceptions to this would be with a quotation or in a series, in the case of "since" acting as a coordinating conjunction in a compound sentence, or in one of the few subordinate clauses that takes a comma for clarity.

Examples: **Because I like books about cats**, I read *The Literary Cat*. (adverb clause at the beginning of the sentence)

I read *The Literary Cat* **because I like books about cats**. (adverb clause that follows the independent clause)

Between (*See* Among and Between)

Bibliographical Forms

These do vary. Use the Modern Language Association form, and you will be safe. Most traditional grammar books have a large list explaining how to write any reference you may need in correct bibliographical form. Just make sure that you insist that students list the books, articles, etc. in their bibliographies in alphabetical order.

Business Letters (Correct Format)

Sender's address
Sender's city, state   zip
Date

Receiver's name
Receiver's address
Receiver's city, state   zip

Dear Sir or Madam:

The bulk of the letter should be written in block style, skipping lines between paragraphs.

Sincerely yours,
Write name here in cursive.
Print or type name here.

Capitalization

Capitalize the following:

1. Abbreviations (*See* Abbreviations for the exceptions.)

2. Beginnings of sentences

3. First word in the greeting and closing of a letter

4. I

5. Names of months and days and holidays

6. Proper nouns and proper adjectives

7. Titles of long works (*see* Titles)

   - Capitalize first and last words.

   - Capitalize all other words in title except prepositions, noun markers (a, an, the), and short conjunctions.

Chronological Order

In writing stories and paragraphs, it is important to narrate the action in a logical order. Chronological order maintains a sequence of time.

Clauses and Phrases

1. **Phrase**: Simply stated, a phrase is a group of words that serves as one part of speech (like a noun or an adjective or an adverb). It lacks a subject or a verb or both. Prepositional phrases are the most common. These are phrases that begin with a preposition and end with a noun (in the dog house).

Examples: in the dog house, to the store, filled with anger, rubbing his ears

2. **Clause**: A clause, on the other hand, is a group of words that contains a subject and a verb. With the removal of a subordinating conjunction that begins it, it could stand on its own as a sentence.

Example: because the dog is lazy (The subject is the word "dog." The verb is the word "is.")

Collective Nouns

Collective nouns are nouns that take a group of something (many) and make that group one thing.

Common collective nouns: crew, class, orchestra, chorus, committee, family, flock, herd, fleet, jury, group, team, majority.

1. Most collective nouns are singular and therefore require the singular form of the verb. Also, any pronoun that refers to such a collective noun must be singular.

Examples: A **flock** of big birds **flies** over her house every autumn. ("Fly" would be the plural form of the verb)

The **group** applauded its leader. "Its" is the singular pronoun; "their" is the plural pronoun and thus is incorrect. This is one of the most common mistakes that people make in speech and in writing.

The girl's **family** took **its** vacation in June.

2. A few collective nouns are plural.

Example: The **people** took **their** dogs to the veterinarian.

Colons

1. Use a colon before a list but never after a verb or a preposition.

Example: It is important to remember to bring the following to class: pencil, paper, and a big grin.

2. Use after the greeting in a business letter.

Examples: Dear Sir or Madam:

To Whom It May Concern:

3. Use a colon to separate the hour from the minute in telling time.

Examples: 5:45 P.M., 6:24 A.M.

4. If the wording that follows a colon forms a complete sentence, do not capitalize the first letter of the sentence.

Example: The question is as follows: do Dobermans like to eat broccoli?

Combining Sentences for Clearer, More Concise Writing

Combine two related sentences into one by making a compound subject and/or a compound verb or by adding an appositive. There are other ways to combine sentences. These are the most common.

Example: Change "The teacher hated spelling. Her students hated spelling." to "The teacher and her students hated spelling." (compound subject).

Change "The Rottweiler loved to sleep. She liked to lick her owner's face in the morning." (compound verb) to "The Rottweiler loved to sleep and liked to lick her owner's face in the morning."

Change "The Doberman had floppy ears. He also had a sweet disposition." to "The Doberman, who had floppy ears, had a sweet disposition." (adding an adjective clause)

Comma Rules

1. Use commas to separate items in a series. There are many different kinds of series, one for each part of speech except conjunctions.

Examples: The teacher **entered** the class, **wrote** on the board, and **sat** down at her desk. (verb series)

The teacher ate **apples, bananas, and cherries**. (noun series)

The **nice, kind**, and **beautiful** teacher assigned no homework for the weekend. (adjective series)

The teacher sat down **quickly, quietly,** and **with great dignity**. (adverb series)

He went **to the store, down the aisle**, and **into the vegetable section**. (prepositional phrase series)

She sat with **him, her**, and **them**. (series of pronouns)

Oh boy, wow, and **whoopee**, the teacher had a great class! (series of interjections)

You also can have a series of predicate nouns and adjectives. (These are just nouns and adjectives that are located after the predicate.)

2. Use commas between two or more adjectives that precede a noun unless one of the adjectives expresses a single idea with the noun (jet plane) or the last adjective tells color (green, etc.) or age (old, young).

Comma needed: The **cute, fuzzy** dog barked at everyone.

Comma omitted: The **cute brown** dog barked at everyone. (color adjective)

The **noisy jet** plane flew overhead. ("Jet plane" is one idea. The adjective is really part of the noun.)

The **ugly young** dog wolfed down its food. (age adjective).

The general "rule of thumb" in this comma rule is to use a comma if it sounds right to use the word "and" instead of a comma.

Examples: The old oaken bucket was covered with wet green moss. (No commas needed as it would be awkward to say "The old and oaken bucket was covered with wet and green moss.")

The **floppy-eared, lazy** Doberman slept all day. (Here you use a comma because it makes sense to say "The floppy-eared and lazy Doberman slept all day.")

3. Use commas to separate the simple sentences included in a compound sentence. (See Compound Sentences)

Example: The teacher wrote the sentence, and she put in a comma because the sentence was compound.

4. Use commas after words, phrases, and clauses that come at the beginning of sentences. "No" and "yes" are included here. They always are followed by a comma.

Examples: **No**, you may not turn in your homework late.

Yes, you may do extra work if you wish.

Wow, the student earned an A+ on his test!

At the end of the phrase, there should be a comma.

If a subordinate clause is at the beginning of a sentence, you have to put a comma after it.

Suddenly, the teacher yelled. (This comma is often debated. Put a comma if a breath or a pause would help clarify the sentence or if you want to accentuate the adverb.)

Well, she said that she would come.

5. Use commas to separate interrupters such as parenthetical expressions, direct addresses, and unnecessary appositives in a sentence.

Examples: Parenthetical expression — The big dog, **of course**, was a wimp.

Direct address: You know, **parents**, it is important to write correctly.

Parents, you know it is important to write correctly.

Unnecessary appositive: My cat, **Skeeter**, likes to sit on my lap as I write. (I have only one cat; therefore his name is not necessary for the meaning of the sentence to be clear.)

My dog Dino has floppy ears. (No commas are needed because I have two dogs, and I need to identify to which dog I refer.)

6. Use commas to separate the month and the day from the year.

Example: September 15, 1945

7. Use commas between the city and the state and after the state as well if the address is within the sentence.

Example: The animal lover lives in **Gainesville, Florida**, and teaches English at a middle school.

8. Use commas after the greeting in friendly letters and after the closing in both friendly and business letters.

Examples: Dear Jane,

Sincerely yours,

9. Use commas with quotation marks to set off what is being said out loud.

Examples: "Get off my foot," she whimpered to the heavy dog.

She whimpered to the heavy dog, "Get off my foot."

"If you don't get off my foot," she said, "I'll step on yours."

Comparisons

Adjectives

1. If you are comparing two or more things and the adjective has fewer than three syllables, add "er" to the adjective.

Example: Florida is **warmer** than Maine in the winter.

2. If you are stating that something is the best (or worst), add "est" to the adjective if it has fewer than three syllables.

Example: Florida is the **warmest** state in the union.

3. Using "more" and "most"

Adjectives of three or more syllables almost always use the words more" or "the most" to state comparison.

Examples: The Rottweiler is **more obnoxious** than the Doberman.

The black and white cat is **the most obnoxious** of all of the animals in her menagerie.

4. When comparing persons or things in the same group, use the word "other."

Example: Jesse can run faster than **any other** boy in his club.

A few adjectives with irregular forms of comparison must be memorized: good-better-best; bad-worse-worst; many, much-more-most; little (quantity only)-less-least; far-farther-farthest.

Adverbs

1. If you are comparing two things, add "er" to the adverb. If you are saying that something is done better than anything else, add "est" to the adverb.

Examples: Planes travel faster than cars.

Rockets travel fastest of all.

2. Using "more" and "most"

There is no steadfast rule as to when you add "er" or "est" or when you use "more" or "most." The best suggestion I can make is to go with what sounds correct. Most adverbs of two or more syllables form comparisons with "more" or "most."

Example: comprehensively, more comprehensively, most comprehensively

Complex Sentences (*See* also Subordinate Clauses)

A complex sentence is a sentence that has one or more independent clauses (a group of words that makes sense by itself) and a subordinate clause (a group of words with a subject and a verb but which does not make sense by itself).

The important thing to remember about a complex sentence is that if the subordinate clause begins the sentence, a comma must follow it.

Example: Although the dog sat on her foot, she did not say a word. (subordinate clause, independent clause)

Compound Sentences

A compound sentence is composed of two complete sentences (related ideas only) joined together with a comma and a coordinating conjunction (and, or, nor, for, so, but, yet) or a semicolon.

Examples: The big dog sat on her foot, **and** she gazed up at her mistress with love. "The big dog sat on her foot" is a complete sentence. "She gazed up at her mistress with love" is a sentence.

I tell my students to put their finger over the coordinating conjunction and check whether there is a complete sentence on either side of the finger. If there are two sentences, a comma has to precede the conjunction because the sentence is compound.

Examples: The big dog licked his paw, **or** he licked his leg.

The big dog did not lick his paw, **nor** did he lick his leg.

The big dog sat on her foot, **for** he loved her.

The big dog ate too much, **so** he was rotund.

The big dog sat on her foot, **but** he didn't put his full weight on it.

The big dog sat on her foot, **yet** he still felt insecure.

Sometimes a compound sentence does not have a coordinating conjunction joining the two sentences. Instead, it has a semicolon.

Example: The big dog sat on her foot; it then licked her knee.

A compound sentence does not occur when the word "that" is included or implied after the word "so." "So that" is a subordinating conjunction of a subordinate clause. If a subordinate clause comes at the end of a sentence, there is no comma.

Examples: She grabbed the bone **so that** the other dog could not get it. ("**So that**" the other dog could not get it, she grabbed the bone.)

She gobbled her food **so** the other dog could not get it. ("That" is implied)

A compound imperative sentence **does not** take a comma because the subjects, while implied, are not stated.

Examples: Get off my feet and go lie down elsewhere. (to the dog)

Stop clawing my legs and settle down. (to the cat)

Compound Subjects and Compound Predicates

These should be recognized if only to ensure that the students know the meanings of the words "compound," "subject," and "predicate." These words appear on the standardized tests. I usually teach these in my diagramming unit. Diagramming makes compound subjects and predicates much clearer.

1. A compound subject is simply more than one thing or person doing the action.

Example: **Rottweilers** and **Dobermans** make wonderful pets.

2. A compound predicate is more than one verb supplying the action.

Example: Rottweilers **love** to eat and **enjoy** being petted.

Conjunctions

A conjunction is a word that joins words or groups of words together. Do not capitalize a conjunction in a title.

Example: The dog **and** the cat are friends.

1. **Coordinating conjunctions**: These are the conjunctions (joiners) which join two complete thoughts (independent clauses) together to form a compound sentence.

List of coordinating conjunctions: **f**or, **a**nd, **n**or, **b**ut, **o**r, **y**et, **s**o. I call these FANBOYS.

It is a good idea to chant these with your students every time you encounter a compound sentence in a Caught'ya.

Example: She loves ice cream, **and** she loves candy, too.

Do not begin a sentence with a coordinating conjunction since they are supposed to join, not begin. Many authors of fiction ignore this rule. This is fine, and it can make for very effective writing. I have to enforce this rule with those students who begin almost every sentence with a conjunction.

2. **Correlative conjunctions**: These are used to join words or word groups. They appear in pairs.

Examples: **Either** you do your homework, **or** your grade will suffer.

Both Dobermans **and** Rottweilers make good companions.

List of correlative conjunctions: either/or, neither/nor, not only/but, both/and, just as/so.

3. **Subordinating conjunctions**: These conjunctions make a clause that was a complete sentence into a clause that cannot stand on its own. In other words, if a subordinating conjunction is placed before an independent clause (complete sentence), the clause becomes a dependent clause (subordinate clause).

Complete sentence: The dog licks the rug.

Dependent clause: **When** the dog licks the rug (no longer a complete sentence)

Subordinating conjunctions begin subordinate clauses. Always set off an intro-ductory adverb clause (another word for a subordinate clause since subordinate clauses act as adverbs) with a comma.

Examples: **After the cat fell asleep**, he twitched his whiskers.

As the man shouted, the two dogs cringed.

Common subordinating conjunctions: after, although, as, as if, as long as, as soon as, as though, because, before, even though, if, in order that, provided that, since, so that, than, till, unless, until, when, whenever, where, whereas, wherever, while.

To make it easier for students to learn the subordinating conjunctions, I call them "White Bus" words, and we memorize them. **A**fter, although, as, **W**hen, while, where, **H**ow, **I**f, **T**han, **E**ven though, **B**ecause, before, **U**ntil unless, **S**ince, so that

Continued Quote

This is a sentence in a quote that is interrupted by identifying the speaker. It is important to recognize that when the quoted sentence continues, quotation marks are necessary, but the first letter should not be capitalized. This is also called an interrupted quote.

Example: "My Doberman is a lazy dog," she said, "but my Rottweiler is even lazier."

Contractions

A contraction is a word made by the shortening of two words into one, eliminating some letters in the process. The two words are then joined by an apostrophe.

1. Contractions can be made by shortening "not" to "n't" and adding to a verb. Sometimes the spelling of the verb changes as when "n't" is added to "shall," "will," or "can."

Examples: is not/isn't; does not/doesn't; cannot/can't; shall not/shan't; will not/won't.

2. It's and its

"Its" is a possessive pronoun that shows that "it" owns something.

Example: The dog ate **its** food.

"It's" is a contraction for "it is."

Example: **It's** a shame that she has so many animals to feed.

3. Contractions are also formed by joining nouns or pronouns with verbs.

Examples: I am/I'm; he is/he's; he had/he'd; you are/you're; she has/she's, let us/let's, they are/they're.

Avoid contractions in formal writing. Contractions render writing informal, and unless a writer is using dialogue or a truly informal style, the use of contractions probably should be avoided.

Dangling Participle

A dangling participle is a participle (present or past form of a verb) used as an adjective that is not adjacent to the noun that it modifies. Dangling participles should be avoided.

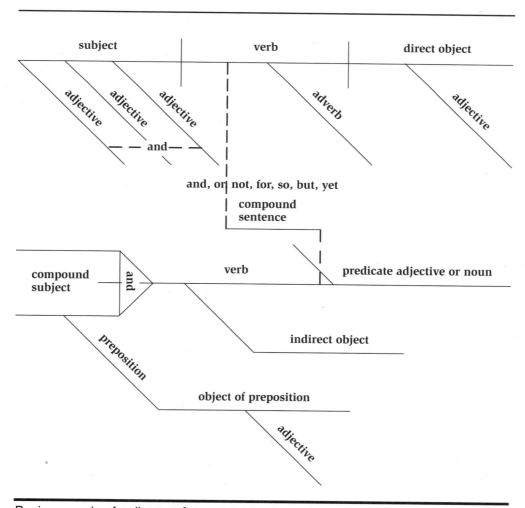

Basic example of a diagram for a compound sentence

Example: **Snoring, the dog's nose** twitched. (The dog's nose did not do the snoring, the dog did. The word "dog" needs to follow the participle "snoring.")

Snoring, the dog twitched his nose.

Dashes   A dash can be used to show a break or a shift in thought or structure. It also can signal an afterthought.

Examples: Now, when I was a boy — (break)

I found her most — well, I didn't like her manner. (shift in structure)

The big Doberman — the one with the floppy ears — leans against walls and people. (break)

My floppy-eared Doberman often leans — you know, all Dobermans lean like that. (shift in thought)

It is important to limit the use of dashes when writing. Too many dashes make the writing seem confused and jerky.

Diagramming Sentences

Sentence diagramming takes every word in a sentence and places it, according to its use, in a diagram-like chart. It is a graphic picture of a sentence. Diagramming sentences is a good skill for students to learn because it forces them to think logically. Diagramming sentences also teaches students good puzzle-solving techniques and makes them practice their knowledge of the eight parts of speech.

If you want students to diagram a few Caught'yas for practice, look at the section on diagramming sentences in any traditional grammar text.

The example shows how a diagram works for a compound sentence.

Dialogues

Begin a new paragraph every time a different person speaks. If a person's speech includes more than one paragraph at a time, do not put quotation marks at the end of the first paragraph. Begin the next paragraph with quotation marks.

Example: (end of paragraph) " . . . and the teacher is always there."

(new paragraph) "Students, on the other hand . . . "

Punctuation of quotes: Put quotation marks around what is said aloud. Capitalize the first letter of a quote unless the quote is a continued one. Set off the quote by commas or by end punctuation. Always put all punctuation inside the quotation marks.

Examples: "Close the window, you outdoor fanatic," she whimpered. "I'm freezing in here."

"Please close the window," she said, "or I'll become an icicle."

She pleaded again, "Close that window."

"Will you please close the window?" she asked.

"Close that window!" she yelled.

Direct Address

A direct address occurs when the writer is speaking directly to someone, telling someone something, and naming that someone.

Direct addresses also are called interrupters because they interrupt the flow of a sentence. Always set a direct address off by commas.

Examples: **Dog**, get off my foot. (talking to the dog)

If you don't get off my foot, **dog**, you are in big trouble.

Get off my foot, dog.

Direct and Indirect Objects

1. **Direct objects** are nouns or pronouns that directly receive the action of the verb. They, therefore, follow only transitive verbs. Direct objects answer the question "whom" or "what" receives the action of the verb.

Examples: The dog licked the **teacher**. ("teacher" answers the question "whom")

Students should do all their **homework**. ("homework" answers the question "what")

The dog licked **me**. (whom)

2. **Indirect objects** are nouns or pronouns that indirectly receive the action. The action happens to them or for them, but the indirect object does not receive the action. This is an important concept to learn if anyone wants to learn a second language. Indirect objects follow only transitive verbs. You must have a direct object before you can have an indirect object. An indirect object answers the questions "to whom" or "for whom" the action is done. (In English, "to" usually is implied for an indirect object, making it more difficult to identify.)

Examples: The teacher gave [to] **the children** (indirect object) **a short homework assignment**. (direct object)

The dog gave [to] **me** (indirect object) **his paw**. (direct object)

End Marks (Punctuation)

Make sure each sentence has one!

1. Use a period at the end of a statement (a sentence that tells something).

Example: Dobermans can be sweet dogs.

2. Use an exclamation mark at the end of a sentence that expresses powerful emotion or strong feeling. You also can use an exclamation mark after an interjection of strong emotion so that the interjection stands all by itself.

Examples: Get out of here!

Wow! I really like that.

3. Use a question mark at the end of an interrogative sentence (a sentence that asks a question).

Example: Will you please get out of here?

Except (*See* Accept/Except)

EXCLAMATION MARKS (*See* End Marks)

Extraneous Capital Letters

Make sure that students eliminate them. Some students throw capital letters around in their writing without any rhyme or reason. If any students do this, put a stop to it.

Farther/Further

These two words are sometimes used incorrectly, but it is really very easy to tell the difference between the two and, therefore, an easy mistake to correct. **Farther** talks about physical distance. **Further** talks about everything else.

Examples: Mark can throw a ball **farther** than Jesse can.

We will discuss this **further** after dinner.

Fewer and Less

Few, fewer, and fewest should be used with things that can be counted. Little, less, and least should be used with things that cannot be counted.

Examples: **Fewer** students are interested in literature these days. (You can count students.)

I have **less** interest in Poodles than I do in Dobermans. (You cannot count an abstract concept like interest.)

Finding and Identifying

It is extremely important that students be able to find and identify the following:

1. **Eight parts of speech**: Noun, verb, adjective, adverb, conjunction, interjection, preposition, pronoun. (*See* each part of speech under its own heading.)

2. **Predicates**

Simple — The main verb or the main verb with a helping verb

Complete — the verb and its complements or modifiers (adverbs, adverb phrases).

3. **Subjects**

Simple — the noun or pronoun that does the action

Complete — the noun or pronoun that does the action and its modifiers (adjectives, adjective phrases)

4. **Synonyms for better writing**

Encourage students to use in their writing the vocabulary words of the *Caught'yas* and encourage them to use a thesaurus when they write.

Footnotes

Today, when a quote is used or referred to in the body of a paper, the trend is to list such a source in the bibliography rather than in footnotes or endnotes (footnotes at the end of a paper). The quote or reference in the text is followed by parentheses containing the author's name and the date of publication. When an author has published two sources within one year, list the title also.

Example: The section on footnotes in Kiester's book says that the trend is not to have footnotes or endnotes in a paper. **(Kiester, 1992)**

Fragments

A sentence fragment is an incomplete thought (either lacking in subject or verb) that is used and punctuated incorrectly as a complete sentence. This is an egregious error. Help students overcome this habit. If students write fragments, then they probably don't understand what a subject and verb are. Frame your discussions accordingly.

Examples: A rather chubby dog on the floor. (no verb)

Slept on the floor by her side. (no subject)

Sticking his paws into the air. (no verb or subject)

Friendly Letters (Correct Format)

> Sender's address
> Sender's city, state   zip
> Date

Dear Jane,

   The bulk of the letter goes here written without skipping lines between paragraphs.

> With love,
> Sign name here

Further (*See* Farther and Further)

Gerund

A gerund is a verb form that ends in "ing" and is used as a noun. A gerund can be used in any way that a noun can be used. Sometimes a gerund serves as the simple subject, direct object, or as the object of a preposition.

Examples: **Snorkeling** is my favorite sport. (subject)

I like **snorkeling**. (direct object)

I think of **snorkeling** a lot when I daydream. (object of the preposition)

Gerund Phrases

Depending on your point of view, gerund phrases are either fun or useless to learn. I believe that the understanding and recognizing of them serves no purpose since no placement of commas is involved. One of my colleagues, on the other hand, maintains that gerunds and gerund phrases are fun. She uses art work to teach the concept to her students. She may well be right.

A gerund phrase is a group of words that includes a gerund and other words that complete its meaning. It can be accompanied by an adjective, an adverb, a direct object, or a prepositional phrase.

A gerund phrase functions as a noun in a sentence. The gerund phrase can be a subject or an object.

Examples: **Speaking softly** was one of the rules. (subject)

She made **speaking softly** a requirement in her class. (object)

Good and Well

These two words often are confused.

1. "Good" is an adjective; it tells about the noun that must follow it.

Example: The **good** dog sat at her feet instead of on them. (adjective — tells what kind of dog)

2. "Well" is the adverb that modifies a verb; it often appears at the end of the sentence.

Examples: He did it **well**. (adverb — tells how he did it)

He did **well** on the test. (adverb — tells how he did)

You can, however, "feel good" because "feel" acts as a verb of being and thus "good" is a predicate adjective.

Example: **I feel good** when I pet my cat.

Helping Verbs

These verbs accompany a past or present participle in a sentence. My students and I call them "dead verbs" or "weak verbs." Help students limit them in their writing.

Common helping verbs: am, are, be, is, have, had, had been, has been, have, have been, was, were, will, and any form of "be" (such as could be, would be, might be, etc.).

Good writing uses strong, active verbs ("screamed" instead of "**was** screaming"). Look at literature!

Sense verbs (look, see, smell, feel, taste) can function as verbs of being or as action verbs.

Example: I **feel** loving today. (verb of being)

The boy **felt** the dog's broken leg. (action verb)

When a sense verb functions as a verb of being, it is often followed by a predicate adjective.

Example: I **feel** bad. (Not "I feel badly" since one would not say "I am badly.")

Homophones

Students need to be able to correctly use the most common ones.

Common homophones: there/their/they're; to/too/two; your/you're; no/know; its/it's; right/rite/write; threw/through; quiet/quit/quite; all ready/already; all together/ altogether; hole/whole; pair/pare/pear; whose/who's

Hyphens

1. Use a hyphen to divide a word at the end of a line. Divide only at syllables. Check a dictionary for syllables.

Example: The two huge dogs ran **around** the yard, terrifying the little girl.

2. Use a hyphen to separate the words in compound numbers from twenty-one to ninety-nine and in fractions that are used as adjectives.

Examples: The teacher had thirty-five pupils in the class.

They ate ten and one-half pizzas for lunch.

3. Use a hyphen in a compound noun that serves as an adjective. More simply stated, use with two or more words that express one thought and serve as one adjective. To test whether a hyphen is needed, simply see if each word alone makes sense in describing the noun.

Examples: an **up-to-the-minute** report

two **star-crossed** lovers

a very **well-known** man

bell-bottom trousers

4. Use a hyphen after the following prefixes: all-, ex-, self-.

Examples: all-knowing, ex-husband, self-deprecating

5. Use a hyphen to separate any prefix from a word that begins with a capital letter.

Example: **pre-Civil** War

Note that except in rare cases (like the example above) when a hyphenated word is capitalized (as in a title), the second part begins with a small letter.

Examples: Stong-verb Paragraphs, Second-grade Story

Imperatives

Imperatives are sentences that are orders. The subject is omitted.

Examples: Get off my feet. (The subject of the dog has been left out.)

Do your homework now! (Again, the subject has been omitted.)

Compound imperative sentences do not take a comma because the subjects are not stated.

Example: Get off my feet and go lie down elsewhere.

Independent Clauses

An independent clause is a sentence within a sentence.

Example: **She petted the dog**, and **she kissed the cat**.

Indirect and Direct Objects (*See* Direct and Indirect Objects)

Indirect Quote

An indirect quote is really a reference to a direct quote. The use of the word "that" turns a direct quote into an indirect one. In an indirect quote, no quotation marks are necessary because a direct quote is being paraphrased. No comma is necessary either

Examples: The student said **that she was hot**.

He told me **that he had a lot of homework to do**.

We shouted to her **that we didn't want to walk the dogs**.

Infinitive

An infinitive is formed from the word "to" together with the basic form of a verb.

Examples: to go, to snore, to eat, to type

Do not split an infinitive with the adverb as in the introduction to the television show *Star Trek*.

Example of what to avoid: " . . . **to** boldly **go** where no one has been before." (Star Trek)

Correction: " . . . **to go** boldly where no one has been before."

You might want to explain the use of "to" as a part of a verb. Most students think it functions only as a preposition.

Infinitive Phrase

This is a group of words with an infinitive and the words that complete the meaning. An infinitive phrase can serve as a noun, an adjective, or an adverb.

Examples:

Noun — To teach grammar is sometimes fun. (noun, subject)

Most students hate **to study grammar**. (object)

The goal of my first book was **to make grammar fun**. (predicate noun)

Adjective — It is now time **to learn your grammar**.

Adverb — The dog turned around six times **to get ready for his nap**.

Intensifier

An intensifier is an adverb that tells to what extent an adjective or another adverb is true. The most common intensifiers are "very" and "extremely."

Examples: an **extremely** angry (adjective) cat

a **very** placid (adjective) dog

The cat wanted to sit on his mistress's lap **very** badly. (adverb)

She spoke **extremely** softly (adverb) because she was afraid to awaken the cat.

Interjection

An interjection is a word or group of words that expresses feeling (anger, surprise, happiness, pain, relief, grief).

Common interjections: ah, aha, awesome, bam, boom, bravo, good grief, goodness, hey, hooray, hurrah, oh, oh boy, oh dear, oh my, oh yes/no, okay, ouch, ow, phew, pow, shhh, ugh, uh oh, well, whee, whoopee, whoops, wow.

Interjections that are at the beginning of the sentence can be followed either by a comma or by an exclamation mark. If an interjection is followed by an exclamation mark, the next word must begin with a capital letter.

Examples: **Well**, what are you doing there?

Okay, let's finish going over your homework.

Wow! Those dogs are big.

Interrupted Quote (*See* Continued Quote)

Interrupters

An interrupter is any word, expression or phrase that interrupts the flow of a sentence. These can be appositives, direct addresses, parenthetical expressions, or any word, phrase, or clause that breaks the flow of a sentence.

Examples: The dog, **however**, refused to get off her foot.

The dog, **I think**, is stubborn.

The black and white cat, **by the way**, is obstreperous.

She loved her only cat, **Skeeter**, very much.

Intransitive Verbs

An intransitive verb never has a direct object. In a sentence where the verb is intransitive, the subject does the acting and does not do anything to anything or anyone else.

Examples: Dogs **bark**.

The teacher **sits** in the chair.

The class **sleeps** during long messages on the loud speaker.

The class **rises** with respect (dream on, fellow teachers) when the teacher enters the room.

The dog **lies** on the floor.

Introductory Words and Phrases

These are simply words and phrases that begin a sentence. The comma after some of these is hotly debated. Using commas makes sentences easier to understand because they signal a separation or a pause between parts. It sounds better to put a comma after an adverb that comes at the beginning of a sentence if that adverb has to do with time. It also helps clarify a sentence if one puts a comma after an introductory prepositional phrase that acts as an adverb and refers to time that has passed in some way.

1. **Adverb** (one-word adverbs): We commonly use a one-word adverb that indicates when the action (the verb) took place. Put a comma after it if you hear a pause when the sentence is spoken aloud.

Examples: **Meanwhile**, the dog's stomach growled.

Tomorrow, she will be fed again.

2. **Adverbial clauses** (subordinate clauses): A comma is needed after an adverbial clause that introduces a sentence.

Example: **After I feed the chubby Rottweiler**, I will feed the rotund Doberman.

3. **Participial phrases**: A comma is needed after a participial phrase that comes at the beginning of a sentence.

Example: **Traveling away from the city**, you can tour some of the beautiful antebellum homes in the country.

4. **Prepositional phrases**: The comma after these, too, is debatable. Many old-fashioned people, like my mother and I, put a comma after a longish prepositional phrase that comes at the beginning of a sentence, particularly if the phrase refers to time. This also can be called an "adverbial phrase."

Examples: **In about two weeks**, she will need to get her shots.

For a very long time, he will be able to exist on the food on the shelves.

A comma is needed after two or more prepositional phrases that follow each other at the beginning of a sentence.

Examples: **At the end of the day**, the fat dog tries to curl up on her "blankey" to go to sleep.

In one hour in the kitchen, the hungry dog will receive a dog biscuit.

In the fall of 1992, a presidential election was held in this country.

5. **Words**: A comma is needed to show a pause after an introductory word. The most common introductory words are "yes" and "no."

Examples: **Yes**, it is necessary to have a comma after introductory words.

No, many dogs do not receive five dog biscuits a day.

Irregular Verb Forms

Instead of forcing students to memorize a list which somehow never transfers to their writing, I teach each verb as it comes up in students' writing. This makes it real to them. They know they made a mistake in a verb and are more receptive to learning the forms of that verb. Plus, overkill (there are so many irregular verbs) only confuses students.

Verbs to stress in Caught'yas: be, do, have, lay, lie, raise, rise, see, set, sit. If you want to teach a unit on irregular verbs, any traditional grammar book will have a complete list for you.

LAY/LIE

Few adults use these verbs correctly. Think about the trouble students must have with them!

1. **lay**: **Lay**, used in the present tense, always has an object, and **laid**, in the past tense always has an object. You lay something on the table. You can't "lay" yourself on the table. That would be awkward as well as ungrammatical.

Principal parts of "lay":

lay (present)

laid (past)

laid (past participle)

Examples: The dog **lay** his head in his owner's lap. (present)

The dog **laid** his head on the rug yesterday. (past)

The dog always **has laid** its bone beside its bed. (past participle)

2. **lie**: Lie means to recline. Lie never takes a direct object. You lie on a bed, but you can never "lie" something on that bed. The confusion **lies** when the past tense of **lie** is used; **lay** used as the past tense of **lie** does not take a direct object.

Principal parts of "lie":

lie (present)

lay (past)

lain (past participle)

Examples: The dog **lies** on the floor today. (present)

The dog **lay** on the floor yesterday. (past)

The dog **is lying** on the floor right now. (present participle)

The dog **has lain** on the floor every day of its life. (past participle)

Less and Fewer (*See* Fewer and Less)

Metaphors

A metaphor is a comparison of two unlike things without using "like" or "as."

Example: The tree **is a ballerina in green**.

Use metaphors in Caught'yas. Have your students write a "Metaphor Paper." (*See* Chapter 5 in *Caught'ya Again*.) Encourage students to write metaphors. They make for beautiful writing. Emily Dickinson used metaphors in almost every poem. Metaphors are a wonderful tool to make writing more sophisticated.

Modifiers and Misplaced Modifiers

1. **Modifiers**: A modifier is simply another word for an adjective. A modifier may be classified as non-restrictive (non-essential) or restrictive (essential). A modifier can be a word, a phrase, or a clause.

An adjective, adjective phrase, or adjective clause is non-restrictive/non-essential when it is not necessary to the meaning of the sentence. The clause gives additional information. Use commas to set off non-restrictive modifiers.

Example: Dino, **who has floppy ears**, won a prize in obedience class. (The name of the dog has been identified, and it is not necessary to add more information about him.)

An adjective, adjective phrase, or adjective clause is restrictive/essential when it is necessary to the meaning of the sentence. Do not set off a restrictive modifier with commas.

Example: The dog **who won a prize in obedience class** has floppy ears. (This information is necessary since there are millions of dogs in the world.)

2. **Misplaced modifiers**: These are simply adjective phrases or clauses that are in the wrong place in a sentence so that they seem to modify the wrong noun. When you use modifiers in sentences, make sure that they are properly placed. The general rule to follow is this: place modifiers as close as possible to the sentence parts they modify.

Examples: The lady watched her dog **driving down the road.** (The dog is not driving down the road; the lady is.)

Corrected sentence: Driving down the road, the lady watched her dog.

After purchasing a skirt, her money was all gone. (The clause "her money was all gone" does not tell more about the skirt. It tells about the **person** "her" refers to and therefore should not come immediately after "skirt.")

Corrected sentence: **After purchasing a skirt**, she had no more money.

Negatives

A negative is a word that expresses the lack of something.

Common negatives: no, not, neither, never, nobody, none, no one, nothing, nowhere, barely, scarcely, hardly.

All you need to stress about negatives is the importance of avoiding the use of two negatives in the same sentence like "don't got no" or "don't have nobody." There should be only *one* negative word per sentence unless you are using the correlative conjunction "neither . . . nor."

Only one negative word is necessary to convey the meaning. There are two ways to correct a sentence with a double negative.

Example: The telephone **isn't no** new instrument.

Corrected sentence: The telephone is **no** new instrument. Or, The telephone is **not** a new instrument.

Noun

A noun is a person, a place, a thing, or an idea. It is important for students to recognize this part of speech and its function as a subject or object. Teach the difference between common and proper nouns.

Common nouns are terms for persons, places, things, or ideas.

Proper nouns are the names of particular persons, places, or things.

Examples:

Common nouns — girl, school, city

Proper nouns — Jane, Westwood School, Gainesville

Nouns have several functions in a sentence.

Subject — the person, place, or thing doing the action

Example: The **dog** yawned.

Direct object — the person, place, or thing who receives the action

Example: She stroked the **cat**.

Object of preposition — the person, place, or thing affected by the preposition

Example: He gave the bone to the **dog**.

Indirect object — the person, place, or thing for whom or to whom the action is done

Example: She gave the **dog** a big bone. ("to" is implied)

Noun Clause

A noun clause is a subordinate clause which is used as a noun. It can be used as a subject, direct object, indirect object, predicate noun, or object of a preposition in a sentence.

Noun clauses usually begin with the following words: how, if, that, what, whatever, where, when, wherever, whether, which, whichever, who, whom, whoever, whomever, why.

Noun clauses take the place of a noun anywhere in a sentence that a noun can be used (subject, direct or indirect object, object of a preposition, predicate noun).

Examples:

Subject — What the dog intended was obvious.

Direct object — I still don't know **why he did it**.

Indirect object — Please give **whichever dog comes up to you** a pat under the chin.

Object of preposition — She tells her stories **to whoever will listen**.

Predicate noun — That is not **what the dog** intended to do.

Noun Markers

This is the term for the three demonstrative adjectives "a," "an," and "the." When I introduce these to the students, I first make my hand into a trumpet, "Toot-te-toot," and then announce, "Noun coming!!!!!!" Students quickly get the idea, and we move on to other things. Young students especially love the drama of the hand trumpet and seem to remember these three little words when they are presented in this fashion.

Example: The lady gave **an** old bone to **a** hungry dog.

Use "a" before a word that begins with a consonant and "an" before a word that begins with a vowel. These demonstrative adjectives are also called "articles." (*See* Articles)

Objects

There are two kinds of objects, direct and indirect. Objects are nouns, noun clauses, or noun phrases that receive the action of the verb either directly or indirectly. They answer the following questions:

1. whom? (direct object)

2. what? (direct object)

3. to or for whom? (indirect object)

4. to or for what? (indirect object)

For further information about objects and for examples, *see* Direct and Indirect Objects

Paragraphs

Discuss the need for a paragraph each time you do a Caught'ya. Correct paragraphing can be learned only through constant practice. While various writers may disagree as to the exact placement of a paragraph, there are some general rules.

1. In general, a new paragraph is needed if there has been a lapse of time, a change of subject, or a change of place. A paragraph is supposed to be about one basic idea. It needs a topic sentence and a concluding sentence (unless it is a quotation).

2. Use a new paragraph in conversations each time a new person speaks. This seems like such a simple thing to grasp, but students have a hard time learning it.

Example:

"Get out of here, you beastly dog!" cried the lady to the big brown Doberman cowering in the kitchen. "You're messing up my floor!"

"Rowrf, Rowrf!" barked back the dog as it slinked sheepishly away.

"Oh, come back here, you poor thing," called the lady. "I'm sorry I yelled at you."

"Rowrf!"

"I like you, too," said the lady.

Parallel Construction

Parallel structure are forms that use similar grammatical constructions. Similar forms of phrases, words, and clauses are used for items that are alike in a sentence.

Parallel construction means that if you begin with a word or a certain part of speech, you have to continue it if you have a series. It can, however, be implied, as in a series of infinitives.

Examples: The big Doberman likes **bananas, tomatoes**, and **broccoli**. (words — these are all nouns)

The two dogs liked **sleeping** and **eating**. (words — gerunds)

The chubby Rottweiler went **to her bowl, to her water dish**, and then **to her bed**. (phrases — prepositional)

She felt **that she was unloved** and **that she was unwanted** because there was no food in her bowl. (clauses)

He likes **to eat**, (to) **sleep**, and (to) **play**. (infinitives)

Parentheses
(As you may have noticed, I abuse these.)

Parentheses enclose information that isn't vital to the meaning of a sentence, but that is nevertheless important to include. Parentheses also can contain information that some of the readers of the sentence already know.

Examples: The author of this book (Jane Kiester) has a thing about animals.

Emily Dickinson (1830-1886) is her favorite poet.

Frequent use of parentheses is not desirable. (Do as I say, not as I do.)

Parenthetical Expressions

Parenthetical expressions are phrases that are thrown into sentences as asides to the reader. They are not necessary to the meaning of the sentence and often interrupt a sentence's flow. Parenthetical expressions also are called interrupters.

Common parenthetical expressions: of course, however, for example, on the contrary, on the other hand, I suppose, in fact, by the way, in my opinion, to tell the truth, nevertheless, I believe, I think, etc.

Parenthetical expressions always are set off by commas no matter where they occur in a sentence.

Examples: The dog, **in fact**, was too chubby for her collar.

To tell the truth, two faithful dogs are a handful.

The cat, **however**, is quite a dapper fellow.

Cats are smarter than dogs, **of course**.

Participial Phrases (also called Participle Phrases)

These are groups of words that have the "ing," the "ed," or the special past form of the verb in them. In other words, they are phrases that contain a participle and its complement and modifiers. Participial phrases can come before or after the word that they modify and can give more information about a noun or an adjective. The participle will be present or past.

1. A present participle is the "ing" form of a verb. It can be used as an adjective by itself or in a participial or gerund phrase.

Examples: The **snoring** (adjective) **dog sleeping on the floor** (participial phrase) is the gentlest of animals.

Cramming before a test is a poor practice. (gerund phrase)

2. A **past participle** is the past tense form of a verb which usually ends in "ed." It can be used with a helping verb or can be used as an adjective or in a participial phrase.

Examples: The chef served the fish **fried in butter**.

That **trained** (adjective) dog who didn't learn anything has barked all morning long.

Participial phrases act as adjectives

Examples: **Rapidly gaining confidence**, the new teacher taught about participial phrases. (more about "teacher")

The new teacher, **feeling more sure of herself**, taught about participial phrases.

If the participial phrase begins the sentence or comes in the middle of the sentence, it usually is set off by commas. If, however, it is at the end of the sentence, it requires no comma.

Examples: **Groaning softly**, the dog kicked out in his sleep.

The dog, **groaning softly**, kicked out in his sleep.

She spied a dog **groaning softly in its sleep.**

Participle

A participle is just a fancy name for a verb form that is used as an adjective. It can be the present participle form of the verb ("–ing") or the past participial form of the verb (usually "–ed").

Examples: The **sleeping** dog blocked the doorway. (present)

A **trained** dog supposedly obeys better than an **untrained** one. (past)

(*See* Participial Phrases. *See also* Dangling Participle)

Parts of Speech

The eight parts of speech are the eight functional categories into which we can divide words. It is important that students learn the eight parts of speech to have a frame of reference and to have a way to understand the finer points of grammar.

The eight parts of speech: adjectives, adverbs, conjunctions, verbs, interjections, nouns, prepositions, pronouns.

I like to use the mnemonic device **NIPPAVAC** to teach them to my students.

Passive Voice (*See* Active vx. Passive Verb Voices)

Periods (*See* End Marks)

Plural

A plural is more than one of a noun. In the *Caught'yas* I covered the common mistakes students make. This is another skill that should be taught individually. When one of your students makes a mistake with the plural of a word, include that word or a similar word in a *Caught'ya* and teach it.

Basic plural rules.

1. Add "s" to most singular nouns.

Examples: dog-dogs; piano-pianos; monkey-monkeys; cat-cats.

2. Add "es" to singular nouns that end in ss, x, ch, sh, or z.

Examples: church-churches; mix-mixes; glass-glasses; buzz-buzzes; wish-wishes.

3. Most nouns that end in "o" add "s" in their plural form, but a few that end in "o" and are preceded by a consonant form their plurals with "es." Some can end in either one.

Examples: tomato-tomatoes, potato-potatoes; BUT hero-heros or heroes

4. Change singular nouns that end in a consonant and a "y" to plural by changing the "y" to an "i" and adding "es." This rule does not apply to proper nouns that end in a consonant and a "y."

Examples: party-parties; baby-babies; BUT Mary-Marys

5. To form the plural of some nouns that end in "f" or "fe," change the "f" to a "v" and add "es."

Examples: calf-calves; knife-knives

6. To form the plural of any proper name, no matter what the end letters, add "s."

Examples: Brady-Bradys; Finch-Finchs

7. There are so many exceptions to these rules that it boggles the mind. If you want a complete list, see a traditional grammar text. Few people can memorize a list one day and then apply it to their writing a month later. Plurals are best taught on the spur of the moment, at the time they are written incorrectly.

Examples: foot-feet; mouse-mice; deer-deer; child-children

Plurals vs. Possessives

For some reason, this is a skill many students find beyond them. No general explanations seem to clear up this problem. Only specific focuses help. I tell my students who put apostrophes on plural nouns to eliminate every apostrophe in their writing for a month. We then slowly put them back in possessives and in conjunctions. This works better than anything else I have tried. I also keep plugging away in the *Caught'yas* by frequently inserting apostrophes correctly and incorrectly in the sentence that is put on the board. This forces students to think each time– "Does that apostrophe belong there? Is the word plural or possessive?" This way, students eventually get the hang of it.

Possessive Nouns

A possessive noun is a noun (a person, place, or thing) that shows ownership of something. Ownership is shown by the use of an apostrophe.

Examples: the dog's bone, the dogs' bones

The rules of possessive nouns are quite simple for something that gives students such anguish.

1. **Singular possessive nouns**: Add "'s" to any singular possessive noun no matter what letter ends it.

Examples: glass's, dog's, cat's, box's, church's, calf's, child's

2. **Plural possessive nouns**: Add an apostrophe to all plural possessive nouns that end in "s."

Examples: glasses', dogs', cats', boxes', churches', calves'

Add "'s" to any plural noun that does not end in "s."

Examples: children's, men's, mice's

Predicate

A predicate is the verb in a sentence and all the words that modify it.

Example: The black and white cat **sat on his mistress's lap**.

Preposition

A preposition is a little word that, with its object, acts either as an adjective or as an adverb in a sentence.

Examples: in the doghouse, on the roof, under the bed

List of prepositions: aboard, about, above, across, after, against, along, among, around, at, before, behind, below, beneath, between, beyond, by, down, during, except, for, from, in, into, like, of, off, on, onto, over, past, since, through, throughout, to, toward, under, underneath, until, up, upon, with, within, without.

Students should memorize the basic list for quick reference. Repeated daily in class, these prepositions are learned in about three weeks. Teach the prepositions early in the year, write poems where every line has to begin with a different preposition, and refer to them often. Once students have memorized the prepositions, they can begin to use them more effectively and capitalize (or not) them correctly in titles.

Do not end a sentence with a preposition. It is uncouth! Do not capitalize a preposition in a title unless it is the first word of that title.

Prepositional Phrases

A prepositional phrase is a preposition and a noun or pronoun plus the adjectives that modify it. It is a group of words that functions as a single word. Prepositional phrases can serve as adjectives to modify a noun or as adverbs to modify a verb.

Examples: I gave a bone **to the dog**. (adverb)

The dog **with the floppy ears** ate the bone. (adjective)

An adjective phrase usually follows the word it modifies.

Example: The dog **on the right** is snoring.

An adverb phrase, like adverbs, may shift position.

Examples: **In the middle**, lies the cat.

The cat lies **in the middle**.

Pronouns

Pronouns are words that take the place of nouns and cause much trouble. They are hateful but necessary. If you think these are bad, try teaching French pronouns!

Especially stress the difference between subject and object pronouns.

Subject pronouns: I, you, he, she, it, we, they

Object pronouns: me, you, him, her, it, us, them.

Include in many *Caught'yas* "My friend and I did something." and "Someone did something to my friend and me."

Students experience much difficulty differentiating subject and object pronouns. They misuse them because they hear them misused all the time in common speech. Model the correct use as often as you can.

Examples of common errors: My friend and **me** went . . .

It is **me**.

She is better than **me**.

Correct examples: My friend and **I** went . . . ("I" is the subject of "went.")

It is **I**. (Implied here is "It is I who does something." "I" is a subject.)

She is better than **I** . . . (Again, something is implied. The word "am" has been left out. "I" is the subject of "am.")

Teach the correct use of the different kinds of pronouns. It is not the name of each that is important; it is recognizing the differences among them.

1. **Personal pronouns**: These are the subject and object pronouns listed above.

2. **Possessive pronouns**: These are pronouns that show ownership of something.

Singular possessive pronouns: my, mine, your, yours, his, her, hers, its

Plural possessive pronouns: our, ours, your, yours, their, theirs

3. **Interrogative pronouns**: These pronouns ask questions: why, what, which, who, whom.

4. **Demonstrative pronouns**: These pronouns point out people, places or things and highlight them: this, that, these, those.

5. **Indefinite pronouns**: These are pronouns that refer to a person or a thing that is not identified. Some indefinite pronouns are singular. Some are plural. Some can act either way.

Singular: another, anybody, anyone, anything, each, either, everybody, everyone, everything, neither, nobody, no one, none, nothing, other, one, somebody, someone, something

Plural: both, few, many, ones, others, several

Either: all, any, most, some

It is important to teach agreement with indefinite pronouns. Many students find it difficult to make a verb or another pronoun agree with the indefinite pronoun.

6. **Reflexive and intensive pronouns**: These usually end in "self" or "selves" and refer to the subject of the sentence. For your trivia information of the day, you need to know that reflexive pronouns are necessary to the meaning of a sentence and cannot be left out. Intensive pronouns, on the other hand, are not necessary and can be left out without hurting the meaning of a sentence.

Examples: The teacher knows **herself** very well. (reflexive)

The teacher **herself** washed the blackboard. (intensive)

7. **Relative pronouns**: These are the pronouns that modify a noun: who, which, that.

There are two big problems with pronouns — using the correct one and making the rest of the sentence agree with it.

Punctuation

Each kind of punctuation is listed under its own heading.

Question Marks (*See* End Marks)

Quotation Marks (In Uses Other Than Conversation)

Use quotation marks around words referred to or letters referred to in the context of a sentence. Use them also with words that are meant tongue-in-cheek.

Periods and commas always go inside quotation marks.

Examples: If you wish to make plural the word **"party,"** take off the **"y"** and add **"ies."**

He loves the poem **"Mother to Son."**

The corpulent Rottweiler has been nicknamed **"Miss Tub."**

Exclamation marks and question marks go outside the quotation marks unless they are part of the words in quotation marks.

Examples: She got an **"A"**!

Did he give an extra bone to **"Miss Tub"**?

Quotations can be avoided with the use of the word "that." Instead of quotation marks, refer to what has been said with the word "that." *See* Indirect Quotes for more information.

Examples: She said that she was hungry and needed refreshments.

Despite her pleas, I told her that she was too chubby to get any more ice cream.

(*See also* Dialogues, Comma Rules, Indirect Quotes, and Titles)

Raise/Rise

These are two more verbs that confuse students. Again, as in "lie" and "lay" and "sit" and "set," one takes an object and the other does not.

1. Raise means "to lift or to grow." It requires an object that has to be "raised."

Example: The cat **raised** his tail and stormed off when no food was offered.

2. Rise means "to get up." It does not take an object.

Example: All students **rise** with a bow of respect when their English teacher enters the room.

Run Ons

A run on is a sentence that contains more than one thought. It goes on and on.

1. Sometimes run-on sentences simply lack punctuation.

Example: The dog lay on the floor she snored loudly.

Corrected: The dog lay on the floor. She snored loudly.

2. Sometimes run-on sentences are a group of sentences joined by coordinating conjunctions into one very long sentence.

Example: She lay on the floor, and she snored, but she didn't groan, and she wiggled her ears.

Corrected: She lay on the floor. She snored, but she didn't groan. She wiggled her ears.

Help your students avoid run ons.

Semicolons

A semicolon is a punctuation mark (;) that is used to separate parts of a sentence.

1. Use semicolons in compound sentences instead of using a conjunction and a comma.

Example: The black cat nuzzled the big dog; it is either very friendly or very stupid.

2. Use semicolons in lists where the use of a lot of commas makes meaning difficult.

Example: Learn the meanings of these homophones: there, their, they're; to, too, two; your, you're; no, know; and hear, here.

3. Use a semicolon to join two independent clauses (two sentences within a sentence) when the second clause begins with however, nevertheless, consequently, besides, therefore, moreover, or furthermore.

Example: The Rottweiler may lick faces**;** however, she is charming.

4. To avoid confusion, use a semicolon to separate two independent clauses that have many commas within one or both of them.

Example: My Rottweiler likes to eat tomatoes, broccoli, and cucumbers**;** my Doberman likes to eat fruit, dog food, and cookies.

Similes

A simile compares two unlike things and uses "like" or "as" in the comparison.

Examples: The cat sprawled on the rug **like a furry throw pillow**.

The leaves, **as agile as ballerinas**, seemed to dance in the wind.

Encourage students to use similes. I have included a plethora of them in the *Caught'yas* so that students can learn to recognize and use them. Point them out to students. Practice coming up orally with other similes.

Simple Sentence

A simple sentence is a sentence with one subject and one predicate. In a simple sentence, the subject

and/or the verb can be more than one thing, as in a compound subject or a compound predicate, but only one idea is expressed.

Examples: The wimpy **Rottweiler sat** on her owner's foot.

The wimpy **Rottweiler** and the brown **Doberman sat** by their owner's feet and **gazed** adoringly into their mistress's eyes. (Two subjects and two verbs, but it is still a simple sentence.)

Since (*See* Because and Since)

Set/Sit

These are two more verbs that students often use incorrectly.

1. Set means to put down. Set always takes an object. You set the sleeping cat in the chair or the milk on the table, but you never set yourself down anywhere. Tell students to think about it. You can't put your hands under your feet and lift your entire body up and set it down on something.

Example: The dumb Doberman **set** his bone down on the floor, and the chubby Rottweiler grabbed it from under his nose.

2. Sit means to place yourself in a seated position. Sit does not take an object. You sit down, but you never sit something down.

Example: The stupid dog always **sits** on its owner's foot.

Spelling Errors, The Most Common

1. All words with "ie" or "ei"

Examples: thief, relief, believe

weird, neighbor, receive

2. Plurals of nouns that end in "y"

Examples: parties, monkeys, babies

3. "A lot" (students write as one word)

Some teachers forbid the use of this in their classrooms. I agree. There are always ways to avoid the use of "a lot."

4. Doubling consonants in words that end in consonant/vowel/consonant plus a suffix that begins with a vowel (like "ed").

Examples: dropped, stopped, petted

5. Any grammar or spelling book will have a long list of commonly misspelled words, but very few people can memorize a long list of words and then remember the spelling of those words when they use them in their writing at a later date. It is better to attack these misspelled words as they appear in students' writings.

Spelling Rules

There are too many spelling rules and exceptions to the spelling rules to list here. See any standard spelling book for a discussion of this subject. The most common ones have been listed by the individual *Caught'yas* in which they appear.

Strong Verbs

These are verbs that are not helping verbs or sense verbs. They show rather than tell what is going on in a sentence. Use of these verbs fosters better writing. You will find the use of strong verbs in literature. There is even a language called E-Prime that is English minus the verb "to be." Try speaking or writing in E-Prime. The results are amazing, and the verb "to be" is only one of the "telling" verbs.

Examples: The dog **stretched** and **rolled** his big brown eyes at me.

He **ambled** to the door and **peeked** outside.

Dead verbs to avoid: to be — be, am, is, are, was, were; to have — has, have, had; become, became.

Sense verbs: sees, looks, feels, sounds, smells.

Any verb ending in "ing"

Subjects

A subject is the noun that performs the action in a sentence and everything that modifies it.

Example: The big black **cat** and his **mistress** like to snooze late on Saturday mornings.

Subject-Verb Agreement

Subject-verb agreement is very important to the coherence of a sentence. The subject of a sentence must agree as to whether it is singular or plural with the verb of the sentence.

If the subject is singular, then the verb should be singular. If the subject is plural, the verb should be plural.

Examples: **He think** he is right. (incorrect)

We goes to the circus every year. (incorrect)

Corrected examples: **He thinks** he is right.

We go to the circus every year.

Subordinate Clause

1. A subordinate clause is a part of a sentence that has a subject and a verb but cannot stand on its own to express a complete thought. A subordinate clause begins with a subordinating conjunction — a conjunction that makes the clause not a complete sentence. *See* Subordinating Conjunctions for a complete list them.

Examples: **When the teacher was funny**, the students laughed. ("The teacher was funny" is a complete

sentence with a subject and a verb. If you add the subordinating conjunction "when," it can no longer stand on its own, and it needs the addition of an independent clause to form a complete sentence.)

While we sit here, I shall tell you my story.

I shall tell you my story **while we sit here**.

2. Subordinate clauses serve in a sentence as adverbs or adjectives. Subordinate clauses that are adverbs (adverb clauses) tell more about the verb and answer one of the following questions about a verb: when it happened, where it happened, how it happened, how often it happened, why it happened.

Examples: *See* Adverb Clauses.

3. Subordinate clauses that are adjectives (adjective clauses) tell more about a noun and answer one of the following questions about it: which one, what kind, how many.

Examples: *See* Adjective Clauses.

4. Punctuation of subordinate clauses is easy. Put a comma at the end of the clause if the clause begins the sentence. Do not put any commas if the clause does not begin the sentence.

Examples: **If you pet the dog**, you will get hairs on your suit.

You will get hairs on your suit **if you pet the dog**.

Subordinating Conjunctions

These are words that make something that was a complete sentence into an incomplete sentence. Subordinating conjunctions begin subordinate clauses (see above).'

Example: **After** the cat fell asleep, he twitched his whiskers.

Common subordinating conjunctions: after, although, as, as if, as long as, as soon as, as though, because, before, even though, how, if, in order that, provided that, since, so that, than, till, unless, until, when, whenever, where, whereas, wherever, while. (*See* Conjunctions for a teaching suggestion.)

Summarizing

To summarize something you write a condensed version of it. This is a skill that is necessary in almost any job. A repair man has to summarize each house call. A doctor has to summarize each patient's problems, and so on. It is a skill that is easily practiced with the Caught'yas. (See #9 of the General Writing Ideas in Chapter 5 of *Caught'ya Again* for ideas to teach summarization skills.)

That

"That" is a relative or a demonstrative pronoun (depending on how it is used). Use "that" in an indirect quote to avoid the use of quotation marks.

Example: She said **that** she was going to feed the dogs.

Do not use "that" as a substitute for "who" or "whom." "That" refers to an object or a thing. "Who" and "whom" refer to people. This is an extremely common mistake.

Example: She is the one **whom** (not "that") I love.

Is feeding two hungry dogs **that** complicated?

She gave the dog the bone **that** seemed the biggest.

Titles

1. Underline titles of long works — books, magazines, newspapers, plays, movies, paintings, and long musical works.

2. Put quotation marks around short works — short stories, poems, chapters of books, magazine articles, songs. It also is important to recall that if a comma or a period follows the quoted work, it must be placed inside the quotation mark. If a question or an exclamation and the end punctuation is not a part of the cited work, then the question mark or the exclamation point goes outside the quotation mark.

Examples: Although she read the article **"Sentence Diagramming,"** she still didn't understand the concept.

She read the article **"Sentence Diagramming."**

Did she read the article **"Sentence Diagramming"**?

3. Do not capitalize prepositions, noun markers, or conjunctions in a title unless they are the first word of the title.

Example: The (noun marker) Dog under (preposition) a (noun marker) Human Roof and (conjunction) the (noun marker) Cat on (preposition) the (noun marker) Lap

The Dog under a Human Roof and the Cat on the Lap

Transitive Verbs

A transitive verb takes a direct object. In other words, it always has to do something to something or someone.

Example: The dog **lay** his **head** on the carpet today.

The cat **set** his **paw** on the table before attacking the plate.

The dog **raised** his **paw** for inspection.

Verb Tense Shift in a Story

Make sure that students stick to the same tense they begin with in any story or paragraph they write. If a story starts in the present tense, it should remain in the present tense. If it begins in the past tense, it should continue in the past tense.

To practice this skill, I frequently have changed the verb tense in the Caught'ya sentences. All of the stories have been told in the past tense, so I sometimes put the verb in the present tense. In the margin I warn the teacher to make sure that the students practice correcting "verb tense shift."

Verbs

For lists of verbs and appropriate forms of regular and irregular verbs, please refer to a traditional grammar text. Otherwise, just correct students as they make the mistakes in their writing. The latter is more effective.

Try to keep students from splitting helping verbs and the participles that follow.

Example: The cat also **has lain** on the carpet all day. (Not "**has** also **lain**") all day.

While splitting helping verbs and the participles that follow is sometimes unavoidable, it is not correct English. Although more rigid grammarians disagree with me on this point, many of my colleagues and I believe that if avoiding the split creates an awkward sentence, the rule should be ignored.

Well (*See* Good and Well)

Who, Whoever, Whom, Whemever

These are relative or interrogative pronouns that are used to refer to people. These four pronouns are so misused in general parlance that to some students the correct form sounds incorrect! Simply correct students every time you hear an error in the use of these four pronouns. You may be making verbal corrections until students feel "grammatically abused," but the more students hear the correct way to use these pronouns, the more they will use them correctly.

Here's a general rule of thumb that works about 95 percent of the time. I tell my students to use "who" and "whoever" if the word after it is a verb. If the word is not a verb but a pronoun or a noun, then they must use "whom" or "whomever."

Another rule that often works even better is to substitute "he" or "she" for "who" and "him" or "her" for "whom" and see if it makes sense. These rules fail when you have one of those weird sentences or phrases that can be turned around like "Who I am" or when you have something else like "I think" between the subject and the verb. (She is the one who **I think** did it.)

1. **Who and whoever**: Used as interrogative pronouns, "who" and "whoever" are the subject of a simple or compound sentence. They should be followed by a verb, the thing that "who" does. Tell students, if they are in doubt, to try substituting "he" or "she" for "who" to see if it makes sense.

Examples: **Who is** that?

Who is sitting on my foot?

All right, **who ate** the dog food?

Whoever broke into the bag and ate the dog food is in big trouble.

Whoever is sitting on my foot had better get off.

Used as a relative pronoun, "who" and "whoever" may be the subject or the predicate noun of a clause.

Examples: **Whoever finishes first** will get extra ice cream for dessert. (subject)

We shall serve **whoever arrives first**. (predicate)

2. **Whom and whomever**: Whom and whomever are relative pronouns that serve as objects of sentences or clauses. They can be direct objects of a verb, indirect objects, or objects of a preposition. Tell students to try substituting "him" or "her" for "whom" to see if it sounds correct.

Examples: He is the one **whom** I love. (object of verb)

With **whom** did you go out last night? (object of preposition)

I will pick the one **whom** I want. (object of verb)

For **whom** does the lady buy diet dog food? (object of preposition)

I will give a dog biscuit to **whomever** I please.

3. **That**: Do not use "that" instead of "who" or "whom." "That" refers to objects or things. "Who" and "whom" refer to people.

Examples: (*See* That)

To reinforce the correct use of "who" and "whom," I tell students that I will give them one point extra credit (three of them erase a zero in my grade book) if they catch someone at home making a "who/whom" error. Students write down the offending sentence, coerce the person into adding a note that he/she did, in fact, make the error, and bring the paper to me. At first I was afraid that I would have angry parents, but it turned out that I received only positive phone calls from grateful parents who were delighted to see their children taking an interest in correct English grammar.

BIBLIOGRAPHY

Note: *A* ❤ *indicates the resource contains excellent suggestions for writing.*

Baars F. J. J en van der School, J.G. *Engels/Nederlands Woordenboek*. Utrecht: Prisma Boeken, 1975.

Baars F. J. J en van der School, J.G. *Nederlands/Engels Woordenboek*. Utrecht: Prisma Boeken, 1975.

Bescherelle 2: L'orthographe pour tous. Paris: Librairie Hatier, 1990.

Blassingame, Wyatt. *Skunks*. New York: Dodd, Mead, & Co., 1981.

Caplan, Rebakah and Catherine Deech. *Showing Writing - A Training Program to Help Students Be Specific*. Berkeley: University of California Press, 1980.

Dingwall, Laima. *Nature's Children: Skunks*. Danbury: Grolier Educational Corporation, 1986.

Elgin, Suzette Haden. *The Great Grammar Myth*. National Writing Project Occasional Paper #5. Berkeley: University of California Press, 1982.

Forney, Melissa. *Dynamite Writing Ideas! Empowering Students to Become Authors*. Gainesville: Maupin House, 1996. ❤

Forney, Melissa. *The Writing Menu: Ensuring Success for Every Student*. Gainesville: Maupin House, 1999. ❤

Freeman, Marcia. *Building a Writing Community: A Practical Guide*. Gainesville: Maupin House, 1995. ❤

Freeman, Marcia. *Listen to This. Developing an Ear for Expository*. Gainesville: Maupin House, 1997. ❤

Freeman, Marcia. *Teaching the Youngest Writers*. Gainesville, Maupin House Publishing, 1998. ❤

French Dictionary. Glasgow: Harper Collins, 1988 ed.

Hacker, Diane. *A Writer's Reference*. Boston: Bedford Books, 1995.

Haley-James, Shirley and Stewig, John Warren. *Houghton Mifflin English*. Boston: Houghton Mifflin company, 1988.

Johnson, Bea. *Never too Early to Write*. Gainesville: Maupin House, 1999. ❤

Kiester, Jane Bell. *Caught'ya! Grammar with a Giggle*. Gainesville: Maupin House Publishing, 1990.

Kiester, Jane Bell. *Caught'ya Again! More Grammar with a Giggle*. Gainesville: Maupin House, 1992. ❤

Kiester, Jane Bell. *Blowing Away the State Writing Assessment Test*. Gainesville: Maupin House, 1996, 2000. ❤

Kiester, Jane Bell. *The Chortling Bard. Grammar with a Giggle for High School*. (Gainesville: Maupin House,) 1997.

Laird, Charlton, preparer. *Webster's New World Thesaurus*. New York: Simon and Schuster, Inc., 1985.

Scarry, Richard. *Mijn Leuk ABC*. Antwerpen: Zuid-Nederlandse Uitgeverij, 1966.

Scarry, Richard. *Mijn Leuk Schooltije*. Antwerpen: Zuid- Nederlandse Uitgeverij, 1969.

Schlein, Miriam. *What's Wrong with Being a Skunk?* New York: Four Winds Press, 1974.

Sherwin, J. Stephen. *Four Problems in Teaching English: A Critique of Research*. Scranton: International Textbook Company, 1969.

Sitton, Rebecca and Forest, Robert. *QUICK-WORD Handbook for Beginning Writers*. Billerica, MA: Curriculum Associates, Inc., 1994. ❤

Sitton, Rebecca and Forest, Robert. *QUICK-WORD Handbook for Everyday Writers*. Billerica, MA: Curriculum Associates, Inc., 1994. ❤

Sitton, Rebecca and Forest, Robert. *QUICK-WORD Handbook for Practical Writing*. Billerica, MA: Curriculum Associates, Inc., 1994.

Stein, Jess, Editor In Chief. *The Random House Dictionary of the English Language* (Unabridged Edition). New York: Random House, 1967.

Stone, Lynn. *Skunks*. Vero Beach: Rourke Corporation, Inc., 1990.

Warriner, John, and Graham, Sheila Laws. *Warriner's English Grammar and Composition, Complete Course*. New York: Harcourt Brace Jovanovich, 1957.

Warriner, John, and Graham, Sheila Laws. *Warriner's English Grammar and Composition, Third Course*, New York: Harcourt Brace Jovanovich, 1977.

Wong, Harry. *The First Days of School: How to Be an Effective Teacher*. Mountain View: Harry Wong Publications, 1998 ed.

Elementary, My Dear

try these other language arts resources
by Jane Bell Kiester

Caught'ya! Grammar with a Giggle

Jane Bell Kiester

One story each for elementary, middle, and high school, easily adaptable to your own classroom needs. Includes plot outlines, tests, answer keys, and spin-off activities. For teachers of grades 3-12. ISBN 0-929895-01-5. #MH07. **$17.95**

The Chortling Bard: Caught'ya! Grammar with a Giggle for High School

Jane Bell Kiester

Do your high schoolers become a pack of **mammering joltheads** when you try to teach them grammar and mechanics? Do they get all **onion-eyed** when you tell them to pull out their handbooks and primers? **Bestill** their **beslubbering mewls**—the popular Caught'ya! technique for teaching grammar and mechanics has taken a Shakespearean twist especially for high school teachers! ISBN 0-929895-25-8. #MH41. **$19.95**

Blowing Away the State Writing Assessment Test

Jane Bell Kiester

A classroom-proven resource that helps students become better writers. Fifty-three reproducible student-written examples cover descriptive, expository, narrative, and persuasive topics for elementary, middle, and high-school students. Students at all levels learn how to cluster ideas, write strong-verb sentences, and compose well developed paragraphs. Grading rubrics are included so students can understand how test samples are scored. Second Edition. ISBN 0-929895-36-3. #MH63. **$19.95**

Maupin House, Inc. • PO Box 90148 / Gainesville, FL 32607
info@maupinhouse.com • www.maupinhouse.com